MAKING TOURISM MORE SUSTAINABLE

A Guide for Policy Makers

United Nations Environment Programme
Division of Technology, Industry and Economics
39-43 Quai André Citroën
75739 Paris CEDEX 15, France
Tel: +33 1 44371450 • Fax: +33 1 44371474
E-mail: unep.tie@unep.fr • www.unep.fr

World Tourism Organization
Capitán Haya 42 · 28020 Madrid, Spain
Tel: +34 91 567 81 00 • Fax: +34 91 571 37 33
E-mail: omt@world-tourism.org • www.world-tourism.org

Foreword

International tourist arrivals have almost quadrupled over the past 30 years and domestic tourism has also intensified in most developed and newly industrialized countries. At the same time, tourist movements have spread geographically to reach practically all countries of the globe, becoming for many of them an important economic sector in terms of income generation, foreign exchange earnings and employment creation.

Awareness about sustainability issues—which referred originally to the natural environment but now also covers the social, economic and cultural spheres as well as the built environment—also developed significantly over those 30 years. Today, most governments, international development agencies, trade associations, academic institutions and non-governmental organizations acknowledge that, without sustainability, there cannot be development that generates benefits to all stakeholders, solves serious and urgent problems such as extreme poverty, and preserves the precious natural and man-made resources on which human prosperity is based.

The tourism sector could not remain indifferent to the sustainability challenge of our times. This is why the World Tourism Organization (WTO) focuses its advisory and technical assistance services on policies, development guidelines, management techniques and measurement instruments that allow national and local governments, as well as the tourism industry, to incorporate sustainability principles into their decision making process and day-to-day operations. This is why the United Nations Environment Programme (UNEP) has initiated a programme that aims at integrating environmental sustainability into decision making in the tourism industry and into consumers' purchasing choices, by disseminating technical know-how and building business networks to catalyse 'sustainability' in the tourism sector.

Making Tourism More Sustainable: a Guide for Policy Makers builds on UNEP and WTO's previous work on different aspects of sustainability, undertaken over the past ten or so years. This is the first time that the two organizations have combined their input in a joint effort to condense all aspects of the sustainability of tourism into a single publication. In addition to earlier work by WTO and UNEP, an extensive research survey was undertaken within WTO Member States, in 2003 and 2004, to identify specific policies and tools applied in their territories that had effectively contributed to making their tourism sector more sustainable. The conclusions drawn and the policies and tools recommended in this Guide are therefore based on real cases, collected from around the world, that have proven to be effective and successful in achieving the aims of sustainable development.

Development of the Guide, which provides a blueprint for governments to formulate and implement sustainable tourism policies, was one of the most important building blocks in the partnership between UNEP and WTO, also benefiting, in this case, from a Ford Foundation grant.

Each national or local government will surely need to select those policies and tools considered most suitable to its particular circumstances, and adapt them to the conditions prevailing in its country, region or local jurisdiction.

Foreword

The Guide defines what sustainability means in tourism, what are the effective approaches for developing strategies and policies for more sustainable tourism, and the tools that would make the policies work on the ground. It shows clearly that there is no 'one-fits-all' solution to address the question of sustainability in tourism development. It does, however, highlight one key universal message: to succeed in making tourism more sustainable it is crucial to work hand in hand with all relevant stakeholders, within and outside government. Therefore—although the report is aimed mainly at governments—public authorities at all levels are encouraged to disseminate its contents to those private and non-governmental organizations that have an interest in ensuring the long-term success of the tourism sector, especially the wide range of tourism businesses and their trade associations.

The long standing partnership between the WTO and UNEP is a living example of the need for and benefits of cooperation.

Francesco Frangialli
Secretary General
World Tourism Organization

Klaus Toepfer
Executive Director
United Nations Environment Programme

Acknowledgements

Conception, technical editing and supervision

Giulia Carbone (UNEP) and Eugenio Yunis (WTO)

Principal consultant

Richard Denman, The Tourism Company, United Kingdom

English language editor

Geoffrey Bird

Design

The Graphic Environment

UNEP and WTO are grateful to the following for their input

For contribution to the case studies:
Australia: Alice Crabtree, David Morgans
Bulgaria: Kamelia Georgieva
Costa Rica: Amos Bien
Egypt: Bill Meade, Ahmed Hassan
Ghana: Wouter Schalken
Mexico: Liliana Garcia Huerta
Kaikoura, New Zealand: Kirsty Quickfall, Ian Challenger
South Africa: Anna Spenceley, Johann Kotze
Calvia, Spain: Rachel Dodds
Scotland, UK: Sandy Dear, Jon Proctor

Additional contributions to the text:
The International Ecotourism Society

Information on specific examples or topics:
Sylvie Barrere, Dirk Belau, Sylvie Blangy, Ralf Buckley, Kelly Bricker, Hugh Cresser, John Downes, Andy Drumm, Steve Edwards, Enzo Finocchiaro, Miriam Geitz, Douglas Hainsworth, Herbert Hamele, Moosa Zameer Hassan, Marion Hammerl, Veronika Holzer, Martha Honey, Maxi Lange, Marcel Leijzer, Manoa Malani, Marie Louise Mangion, Salvador Semitier Marti, Rabi Jung Pandey, Anna Quartucci, Laure Sagaert, Jennifer Seif, Mercedes Silva, Murray Simpson, Claire Stott, Richard Tapper, Jean-Paul Teyssandier, Yara Zuniga.

UNEP and WTO are grateful to the Ford Foundation for its financial support which has made this project possible.

Table of Contents

Table of Contents

List of Abbreviations

CBD	Convention on Biological Diversity
CFCs	Chlorofluorocarbons
CSD	Commission on Sustainable Development
CSR	Corporate social responsibility
EIA	Environmental impact assessment
GRI	Global Reporting Initiative
ICZM	Integrated coastal zone management
ILO	International Labour Organisation
IUCN	International Union for the Conservation of Nature and Natural Resources (World Conservation Union)
LA21	Local Agenda 21
LAC	Limits of acceptable change
MSME	Micro, small and medium sized enterprise
NGO	Non-governmental organisation
SEA	Strategic environmental assessment
TIC	Tourist information centre
TOI	Tour Operators' Initiative
UNDP	United Nations Development Programme
UNEP	United Nations Environment Programme
UNESCO	United Nations Educational, Scientific and Cultural Organisation
USAID	The US Agency for International Development
WSSD	World Summit on Sustainable Development
WTO	World Tourism Organization
WTTC	World Travel and Tourism Council

Introduction

Tourism is an activity that has grown by around 25 per cent in the past 10 years. It now accounts for around 10 per cent of the world's economic activity and is one of the main generators of employment. However, it also has major impacts on the natural and built environments and on the wellbeing and culture of host populations. In roughly that same period, the concept of sustainable development has become widely accepted as the way to a better future, even though its roots go back to the 1980s.

It is against this background that *Making Tourism More Sustainable: A Guide for Policy Makers* views the effects of tourism, both positive and negative. In this context, the Guide examines ways in which principally governments but also other stakeholders can develop strategies, policies and tools to maximize the industry's positive effects while minimizing the negative impacts.

Tourism can play a significant role in sustainable development and the United Nations Environment Programme (UNEP) and the World Tourism Organization (WTO) wish to encourage all countries to make sure that their policies and actions for its development and management fully embrace the principles of sustainability. Likewise, policies to promote sustainable development should take full account of the opportunities offered by tourism.

Various international conventions and declarations have put forward principles and guidelines for sustainable tourism and the importance of tourism and its sustainability was underlined at the 2002 World Summit on Sustainable Development. Many countries declare that they are pursuing, or wish to pursue, policies for 'sustainable tourism'. Despite this interest, there remains a degree of uncertainty over the scope and priorities for making tourism more sustainable and only partial appreciation of how to put this into practice.

All tourism should be more sustainable

Sustainable tourism is not a discrete or special form of tourism. Rather, all forms of tourism should strive to be more sustainable.

Making tourism more sustainable is not just about controlling and managing the negative impacts of the industry. Tourism is in a very special position to benefit local communities, economically and socially, and to raise awareness and support for conservation of the environment. Within the tourism sector, economic development and environmental protection should not be seen as opposing forces—they should be pursued hand in hand as aspirations that can and should be mutually reinforcing. Policies and actions must aim to strengthen the benefits and reduce the costs of tourism.

Big issues are at stake here. Further massive growth is predicted for tourism between now and 2020, providing excellent opportunities for spreading prosperity but presenting considerable challenges and potential threats to the environment and local communities if not well managed. Climate change is recognized as a major global issue, with significant implications for tourism. There is also an increasing appreciation of the potential role of tourism in addressing world poverty, by bringing sources of income to the heart of some of the poorest communities.

Stakeholders in sustainable tourism

Many different interests can benefit from tourism being made more sustainable:

- Tourism enterprises, while seeking long term profitability, should be concerned about their corporate image, the relationship with their staff, and their impact on the global environment and that immediately around them.
- Local communities are seeking increased prosperity but without exploitation or damage to their quality of life.
- Environmentalists are concerned about the harmful impacts of tourism but also see it as a valuable source of income for conservation.
- Tourists are seeking a high quality experience in safe and attractive environments; they are becoming more aware of the impacts of their travelling.

In seeking more sustainable tourism, governments must recognize the different positions and motivations of these stakeholders and work with them to achieve common goals.

Governments play a leading role

Sustainability is the responsibility of all those involved in tourism. Most of the impacts of tourism are the result of actions taken by private sector enterprises and by tourists themselves. However, there is a clear need for governments to take a leading role if truly significant progress is to be achieved in making tourism more sustainable. This is because:

- The tourism industry is very fragmented. It is difficult for the individual actions of many micro and small businesses to make a positive difference and coordination is required.
- Sustainability relates to areas of public concern—air, water, natural and cultural heritage and the quality of life. Moreover, many of the relevant resources are managed by governments.
- Governments have many of the tools that can be used to make a difference—such as the power to make regulations and offer economic incentives, and the resources and institutions to promote and disseminate good practice.

Governments should provide an environment that enables and encourages the private sector, tourists and other stakeholders to respond to sustainability issues. This can best be achieved by establishing and implementing a set of policies for tourism development and management, drawn up in concert with others, that place sustainability at its centre.

The principles of sustainable development put emphasis on local determination and implementation of policies and actions. This should be placed within a supportive national policy framework.

Who this Guide is for

The Guide is primarily aimed at governments, at both national and local levels. It is also relevant to international development agencies, NGOs and the private sector, to the extent that they are affected by, and can affect, tourism policy and its implementation.

Introduction

The sustainability of tourism is an issue of equal importance in both developed and developing countries. This document is aimed at both. However, the balance of priorities may vary between them.

Purpose and scope of the Guide

The purpose of this document is to provide governments with guidance and a framework for the development of policies for more sustainable tourism as well as a toolbox of instruments that they can use to implement those policies.

The Guide contains five chapters:

1) Tourism and sustainability. This looks closely at what sustainability means for tourism and why governments need to address it. It introduces some key principles and an agenda for more sustainable tourism, framed around a set of 12 Aims.

2) Policy implications of a sustainable tourism agenda. The 12 Aims for more sustainable tourism are discussed in turn and policy areas relevant to each of them are identified.

3) Structures and strategies for more sustainable tourism. This chapter is about establishing the right structures through which governments can work with others towards more sustainable tourism, and about the strategies that are required to develop and drive policies and actions. Particular attention is paid to the relationship between national and local structures and strategies for sustainable tourism.

4) Shaping sustainable tourism. This chapter looks at the process of developing a tourism strategy that embraces sustainability and identifies some of the strategic choices that need to be made. It looks at product and market selection, and introduces the tools that may be used to influence tourism development, the operation of tourism enterprises and the behaviour of visitors.

5) Instruments for more sustainable tourism. A detailed description is given of a set of tools, and of how they can be applied by governments. They include the use of sustainability indicators, planning, infrastructure provision, legislation and regulations, and a set of voluntary and facilitating instruments.

Both tourism and sustainable development are subjects that relate to a broad spectrum of topics and a Guide such as this one inevitably makes passing reference to many of them. To assist readers wishing to expand their background knowledge, the final section of the Guide provides a comprehensive list of relevant sources of further information from UNEP and WTO.

Gathering information for the Guide

This document has been informed by looking at a wide variety of different practices by governments around the world, in the development of policies and the application of instruments.

Initially, a postal survey was carried out by the WTO asking governments to submit information about their existing policies and initiatives relating to the sustainability of tourism. This was supplemented by a survey of experts and practitioners known by UNEP and the WTO to be working in this field. They were asked to recommend examples of good practice against a checklist of instruments. A call for examples was also issued through the regional offices of UNEP, at a number of relevant international conferences, and through publications such as the newsletter of The International Ecotourism Society.

Box I.1: Initial motivations and triggers

It is instructive at the outset to consider the kinds of motivational factors that might lead a country or local destination to pay more attention to sustainability issues in its policy making for tourism.

- A fundamental, overarching national policy position, putting sustainability at the top of the public agenda.
  In South Africa, all recent policies seek to support a process of reconstruction and development, with social empowerment and transformation being driving forces.

- A perceived need to change direction from high impact tourism in order to reduce impacts on the local environment and improve quality of the product offer in line with new market trends.
  Calvià (Spain), Mexico and Egypt provide examples of destinations with established or developing coastal resorts and heritage towns where it was realized that better planning and reduced environmental impact were essential for long term economic as well as environmental sustainability.

- A need to back up a tourism product and market position that is based on the appeal of the area's natural environment with policy to underpin its good management and future sustainability.
  In Costa Rica, early success with ecotourism defined the market positioning of the country as a nature based destination and has stimulated an emphasis on sustainability in the country's tourism strategy. In Kaikoura (New Zealand) the focus on environmental management underpins the town's appeal as a green destination based on a stunning coastal setting and a whale watching product. In Scotland and Australia, the initial interest stemmed from the importance of the fine natural environment for the country's tourism.

- The need and opportunity to develop a form of tourism which would bring income to rural communities and benefit conservation, with a supportive policy framework.
  This is the situation in Bulgaria, where individual ecotourism projects were failing through lack of coordination and marketing. In Ghana the creation of a network of community-based tourism projects has raised the level of interest in tourism as a tool for sustainable development and the fight against poverty.

Case Studies

Ten Case Studies have been prepared from the material collected, and are presented at the end of the document. Rather than focusing on individual policies or instruments, they illustrate the more comprehensive approaches adopted by different countries or destinations. They have been chosen to represent different types of destinations, facing a variety of challenges and with contrasting motives for seeking more sustainable tourism. Most employ a range of instruments and the Case Studies illustrate how they can be used together. The Case Studies illustrate a broad range of situations that may be reflected in many other destinations. Linkages to the Case Studies also punctuate the text, at points where they throw additional light on the subject under discussion.

The text is further illustrated by Boxes, like the one below, which describe individual instruments and approaches by giving specific examples from around the world.

Tourism and Sustainability

This chapter examines two basic questions:

- What is meant by making tourism more sustainable? and
- Why should governments be concerned about it?

In developing an answer, the chapter outlines why tourism is in a special position with respect to sustainable development; discusses some of the key challenges that need to be addressed; and reviews the international recognition that is being given to the sustainability of tourism. Using this as a basis, it goes on to outline some guiding principles that should be observed and then presents an agenda for sustainable tourism, in the form of twelve aims. Finally, it is shown that, although visitors and the tourism industry are becoming increasingly responsive to these issues, governments nevertheless have a critical role in creating the context and stimulating actions to ensure that tourism is more sustainable in the future.

1.1 Tourism: dynamism and growth

With 760 million international arrivals recorded in 2004, accounting for almost US$622 billion of receipts, tourism is a major global activity that has grown by 25 per cent in the past 10 years.[1]

Predicted growth rates remain high and, although global and regional patterns have fluctuated from year to year (most recently owing to fears over terrorism, health crises (e.g. SARs) and natural disasters), tourism has shown a strong and rapid ability to recover. More and more people have the desire and means to travel and the World Tourism Organization (WTO) is predicting over 1 500 million international arrivals by 2020, more than double the current level.[2]

Forecasts to the year 2020 predict growth in tourism in all regions of the world, with the strongest relative growth occurring in parts of the developing world. Although Europe, the Americas, and East Asia and the Pacific will account for 80 per cent of total arrivals, and thus continue to dominate in terms of volume, international tourist arrivals to Africa are forecast to grow, on average, by 5.5 per cent per year during this period and those to South Asia by more than 6 per cent, compared with a world average of just over 4 per cent.[3]

International travel is only one aspect of tourism. In many countries, domestic tourism outweighs international arrivals in terms of volume and income generated. This is also predicted to grow strongly.

Tourism is also a major source of employment, supporting 74 million jobs directly according to a World Travel and Tourism Council (WTTC) estimate, and 215 million (8.1 per cent of the world total) if all the indirect economic effects of the sector are taken into account. It represents US$4 218 billion of GDP (10.4 per cent of the world total), with travel and tourism making a particularly significant contribution to international trade, at over 12 per cent of total exports.[4]

1.2 Sustainable development: an evolving agenda

The most commonly used definition of sustainable development is still that given in the report of the World Commission on Environment and Development (1987), i.e. sustainable development is *'a process to meet the needs of the present without compromising the ability of future generations to meet their own needs.'*

Sustainable development is therefore about creating a better life for all people in ways that will be as viable in the future as they are at present. In other words, sustainable development is based on principles of sound husbandry of the world's resources, and on equity in the way those resources are used and in the way in which the benefits obtained from them are distributed.

The concept has evolved since the 1987 definition, notably through Agenda 21, the plan of action which emerged from the UN Conference on Environment and Development (Rio, 1992), and the plan of implementation from the World Summit on Sustainable Development (Johannesburg, 2002). Three dimensions or 'pillars' of sustainable development are now recognized and underlined. These are:

- Economic sustainability, which means generating prosperity at different levels of society and addressing the cost effectiveness of all economic activity. Crucially, it is about the viability of enterprises and activities and their ability to be maintained in the long term.

- Social sustainability, which means respecting human rights and equal opportunities for all in society. It requires an equitable distribution of benefits, with a focus on alleviating poverty. There is an emphasis on local communities, maintaining and strengthening their life support systems, recognizing and respecting different cultures and avoiding any form of exploitation.

- Environmental sustainability, which means conserving and managing resources, especially those that are not renewable or are precious in terms of life support. It requires action to minimize pollution of air, land and water, and to conserve biological diversity and natural heritage.

It is important to appreciate that these three pillars are in many ways interdependent and can be both mutually reinforcing or in competition. Delivering sustainable development means striking a balance between them.

1.3 Tourism and sustainable development: a special relationship

Tourism is in a special position in the contribution it can make to sustainable development and the challenges it presents. Firstly, this is because of the dynamism and growth of the sector, and the major contribution that it makes to the economies of many countries and local destinations. Secondly, it is because tourism is an activity which involves **a special relationship between consumers (visitors), the industry, the environment and local communities**.

This special relationship arises because, unlike most other sectors, the consumer of tourism (the tourist) travels to the producer and the product. This leads to three important and unique aspects of the relationship between tourism and sustainable development:

- Interaction: The nature of tourism, as a service industry that is based on delivering an experience of new places, means that it involves a considerable amount of interaction, both direct and indirect, between visitors, host communities and their local environments.

- Awareness: Tourism makes people (visitors and hosts) become far more conscious of environmental issues and differences between nations and cultures. This can

Tourism and
Sustainability

affect attitudes and concerns for sustainability issues not only while travelling but throughout people's lives.

• Dependency: Much of tourism is based on visitors seeking to experience intact and clean environments, attractive natural areas, authentic historic and cultural traditions, and welcoming hosts with whom they have a good relationship. The industry depends on these attributes being in place.

This close and direct relationship creates a sensitive situation, whereby tourism can be both very damaging but also very positive for sustainable development.

On the positive side, tourism can:

• Provide a growing source of opportunities for enterprise development and employment creation as well as stimulating investment and support for local services, even in quite remote communities.
• Bring tangible economic value to natural and cultural resources. This can result in direct income from visitor spending for their conservation, and an increase in support for conservation from local communities.
• Be a force for inter-cultural understanding and peace.

Conversely, tourism can:

• Place direct pressure on fragile ecosystems causing degradation of the physical environment and disruption to wildlife.
• Exert considerable pressure on host communities and lead to dislocation of traditional societies.
• Compete for the use of scarce resources, notably land and water.
• Be a significant contributor to local and global pollution.
• Be a vulnerable and unstable source of income, as it is often very sensitive to actual or perceived changes to the environmental and social conditions of destinations.

The net result is that all those involved in tourism have a huge responsibility to recognize the importance of its sustainable development. Tourism has immense power to do good. Yet it can also be the vector for the very pressures that may destroy the assets on which it relies. Developed without concern for sustainability, tourism can not only damage societies and the environment, it could also contain the seeds of its own destruction.

For governments, tourism policies that address economic, social and environmental issues, and which are developed with an awareness of the potential both for harm and for benefit, can channel the forces resulting from the sector's dynamic growth in a positive direction. For the tourism industry, accepting this responsibility is not only about good citizenship, it should also be fuelled by a strong element of self-interest, since any harm that is inflicted to the natural, cultural or social environment of destinations can lead to their eventual destruction or loss of value as a tourism product. In economic terms, sustainability can guarantee that crucial factor already mentioned: 'the viability of enterprises and activities and their ability to be maintained in the long term'.

1.4 Making all tourism more sustainable

Some commentators and institutions have implied that sustainable tourism is a particular kind of tourism appealing to a market niche that is sensitive to environmental and social impacts, serviced by particular types of products and operators, and usually—in contrast with high-volume tourism—implying small in scale. This is a dangerous misapprehension. It must be clear that the term 'sustainable tourism'—meaning 'tourism that is based on the principles of sustainable development'—refers to a fundamental objective: to make **all** tourism more sustainable. The term should be used to refer to a condition of tourism, not a type of tourism. Well-managed high-volume tourism can, and ought to be, just as sustainable as small-scale, dispersed special interest tourism.

Box 1.1: The World Tourism Organization's definition of sustainable tourism

Sustainable tourism development guidelines and management practices are applicable to all forms of tourism in all types of destinations, including mass tourism and the various niche tourism segments. Sustainability principles refer to the environmental, economic and socio-cultural aspects of tourism development, and a suitable balance must be established between these three dimensions to guarantee its long-term sustainability.

Thus, sustainable tourism should:

1) Make optimal use of environmental resources that constitute a key element in tourism development, maintaining essential ecological processes and helping to conserve natural resources and biodiversity.

2) Respect the socio-cultural authenticity of host communities, conserve their built and living cultural heritage and traditional values, and contribute to inter-cultural understanding and tolerance.

3) Ensure viable, long-term economic operations, providing socio-economic benefits to all stakeholders that are fairly distributed, including stable employment and income-earning opportunities and social services to host communities, and contributing to poverty alleviation.

Sustainable tourism development requires the informed participation of all relevant stakeholders, as well as strong political leadership to ensure wide participation and consensus building. Achieving sustainable tourism is a continuous process and it requires constant monitoring of impacts, introducing the necessary preventive and/or corrective measures whenever necessary.

Sustainable tourism should also maintain a high level of tourist satisfaction and ensure a meaningful experience to the tourists, raising their awareness about sustainability issues and promoting sustainable tourism practices amongst them.

Moreover, sustainable tourism should not be taken to imply a finite state of tourism. In fact, it is often argued that tourism may never be totally sustainable—sustainable development of tourism is a continuous process of improvement.

Confusion over the meaning of sustainable tourism has been compounded in some countries by use of the term 'ecotourism' as meaning the same as 'sustainable tourism'. Ecotourism does indeed embrace the principles of sustainability, but it refers explicitly to a product niche. It is about tourism in natural areas, normally involving some form of interpretative experience of natural and cultural heritage, positively supporting conservation and indigenous communities, and usually organized for small groups. The development of ecotourism can provide a useful tool within wider strategies towards more sustainable tourism, as was expounded in the Quebec Declaration on Ecotourism, 2002.[5]

The WTO has given the full definition of sustainable tourism presented in Box 1.1 emphasizing the need to make all tourism sustainable. Expressed simply, sustainable tourism can be said to be:

'Tourism that takes full account of its current and future economic, social and environmental impacts, addressing the needs of visitors, the industry, the environment and host communities.'

Making tourism more sustainable means taking these impacts and needs into account in the planning, development and operation of tourism. It is a continual process of improvement and one which applies equally to tourism in cities, resorts, rural and coastal areas, mountains, and protected areas. It can apply to all forms of business and leisure tourism.

1.5 Key challenges for more sustainable tourism

Tourism, like others sectors, faces major global challenges. Five of these are discussed below. Although they do not encompass all of the challenges facing the sector, all are important issues recognized around the world. They serve here to illustrate the range of impacts and opportunities that relate to tourism, and also to highlight some of the many reasons why governments should pay serious attention to its sustainable development.

Managing dynamic growth

The doubling of international tourist movements predicted for the next 15 to 20 years will bring considerable pressures. If serious harm to the very resources on which tourism depends is to be avoided, this growth must be well managed. This will require careful planning of the location and types of new development, improved environmental management practices and influencing consumption patterns.

Certain types of location, including those listed below, are particularly vulnerable to pressure:

- Marine and coastal environments, where badly sited development, poor management of waste from resorts and cruise shipping, and general over-use by

tourists leads to serious loss of amenity and natural habitats.
- Historic towns and cities and cultural heritage sites, where pressures and congestion from visitors and their traffic affect overall amenity and residents' quality of life.
- Fragile natural environments, where even quite low levels of visitation can threaten biodiversity.

Climate change

Climate change is a major issue for the long term sustainability of tourism in two senses: climate change will have consequences for tourism, and tourism is a contributor to climate change.

Effects of climate change, such as rising sea levels, increased frequency and energy of surges and storms, beach erosion, coral bleaching, and disrupted water supply threaten many coastal destinations. Mountain resorts will also suffer, from rising snow lines and shortening winter sports seasons. Changes in temperature and rainfall will affect market appeal in most parts of the world, although in different ways, depending on the interplay of push and pull effects in countries of origin and destination. Tourism may also be affected by other factors such as the spread of tropical diseases and the availability of water. Some of these impacts are already being felt.

It is estimated that tourism may contribute up to 5.3 per cent of global anthropogenic greenhouse gas emissions, with transport accounting for about 90 per cent of this.[6] Estimates suggest that aviation accounts for 2–3 per cent of the world's total use of fossil fuels and up to 3.5 per cent of the anthropogenic greenhouse effect. More than 80 per cent of this is due to civil aviation.[7] Based on current trends, these impacts are set to increase significantly as air transport is one of the fastest growing sources of greenhouse gas emissions.

Poverty alleviation

Halving world poverty by 2015 is the foremost UN Millennium Goal. The potential for tourism to contribute to this reduction is increasingly recognized, partly because it is one of the few sectors in which poor countries' cultural and natural resources give them a comparative economic advantage. The development of tourism provides a good opportunity to help alleviate poverty because it is often a new source of revenue in rural areas, where three-quarters of the world's poor are to be found. It is also a labour intensive activity and one that has low entry barriers. The challenge is to find better ways of channelling visitor spending towards poor people, including through the informal economy.

There is a parallel challenge here: to reverse the tendency for tourism jobs to be low paid. All countries need to ensure that people employed in tourism are properly remunerated, receive proper treatment and are given opportunities for advancement.

Support for conservation

The need to find more financial resources to support conservation is a worldwide issue, although the severity of the problem varies from country to country. Protected

Tourism and
Sustainability

areas in developing countries receive less than 30 per cent of their basic funding needs, and some governments have cut spending on conservation by over 50 per cent in the past decade.

Tourism already makes a major direct contribution to income for protected areas and heritage sites, through entry fees, permits, concessions, etc. and this can be extended. More widely, tourism can become a force for more sustainable land management in all parts of the world by providing an additional or alternative form of livelihood for farmers and rural communities that is dependent on well maintained natural resources.

Health, safety and security

In recent years, uncertainty about the health and safety of travel and of certain destinations has caused significant fluctuations in tourism flows. Although this may be a short term phenomenon and recovery is often fast, it should be regarded as a global issue for the sustainability of tourism. There are policy implications for image, for management of information, and for specific measures to improve the safety and security of tourists.

1.6 International recognition

The importance of tourism to sustainable development and of the need for tourism to integrate sustainability principles has been increasingly recognized in international fora, and echoed in policy statements.

The UN Commission on Sustainable Development, 7th session, 1999

The seventh session of the UN Commission on Sustainable Development (CSD) urged governments to advance the development of sustainable tourism. Particular emphasis was placed on the need for the development of policies, strategies and master plans for sustainable tourism based on Agenda 21, as a way of providing focus and direction for relevant organizations, the private sector and indigenous and local communities. It underlined the need for consultation with all the above stakeholders and for working in partnership with them. It called for capacity building with local communities and for the deployment of a mix of instruments including voluntary initiatives and agreements. Clauses included support for small and medium sized enterprises and appropriate information for tourists.

The WTO Global Code of Ethics for Tourism, 1999

This code was endorsed by the UN General Assembly in 2001 which invited governments and other stakeholders in the tourism sector to consider introducing the contents of the code into relevant laws, regulations and professional practices. The code contains many of the principles of sustainable development of tourism articulated by the CSD and others. It also places particular emphasis on the special role of tourism in contributing to mutual understanding and respect between peoples and as a vehicle for individual and collective fulfilment. Separate articles set out the right to tourism ('The prospect of direct and personal access to the discovery and enjoyment of the planet's resources constitutes a right equally open to all the world's inhabitants') and freedom of movement of tourists, based partly on the Universal Declaration of Human Rights. It also sets out the rights of workers and entrepreneurs in the tourism industry with regard to recognition, training, social welfare and other matters.

Convention on Biological Diversity, Guidelines on Biodiversity and Tourism Development, 2003

These guidelines were adopted in 2003 by the Conference of the Parties to the Convention on Biological Diversity (CBD). Governments are invited to integrate them into the development or review of their strategies and plans for tourism development, national biodiversity strategies and action plans, and other related sectoral strategies, in consultation with interested stakeholders. The guidelines set out a 10-stage process for policy making, development planning and management of tourism in destinations or sites. This includes data gathering, identifying visions and objectives, review of legislation, impact assessment and management, decision making, implementation, monitoring and adaptive management. The guidelines also set out requirements for notification of any intended development and for capacity building to strengthen the overall process.

Quebec Declaration on Ecotourism, 2002

This is the declaration of the World Ecotourism Summit, which was the peak event of the International Year of Ecotourism, 2002, as designated by the United Nations. It sets out recommendations, from the participants in the summit, to governments, the tourism industry and other stakeholders, on the various measures they should take to foster the development of ecotourism. A number of these include recommendations on specific instruments considered elsewhere in this publication. The declaration explicitly recognizes the relevance of approaches developed for ecotourism to the wider task of making all tourism more sustainable.

World Summit on Sustainable Development, Johannesburg, 2002

In its Plan of Implementation, the WSSD specifically called for the promotion of sustainable tourism as one of a number of strategies for protecting and managing the natural resource base of economic and social development. Although not very prescriptive, the plan (in its Article 43) places emphasis on international cooperation, technical assistance to communities, visitor management and improved market access. Tourism development was also specifically referred to amongst measures for the sustainable development of small island states and for Africa, and in relation to the management of energy and biodiversity conservation.

1.7 Guiding principles and approaches

The development and implementation of policies for sustainable tourism should be based on a number of overarching principles and approaches. Some of these are inherent to the principles of sustainability while others have been identified over time by those working in the field. Guiding concepts and principles are presented below.

Tourism and Sustainability

Setting the course

Taking a holistic view

Planning and development of tourism should not take place in isolation. Tourism should be considered as part of the sustainable development of communities, alongside other activities. Its impact on other sectors, in terms of competing resource use and mutual support, should be considered. Over-dependency of an economy and society on tourism should be avoided. A holistic approach is also about taking account of all impacts and relationships within the tourism sector itself, and considering how all public policies may affect or be affected by tourism.

Pursuing multi-stakeholder engagement

Sustainable tourism is about local control, but also about working together. All those implicated by tourism should have an opportunity to influence its development and management. This may involve formal partnerships or looser arrangements, as well as strengthening and utilizing local democratic structures.

Planning for the long term

Short term approaches should be avoided and the long-term view encouraged, with resources committed accordingly. Where possible, actions should be self-sustaining. Projects that are structured around short term inputs and finance must take account of how initiatives, once started, can be maintained into the future.

Addressing global and local impacts

Impacts on the local environment and communities are often apparent. It can therefore be easier to gain support for policies that address these local impacts rather than for policies that address global issues. However, the sustainable development of tourism should pay equal attention to global impacts, especially with respect to pollution from tourism (such as greenhouse gas emissions) and the use of non-renewable resources. Such global impacts also have a direct effect on tourism itself (e.g. climate change).

Promoting sustainable consumption

Sustainability is not just about the supply side. Equal consideration should be given to influencing the pattern and impact of consumption. This means influencing the volume and nature of tourism demand, the choices made by tourists (such as products selected and mode of travel), and their activities and behaviour.

Equating sustainability and quality

It should be increasingly accepted that a quality tourism destination or product is one that addresses the full range of sustainability issues rather than simply concentrating on visitor satisfaction. Indeed, tourists should themselves be encouraged to think in these terms—a place that cares for the environment and its workforce is more likely also to care for them.

Developing the approach

Reflecting all impacts in costs—polluter pays principle

Under the polluter pays principle it is the perpetrator of environmental impacts who bears the responsibility for costs incurred which, where possible, should be reflected in financial costs. This principle has strong implications both for policies and for the use of economic instruments to influence consumption and pollution. In tourism it has implications, for example, for charges for activities such as transport, admission to sites and waste disposal.

Minimizing risk taking—precautionary principle

Careful risk assessment is an important component of sustainable tourism development. Where there is limited evidence about the possible impact of a development or action, a cautious approach should be adopted. The precautionary principle means putting in place measures to avoid damage before it occurs rather than trying to repair it afterwards.

Taking a life cycle perspective

Life-cycle assessment means taking full account of impacts over the entire life of a product or service, including initial resources used, siting and design, development and construction, all inputs to its operation, and disposal and after-use implications.

Considering functional alternatives

Consideration should be given to whether the same function can be performed and the same result achieved by doing things in a way that has more positive and less negative impacts on resources. For example, in a strategy to improve visitor satisfaction by adding further recreational opportunities, preference should be given to those options that bring the least environmental and social impacts and the highest economic returns.

Respecting limits

The readiness and ability to limit the amount of tourism development or the volume of tourist flows in a destination or site are central to the concept of sustainable tourism. Limiting factors may be ecological resilience, resource capacity, community concerns, visitor satisfaction, etc. These factors should be taken into account in setting limits that are respected by all concerned.

Ensuring ongoing progress

Adapting to changing conditions

Adaptive response and management is an important aspect of sustainable development. Tourism is sensitive to external conditions in terms of its performance and the level of its impact. Global threats, such as climate change and terrorism need to be considered in planning for future tourism and in introducing risk management policies.

Undertaking continuous monitoring using indicators

Sound management of tourism requires readily available evidence of changes in impact over time, so that adjustments to policies and actions can be made. Indicators that relate to sustainability aims and objectives should be established to monitor the condition, performance and impact of tourism. Cost effective monitoring programmes should be put in place.

1.8 An agenda for sustainable tourism

Consideration of the general concept of sustainable development, the special position of tourism and the agreements reached at international fora, helps to set an agenda for more sustainable tourism.

This agenda needs to embrace two, interrelated, elements of the sustainability of tourism:

- the ability of tourism to continue as an activity in the future, ensuring that the conditions are right for this; and
- the ability of society and the environment to absorb and benefit from the impacts of tourism in a sustainable way.

Based on this, an agenda for sustainable tourism can be articulated as a set of twelve aims that address economic, social and environmental impacts. The agenda formulated in this way can then be used as a framework to develop policies for more sustainable tourism that recognize the two directions in which tourism policy can exert an influence:

- minimizing the negative impacts of tourism on society and the environment; and
- maximizing tourism's positive and creative contribution to local economies, the conservation of natural and cultural heritage, and the quality of life of hosts and visitors.

The twelve aims for an agenda for sustainable tourism are:

1) Economic Viability
   To ensure the viability and competitiveness of tourism destinations and enterprises, so that they are able to continue to prosper and deliver benefits in the long term.

2) Local Prosperity
   To maximize the contribution of tourism to the economic prosperity of the host destination, including the proportion of visitor spending that is retained locally.

3) Employment Quality
   To strengthen the number and quality of local jobs created and supported by tourism, including the level of pay, conditions of service and availability to all without discrimination by gender, race, disability or in other ways.

4) Social Equity
   To seek a widespread and fair distribution of economic and social benefits from tourism throughout the recipient community, including improving opportunities, income and services available to the poor.

5) Visitor Fulfillment
   To provide a safe, satisfying and fulfilling experience for visitors, available to all without discrimination by gender, race, disability or in other ways.

6) Local Control

To engage and empower local communities in planning and decision making about the management and future development of tourism in their area, in consultation with other stakeholders.

7) Community Wellbeing

To maintain and strengthen the quality of life in local communities, including social structures and access to resources, amenities and life support systems, avoiding any form of social degradation or exploitation.

8) Cultural Richness

To respect and enhance the historic heritage, authentic culture, traditions and distinctiveness of host communities.

9) Physical Integrity

To maintain and enhance the quality of landscapes, both urban and rural, and avoid the physical and visual degradation of the environment.

10) Biological Diversity

To support the conservation of natural areas, habitats and wildlife, and minimize damage to them.

11) Resource Efficiency

To minimize the use of scarce and non-renewable resources in the development and operation of tourism facilities and services.

12) Environmental Purity

To minimize the pollution of air, water and land and the generation of waste by tourism enterprises and visitors.

The order in which these twelve aims are listed does not imply any order of priority. Each one is equally important.

Many of the aims relate to a combination of environmental, economic and social issues and impacts, as illustrated by Figure 1.1 and by the examples below:

* Economic viability of tourism depends strongly on maintaining the quality of the local environment.
* Visitor fulfilment is about meeting visitors' needs and providing opportunities (a social aim), but is also very important for economic sustainability.
* Cultural richness is often considered to be in the social sphere of sustainability, but it has a strong bearing on environmental aspects in terms of the built environment and cultural dimensions of society's interaction with nature.
* Community wellbeing, which can be seen mainly as a social aim, is strongly related to environmental resource management, for example with respect to access to fresh water.
* Employment quality and social equity issues, such as poverty alleviation, relate closely to both economic and social sustainability issues.

Figure 1.1: Relationship between the 12 aims and the pillars of sustainability

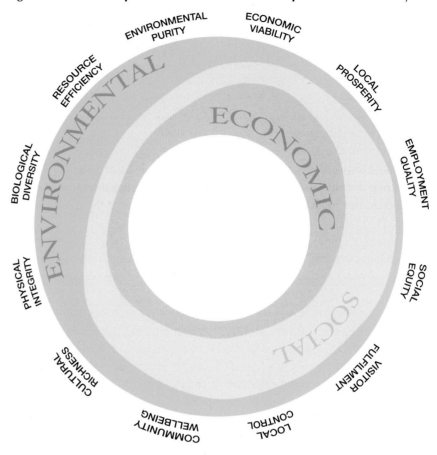

1.9 Governments, the market and the industry's view

Governments should recognize that interest in the sustainability of tourism is growing amongst many private sector enterprises and within visitor markets. They should take account of this when seeking to persuade the tourism industry to take sustainability more seriously, pointing out the advantages for attracting new business and the overall profitability of a more sustainable approach.

Understanding tourists' attitudes—more than a niche market response

Governments need to understand what is important to tourists if they are to influence their behaviour effectively. It has been suggested that tourists are not generally interested in the sustainability of the trips they take, and that this is a major constraint on the pursuit of more sustainable tourism. However, the interpretation of tourist response depends on the nature of the questions asked.

For example, although studies of the ecotourism market (e.g. those carried out by the WTO[8]) have concluded that this is indeed a small (albeit growing) niche market, such surveys attempted specifically to identify tourists and tour operators that were looking for, or selling, special interest holidays involving nature observation and concern for conservation as a primary motivation for the trip. Wider surveys that have attempted to assess the degree to which general consumers are interested in the interrelationship between their activities as tourists and the environment and host communities (rather than their response to the concept of sustainability as a whole) suggest a far wider relevance in the market place. They point to:

- Very high levels of concern for environment and society in destinations, where the issue is likely to directly affect the tourist's own wellbeing (e.g. cleanness of the water and levels of safety).
- High and growing levels of interest by tourists in visiting natural and cultural sites during their holidays, and the authenticity and educational value of such experiences. This applies to general holidaymakers as well as to those with a specialist interest.
- Large numbers of tourists expressing concern about the impact of their travelling, both through their own actions and in their choice of tour operator or service provider.
- Considerable willingness to pay more to support local environments and communities.

Some statistical evidence backing up these conclusions is presented in Box 1.2.

Despite this positive feedback, it is important to be realistic about the balance of influences on holiday choice. Visitor surveys and practical experience suggest that overall perceived attractiveness of a destination, climate, convenience, quality of facilities, and price still far outweigh concerns for the impact of travel. However, the latter concerns do make a difference to holiday choices if the former factors are considered equal. It also appears that tourists are more likely to be concerned about impacts on the local environment and the quality of life of their hosts than about global issues. Finally, there is less evidence that tourists have actually taken actions to change their travel and consumption patterns, despite their expressed concern and interest.

The challenge therefore remains to provide more leadership, incentives and information to ensure a genuine response. In line with the broad approach advocated in this Guide, the strategy should be to encourage all tourists to be more aware of the impacts of their travelling and be more interested and concerned about host populations, rather than to try to seek out the 'sustainable tourist'.

Corporate Social Responsibility in the tourism sector

There is a general trend amongst private sector businesses to recognize their responsibilities to society beyond their traditional functions of generating wealth and profit. Governments can use this growing awareness when developing industry-related policies and activities and as a lever to achieve industry involvement and buy-in.

In companies, the concept of Corporate Social Responsibility (CSR) means adopting transparent business practices that are based on ethical values. It has started to gain ground and many companies already include social and environmental commitments in their core mission statements. Some adopt triple bottom line reporting, whereby social and environmental results are measured and reported next to financial results.

Box 1.2: Statistical evidence of market response

a) Anxieties about visitors' own wellbeing
- 83 per cent of British package holidaymakers say that a dirty beach or polluted sea matter a great deal to them when choosing a destination. 74 per cent are similarly influenced by levels of crime, and 62 per cent by incidence of local illness.[9]
- 60 per cent of German tourists are concerned about litter, 51 per cent about noise pollution and 46 per cent about good nature protection in the destination.[10]

b) Interest in a diversified experience
- 61 per cent of US tourists are looking for travel experiences involving well-preserved natural, historical or cultural sites. 53 per cent agree that they have a better travel experience when they learn as much as possible about their destination's customs, geography and culture.[11]
- Three in four British tourists agree that their trip should include experiences of local culture and food.[12]

c) Concern for the impact of their actions
- Three-quarters of US travellers feel that it is important that their visits do not damage the environment.[13]
- 51 per cent of British tourists say that food or water shortages for local residents matter a great deal to them in their choice of destination.[14]
- 65 per cent of British tourists feel that the reputation of the holiday company on environmental issues is important.[15]
- 82 per cent of Dutch tourists believe that integrating environmental information into travel brochures is a good idea.[16]

d) Willingness to pay more
- 53 per cent of British tourists would be prepared to pay more for their holiday in order that workers in the destination could be guaranteed good wages and working conditions. 45 per cent would be prepared to do so to support preservation of the local environment and reverse the negative environmental effects of tourism. The average additional sum indicated is about 5 per cent of the holiday price.[17]
- 69 per cent of Danish tourists staying in eco-labelled hotels are willing to pay more for such hotels owing to their environmental designation.

In the tourism sector, some companies now have an environmental management system and have established foundations or other mechanisms for supporting social and environmental projects in the communities in which they operate.

Tour operators have been quite active in embracing sustainability principles in the design of tour programmes, selection of suppliers, work with local communities, and information for tourists, but this has applied mainly to smaller, specialist operators. Networks of operators committed to this approach exist in France, Germany, the Netherlands and some other countries. The Tour Operators' Initiative, supported by UNEP, UNESCO and the WTO, has members from a number of different countries and has pioneered good sustainability practice, both by tour operators and within the destinations in which they operate[18].

The response of small independent service providers is difficult to determine. Their reaction to issues such as environmental management often depends on the personal interest of the proprietor. The proportion of individual accommodation enterprises participating in eco-labelling (certification) is only between 1 and 10 per cent of the total of enterprises in countries where labelling exists. Nevertheless, there are some really excellent examples of individual enterprises supporting local environment and community projects. Governments can play a crucial role in stimulating widespread recognition and response across the industry.

1.10 The crucial role of government

Governments have a crucial role to play in the development and management of tourism and in making it more sustainable. The level of government engagement in tourism varies considerably across the world. Contacts with governments on sustainability nevertheless reveal that most are, at least nominally, seeking to pursue sustainable tourism. This applies equally to developed and developing countries, though the emphasis may be different. In developing countries, interest in sustainable tourism is more likely to be linked to poverty alleviation and the funding of conservation; in the developed world, issues of rejuvenation and visitor management are more prominent.

Whatever the motivation of governments, their role relates only partly to their own actions. Tourism is primarily an activity carried out by private sector enterprises, and it is their actions, together with those of tourists, that are responsible for most impacts, positive and negative. A primary function of government in fostering more sustainable tourism is therefore to create an environment that enables or influences the private sector to operate more sustainably, and influences patterns of visitor flows and behaviour so as to maximize the benefits and minimize the negative impacts of tourism.

The key reasons for the importance of the role of government are as follows:

- Much of the sustainability agenda is about areas of public rather than private concern. Although the private sector is beginning to recognize its responsibility, it cannot, on its own, be expected to take a lead on these issues.
- In all countries, the tourism sector is fragmented into many thousands of businesses, mainly micro or small enterprises. Collectively their actions can make a difference, while individually they cannot, so coordination is needed. Furthermore, very small businesses often need external support and advice if they are to change their operations successfully to meet a new agenda.
- Governments are responsible for many functions that are fundamentally important to the sustainable development of tourism, such as land use planning, labour and environmental regulations, and the provision of infrastructure and social and environmental services.
- Many governments are already actively engaged in supporting tourism through marketing, information services, education and in other ways, often through joint public-private frameworks. These functions need to continue and to be more closely aligned with sustainability objectives.

These arguments and functions are applicable at both national and local government levels.

In many countries, many of the objectives and actions that governments are pursuing can be said to be in line with sustainability, and there is considerable recent interest in relating tourism policies to wider sustainable development or poverty reduction strategies. However, as has already been pointed out, the understanding of what the sustainable development of tourism entails, and even the terminology, is not consistent between governments. A more systematic approach to link sustainability aims and principles to policies and tools is needed.

Notes

1 WTO World Tourism Barometer, June 2005.
2 WTO Tourism 2020 Vision, 2004.
3 WTO Tourism 2020 Vision, 2004.
4 WTTC, World Travel and Tourism Forging Ahead, 2004.
5 The definition of ecotourism promoted by The International Ecotourism Society is 'responsible travel to natural areas that conserves the environment and sustains the well-being of local people'. The Quebec Declaration on Ecotourism (2002) recognizes that ecotourism embraces the following specific principles which distinguish it from the wider concept of sustainable tourism:
   • Contributes actively to the conservation of natural and cultural heritage;
   • Includes local and indigenous communities in its planning, development and operation, and contributes to their well-being;
   • Interprets the natural and cultural heritage of the destination to visitors;
   • Lends itself better to independent travellers, as well as to organized tours for small size groups.
6 Gössling, S. (2002) Global environmental consequences of tourism. Global Environmental Change 12, 283 – 302.
7 International Panel on Climate Change, Special Report on Aviation and the Global Atmosphere (Penner et al.,1999).
8 WTO surveys, conducted in seven countries in 2001, indicated that this market niche accounted for no more than 2–5 per cent of organised or packaged leisure tourism.
9 ABTA survey, 2002.
10 Ecotrans/FUR Reiseanalyse, 2002.
11 Travel Industry Association of America and National Geographic Traveller, The Geotourism Study 2002.
12 Harold Goodwin and Justin Francis 'Ethical and responsible tourism: consumer trends in the UK', Journal of Vacation Marketing, Vol 9(3), 2003.
13 Travel Industry Association of America and National Geographic Traveller The Geotourism Study 2002.
14 ABTA survey, 2002.
15 Goodwin and Francis (2003).
16 FEMATOUR market study, 2000.
17 ABTA survey, 2002.
18 The Tour Operators' Initiative is a voluntary network of tour operators committed to integrate sustainable development in their operations. For more information visit http://www.toinitiative.org.

Policy Implications
of a Sustainable Tourism Agenda

The previous chapter presented twelve aims for sustainable tourism. In this chapter, the aims are used to identify **policy areas** to be addressed so that specific policies and actions to meet the aims can be formulated. The focus is on policy areas rather than on specific policies as it is governments and their partners who will develop the actual policies appropriate to local circumstances.

All of the policy areas identified relate to the overall performance and impact of tourism and are therefore areas in which both national and local governments and other stakeholders are, or should be, interested. In many cases, actions on the ground will be taken by the private sector. The role of government is to develop and implement policies that create an enabling environment, encouraging such actions and influencing them towards sustainability.

2.1 Economic Viability

To ensure the viability and competitiveness of tourism destinations and enterprises, so that they are able to continue to prosper and deliver benefits in the long term

Successful tourism businesses are vital if the sector is to deliver tangible benefits to host populations. Despite growing global tourism markets, many enterprises struggle and there is a considerable rate of business turnover in the sector. Many of the businesses may be micro, small and medium-sized enterprises (MSMEs) with limited skills and market access. There are also numerous examples around the world, especially in developing countries, of projects aiming at delivering sustainable tourism products (sometimes initiated or supported by NGOs or donors) that fail through lack of good, long term business assessment and planning.

Policy areas to address:

Understanding the market

The viability of tourism destinations and individual enterprises depends on an ability to identify markets that will continue to deliver business in the long term; to understand what potential consumers are looking for; and to adapt to trends and changes in source market conditions, travel patterns and tastes. This requires effective and ongoing market research to guide tourism development in the destination as a whole, and realistic market assessment for individual project proposals.

Delivering visitor satisfaction

Long-term viability needs satisfied visitors who return and who recommend others to visit. This means delivering an experience that meets or exceeds expectations. It requires:

- An emphasis on the quality of every component of the visitor experience, including mechanisms for checking, identifying and improving it.
- Attention to value for money and the overall competitiveness of the destination.
- Obtaining regular feedback from visitors.

Maintaining good trading conditions

A number of factors need to be in place if trading is to be carried out successfully and tourism enterprises are to remain viable. These include:

- An enterprise culture and a stable business climate. There should, therefore, be no unnecessary regulatory burdens on enterprises or administrative inefficiency, and the taxation system must be fair. A stable and supportive political climate is a prerequisite for economic sustainability.
- Effective market access and promotion. Enterprises must be able to maintain cost effective ways of communicating with markets, directly or through intermediaries. For small, individual enterprises, this is often a significant challenge which can

be eased through working in partnership and through channels developed at destination level. Opportunities include adapting to new forms of market access and making the best possible use of information technology.

- A reliable labour supply. In many parts of the world, staff recruitment has proved to be a considerable problem for tourism enterprises. This may be addressed by policies relating to employment quality (discussed further under Aim 2.3, below).
- Good accessibility. Reasonably swift and inexpensive access to markets is often a key determinant of the viability of tourism enterprises. This is a particular issue in many developing countries where road access may be poor and other transport options limited, and where the cost and convenience of air services is a primary determining factor for a destination's competitiveness. The requirement for accessibility may be in conflict with the need to minimize environmental pollution from tourism transport (discussed under Aim 2.12, below) and a balance will need to be struck. Other aspects of accessibility, such as telecommunications, are also key factors in some developing countries.

Maintaining and projecting an attractive destination

The viability of individual enterprises is also considerably affected by how the destination as a whole is perceived by visitors. Three critical aspects of this are:

- A positive and consistent image. Effective destination branding, promotion of the brand and the ability to ensure that the nature and quality of experience match the brand image have become principal concerns of many tourism destinations in recent years. Media management is an important part of this.
- Safety and security. Viable destinations need to be safe and secure, and to be perceived as such. This requires attention to matters such as levels of policing, health care available to visitors, quality of information available and support services for visitors in need of assistance. Travel advice relating to safety, issued by governments in source countries, can have a considerable impact on the performance of the tourism economy in recipient countries.
- Overall environmental quality. The attractiveness of the natural and cultural environment in a destination and the general level of amenity and maintenance are of fundamental importance to the viability of tourism enterprises. When asked how the public sector can best support their business, tourism enterprises often suggest that a highest priority should be given to maintaining an attractive environment. As already pointed out, the importance of the environment to the economic sustainability of the industry is a particular feature of tourism.

Delivering business support

Enterprise viability can be underpinned by policies on business services, such as training or advice in management and marketing skills. It is important that these are tailored to needs. A particular requirement for long-term economic sustainability is to avoid a culture of dependency on financial assistance. Funding schemes should be designed to help businesses and projects towards self-sufficiency.

2.2 Local Prosperity

To maximize the contribution of tourism to the economic prosperity of the host destination, including the proportion of visitor spending that is retained locally

Ensuring that economic benefits are secured at the place where costs are incurred is an important principle of sustainable development. As local communities have to meet a number of external costs associated with tourism, it is important that policies seek to maximize the economic returns to the community. This is partly about securing reliable tourism growth, but equally about processes to maximize visitor spending per head and to reduce leakages, as well as developing linkages in the local economy. The fact that tourists, and the enterprises that serve them, make a very large number of purchases from a range of suppliers (tour operators, food producers, transport services, guides, etc.) means that there are often many opportunities to strengthen the level of income retained locally.

Local prosperity means ensuring that tourism is well integrated within the economy and is developed alongside other sectors. It is also important to avoid over-dependency on tourism, while ensuring that it can provide a consistent and reliable source of income.

Policy areas to address:

Reducing leakages

Leakages can occur through the repatriation of profits by external investors or owners; by purchases made by tourists outside the destination (i.e. from international tour operators); and by purchases by tourists and enterprises of imported goods. Second round leakages may occur if income earned within a community is spent outside of it. Policies may seek to:

- Support locally owned businesses. When businesses are locally owned, a higher proportion of profits is likely to be retained within the community. In many areas, locally owned businesses are likely to be MSMEs, and policies in support of them may point to capacity building and financial support programmes specifically related to their needs. This should be weighed against the advantages that external or multinational business may bring in terms of investment, skills, employment generation, etc.
- Ensure that a fair proportion of total travel expenditure is received locally. International tour operators have a very important role to play in the effective promotion of tourism and in reaching new markets, but they should not take an undue proportion of total visitor spending. The Internet has provided new opportunities for direct contact and booking, enabling a higher percentage of holiday spending to be retained locally. In the face of this, international tour operators will need to actively demonstrate the added value they can offer in terms of market access, creative programmes and visitor assurance.
- Encourage employment of local labour. This can have a significant effect on local prosperity. It has further policy implications relating to nurturing and facilitating a local labour supply, such as the local provision of education and training, transport to work, etc. (see Aim 2.3).

Strengthening links between businesses

Strengthening links between businesses means addressing the local supply chain. Policies may seek to:

- Encourage and facilitate local sourcing of supplies. Tour operators should be encouraged to use locally based service providers and products that are most likely to benefit local communities. Service providers should be encouraged to undertake an audit of sources used (such as food producers) and to seek to maximize the proportion of local suppliers. Using local products can greatly enhance the authenticity of the tourist offer and the multiplier effect of tourism in local economies. Achieving a consistent supply of high quality local goods can be a challenge, but is necessary to reduce the need for imported goods and thus reduce leakages. This can be facilitated by the creation of wholesale markets or consortia.
- Encourage clusters and networking of businesses. This means getting businesses to work more closely together, thereby achieving more for themselves and for the local community. It can be achieved through planning policies that encourage geographical clustering and through capacity building or marketing to support trade associations. Networks may be formed between similar service providers, for mutual support and cost and benefit sharing; between providers of different kinds of tourism service, to strengthen packaging of offers; and between enterprises in different sectors (e.g. between accommodation operators and suppliers of food or handicrafts), to strengthen the supply chain.
- Recognize the needs of multiple occupations, including tourism. Many parts of the world have a tradition of local people being involved in a variety of different occupations at the same time, either as employees or running a number of businesses together, sometimes on the same land holding. This can fit well with the seasonal nature of tourism. Supporting such activity is very much in line with the holistic principles of sustainable development. Policies relating to taxation and business practice should facilitate and not penalize this.

Influencing levels of visitor spending

Local prosperity can be strengthened by demand-side policies, which seek to:

- Attract higher spending markets. Some market segments are more likely than others to spend money within destinations visited.
- Increase length of stay as well as the availability of spending opportunities and visitors' awareness of them. This can be achieved by promoting longer-stay markets and encouraging existing visitors to stay longer, at the time or on return visits. It may involve seeking an optimum level of attractions, events and other activities and outlets to retain visitor interest. Extending the opening hours of attractions can also make a difference. The provision of effective local information services can increase visitors' awareness of places to visit and things to do, thereby raising the level of spending.
- Promote the purchasing of local products. This means strengthening the whole retailing process as well as the quality, price, distribution and display of local products such as food, drink and handicrafts.

2.3 Employment Quality

To strengthen the number and quality of local jobs created and supported by tourism, including the level of pay, conditions of service and availability to all without discrimination by gender, race, disability or in other ways

Providing employment is one of the major ways in which tourism can contribute to the quality of life in host communities. However, in spite of the importance of human resources in tourism and the sector's contribution to the global economy, tourism jobs are often quite low paid, with poor conditions and little security of employment. This is partly due to the fragmentation of the sector which is characterized by seasonal, part-time and often family-based employment, but also to the view that service industry jobs are non-professional or casual work. There is a very high turnover of workers in some sectors of the industry. Improved conditions for workers can lead to better performance, increased staff retention, and greater efficiency and productivity. The resulting change in staff-customer relationships can lead to greater satisfaction with the overall holiday experience.

Policy areas to address:

Increasing employment opportunities and the proportion of year round, full-time jobs

High priority should be given to the creation of jobs that are stable, permanent and full-time, and that provide fair salaries and benefits. One of the main reasons why the tourism sector fails to deliver quality employment is the significant seasonal nature of demand in many destinations. This calls for clear policies to extend the season through measures such as: targeting markets most likely to travel in the off-season; discounted seasonal offers; organizing events at less busy times of the year; encouraging attractions to stay open longer; and seeking to influence the root causes of seasonality, such as the timing of the school year.

Where year-round full-time employment cannot be achieved, alternative solutions may prove possible. For instance, working hours could be adapted to suit seasonal patterns while maintaining benefits, or seasonal workers could be ensured jobs with the same employers each season.

Ensuring and enforcing labour regulations

At a minimum, the International Labour Organization's (ILO) 'core labour standards' should be observed in all countries, irrespective of their level of development. These standards, which reflect basic human rights, stipulate: the right of workers to associate and to bargain collectively; the prohibition of forced labour and of exploitative child labour; and non-discrimination in employment.

Equity issues associated with sustainable development suggest that good employment practice goes beyond these core standards, promoting economic and social welfare, and leading to the improvement of living standards and the satisfaction of basic

Box 2.1: Principles for good employment practice

Employment promotion
Promoting full, productive and freely chosen employment.

Equality of opportunity and treatment
Eliminating any discrimination based on race, colour, sex, religion, political opinion, national extraction or social origin.
Accommodating the cultural customs, traditions and practices of employees.

Security of employment
Offering formal employment contracts and focusing on the long-term development of tourism enterprises.

Training
Encouraging skill formulation and development, complemented by vocational training and guidance closely linked with employment.

Conditions of work and life
Providing the best possible wages, benefits and conditions of work within the framework of government policies. Employee benefits can be extended to include contributions to health care, disability, maternity, education and retirement, where these are not legally mandated. Amenities such as housing, food and medical care should be provided where needed and should be of a good standard. Service charge distribution should be a well-documented and transparent process.

Minimum age
Respecting the minimum age for admission to employment or work in order to secure the effective abolition of child labour.

Safety and health
Providing adequate safety and health standards and programmes for employees.

needs. A set of principles, reflecting such good practice, and based on the ILO's Tripartite Declaration of Principles, is given in Box 2.1.

It is important to set labour standards that can be realistically attained by both domestic and international operators, providing a level playing field between them and ensuring maximum compliance by everyone.

Encouraging enterprises to provide skills training programmes and career advancement

A high quality, loyal labour force is a great asset to an enterprise and to the reputation of a destination. This can be achieved through investment in skill development and vocational training, and reinforced by occupational development and opportunities for promotion and advancement. Policies should be concerned with:

- Influencing enterprises to provide training, e.g. through incentives.
- Establishing publicly driven and supported human resource development and training programmes, in local destinations or for groups of enterprises.

- Working with national technical and vocational schools to improve their standards and outreach.

Concern for the wellbeing of workers who lose their jobs

The tourism sector is particularly vulnerable to many kinds of crisis—including disease, natural disasters, war and terrorism—that can occur without warning and have an immediate effect. Many workers including, but not only, the high numbers of part-time or casual workers may have no right to benefit or support when jobs are withdrawn. This could be overcome by introducing contracts that require adequate provision for advance notice of termination of employment, severance pay, etc. Government policy on social security support for people made redundant is also relevant here.

2.4 Social Equity

To seek a widespread and fair distribution of economic and social benefits from tourism throughout the recipient community, including improving opportunities, income and services available to the poor

Tourism policies concerned with social equity should seek to benefit disadvantaged people by delivering economic and social benefits to them. A particular focus should be on tackling poverty, an aim that is given clear prominence in international declarations and related agendas for sustainable development. However, policies should also address a wider constituency and aim to improve the circumstances of those who have been historically disadvantaged or who have limited access to power. For example, in many developing countries, indigenous and traditional communities can be said to be historically disadvantaged, and there is often a need to improve the position of women and the income earning options open to them. Social equity is also an issue in developed countries, an example being the need to provide opportunities for unemployed urban youth.

There are many reasons why tourism is well placed to reach disadvantaged people, mainly because it is a labour intensive service industry with relatively low entry barriers and an activity that takes place in situ within communities. In addition to bringing income, the interaction it entails between people can bolster dignity and self-esteem.

Policy areas[1] to address:

Developing income earning opportunities for disadvantaged people

Policies relating to local prosperity and employment quality are relevant here, but should be more focused and extended when seeking especially to benefit disadvantaged people. Areas of action include:

- Encouraging employment practices that provide opportunities for disadvantaged people. Factors that can have a positive effect include locating new enterprises closer to poor areas; providing education and training that is relevant and accessible to disadvantaged people in such areas; and adopting open recruitment policies.
- Engaging disadvantaged people more directly in the supply of goods and services.

This means encouraging tourism enterprises to pay particular attention to the nature of their sources, and to work with poor communities (e.g. marginal farming communities) on developing reliable supply streams for the tourism industry.

- Bringing more benefit to the informal economy from tourism. Disadvantaged people often gain access to visitors and seek to earn income from them through activities such as street trading, personal guiding services or providing simple accommodation, etc. This can be strengthened through capacity building, attention to quality, licensing, better information for tourists, etc.

- Supporting the development of enterprises by disadvantaged people. This requires policies to encourage the development of small, individual or community-owned tourism businesses within disadvantaged communities. There are many good examples of joint ventures between private operators and disadvantaged communities; policies should seek to provide the right conditions for such ventures.

Utilizing income from tourism to support social programmes

Income from tourism can be used to tackle social issues and benefit disadvantaged people indirectly, whether or not they are themselves engaged in the sector. This can involve development of pools of funding that can then be directed towards social and community schemes, such as education, health and social welfare. Funds can be raised by:

- Taxation or compulsory levies or charges on tourists or tourism enterprises.
- Voluntary giving and sponsorship by tourists or by tourism enterprises, including help in kind.

Investment in tourism in a destination area can result in the provision of additional services, such as water, electricity and health care, which can be of particular benefit to disadvantaged communities.

2.5 Visitor Fulfilment

To provide a safe, satisfying and fulfilling experience for visitors, available to all without discrimination by gender, race, disability or in other ways

The social dimension and equity principles associated with sustainable development should apply to tourists as well as to the host population. The great recreational and educational benefits brought by tourism should be respected and made as widely available as possible without discrimination. This implies viewing visitor satisfaction and fulfilment as an aim in its own right, rather than simply as a means to economic benefit. It is also about the responsibilities that destinations have towards the wellbeing of their guests.

Policy areas to address:

Improving access for all

Improving access for all means ensuring that tourism facilities and infrastructure are accessible and usable by people with disabilities[2]. It should be borne in mind that, in most countries, a large part of the population is affected in some way by disability—for instance having a disabled person within the family group. Consideration needs to be given both to those with physical disabilities, including wheelchair users, and to those with sensory and learning difficulties. Good physical access can also benefit other categories, such as families with small children. Issues to address include the design and layout of buildings and sites, access to public transport, and the provision of effective information to such groups.

Providing holiday opportunities for the economically and socially disadvantaged

Low income or other social disadvantages affect many people's ability to take holidays. Policy in this area should aim to provide people with opportunities to take inexpensive holidays. This may be particularly relevant when seeking to provide recreational and vacation opportunities for the domestic population in developing countries. Policies could address pricing, including differential pricing for disadvantaged groups. People without cars are also often disadvantaged where tourism facilities are not accessible by public transport.

Maintaining a duty of care to visitors

Duty of care to visitors means being concerned for their safety and security in the destination and in enterprises. Issues include fire prevention, health and hygiene, awareness raising, prevention and preparedness for disasters (natural and industrial) adaptation to the effects of natural hazards and protection from crime and terrorism. Ensuring accuracy of marketing and information and avoiding misleading and false descriptions are other important aspects. There should also be clear procedures for registering and handling visitors' complaints and for solving problems that they encounter such as loss of possessions or the need for emergency medical attention.

Monitoring and addressing visitor satisfaction and the quality of experience

Policies that seek to promote quality and to monitor and deliver visitor satisfaction in general are relevant to this aim. This includes maintaining a regular survey of visitors to destinations and encouraging enterprises to obtain feedback from their guests.

Although tourists' motivations for travel vary, particular attention should be paid to encouraging and enabling them to learn about and appreciate the cultures and environments they visit. This is an important part of meeting the aim of visitor fulfilment; it also assists in meeting other aims relating to social and environmental impact within the host destination.

2.6 Local Control

To engage and empower local communities in planning and decision making about the management and future development of tourism in their area, in consultation with other stakeholders

Giving people responsibility and control over their lives is a fundamental principle of sustainable development. Moreover, tourism projects that engage local communities directly in their planning and implementation are much more likely to be successful in delivering local benefits and to be sustained over time. Policy in this area is not, however, just about engagement through consultation processes; it is also about empowering communities to influence decisions about the developments and activities that will affect their future while enabling the needs of other legitimate interests to be taken into account.

Policy areas to address:

Ensuring appropriate engagement and empowerment of local communities

Given the widely differing social structures and forms of governance around the world, it is difficult to be prescriptive about ensuring appropriate engagement and empowerment. However, in principle, decisions should be made about tourism development at the lowest appropriate level of governance. Where it is appropriate to make decisions centrally, the local stakeholders affected should be consulted and encouraged to participate. It is important to:

- Fully engage the local community in the development of tourism policies and plans. This should involve local government institutions and there should be a process of wider consultation and participation for the community and other stakeholders. Community engagement structures and processes are discussed further in Chapter 3.
- Empower local communities to influence decisions on tourism development in their area. This process covers both the ongoing direction of tourism and determination of individual development proposals. In some countries it may be achieved through democratic development control systems that are within the land use planning process and which involve decisions made by local elected representatives, based on evidence obtained from all of those likely to be affected by a project.

Improving the conditions for effective local decision making

An important aspect of local empowerment is to provide the skills and knowledge that people need to participate effectively in decision making at the local level. Policies in this area should aim to:

- Strengthen the capacity of local governance bodies and improve their knowledge of tourism and its sustainability.
- Raise public awareness of the ways in which tourism can affect communities.
- Involve communities in the development and maintenance of a system of indicators for sustainable tourism.
- Ensure that objective and transparent information on proposed new developments is available locally.

Addressing the specific position of indigenous and traditional communities with respect to local control

In many developing countries, indigenous communities are in a unique and often vulnerable position with respect to the potential impact of tourism on their culture and livelihoods. It is important to empower indigenous communities and to engage them in decision making processes. Local control can be enhanced by:

- Respect and recognition of traditional tribal empowerment, backing this up with legal empowerment.
- Guaranteeing the individual and collective rights of indigenous people regarding the land that they occupy. This allows them to control tourism within their lands and to negotiate.
- Respect for indigenous people's beliefs and traditions and consulting with them on how to portray their culture to tourists.

2.7 Community Wellbeing

To maintain and strengthen the quality of life in local communities, including social structures and access to resources, amenities and life support systems, avoiding any form of social or environmental degradation or exploitation

Tourism can impact the social wellbeing of communities in many ways, both positively and negatively. As well as providing jobs, the additional investment and spending brought by tourism can support a wide variety of amenities that add to the quality of local people's lives. These include essential services such as water and energy, roads and transport services, health services, shops, garages, leisure and entertainment facilities, and outdoor amenities. Conversely, the presence of visitors can put pressure on facilities and services, adding to the cost of their provision and maintenance, reducing the enjoyment of them by local people and making access to them difficult or even impossible. Tourism developments and activity also sometimes interfere with other sources of livelihood and disrupt access to them.

Tourism can be socially disruptive in other ways. It may stimulate an abnormal rise in house and land prices and in the general cost of living. Visitors may cause noise and general disturbance, leave litter and on occasion may be the source of crime. Forms of behaviour that may be alien to host communities can lead to unacceptable social practices amongst tourists and local people, such as an increase in prostitution and drug use. Child sex tourism, which is a clear violation of human rights, is of considerable global concern and is the subject of an international campaign for its eradication[3].

Policy areas to address:

Getting the balance right in the volume, timing and location of visits

The difference between a negative and a positive community reaction to tourism depends to a significant extent on the volume of visitors in an area at any one time and how this relates to the size of the local population. It may also be affected by the degree of concentration or geographical spread. The concept of the social carrying capacity of a destination is relevant here, and policies should maintain an optimum number of visitors. This can be done by keeping abreast of community reactions and using appropriate indicators such as volume of visits, traffic counts, number of complaints from local people, level of litter, etc.

Reducing congestion

Congestion, especially at peak times, caused by the volume of visitors and/or their vehicles, can be a primary threat to community wellbeing. It can be addressed by visitor management policies and actions including:

- Managing demand and reducing seasonality by marketing and pricing techniques to promote off-season visits, or by promoting alternative locations to spread visits within and outside of the destination.
- Improving traffic management through physical changes, signage, information, and promotion of alternative transport options.
- Addressing specific types of activity that may bring large influxes of visitors at certain times (e.g. management of cruise ship arrivals).

Careful planning and management of tourism enterprises and infrastructure

Forward thinking in the layout and design of tourist destinations and in the provision of services can make a significant difference to the impact on communities. Relevant approaches include:

- Planning the scale, design and siting of new tourism development, to take account of the overall amenity of the destination and the location of residential areas and other activities within the community.
- Planning the development of infrastructure, including transport, water and energy supplies, which should be designed to meet the combined needs of visitors and the community.
- Maximizing the availability of open space and other amenity areas, including beaches, that are accessible for use by residents and visitors.
- Where appropriate, encouraging tourism enterprises and their visitors to minimize water consumption.

Promoting mutual use of facilities and services by residents and tourists

Where possible, facilities and amenities developed for tourists should also be made available to members of the local community. In some locations, visitor spending can make the difference in ensuring viability of community services and facilities, such as local shops and village halls. Use of such services by tourists should be encouraged through information, events, etc.

Influencing the behaviour of tourists towards local communities

Many of the more specific and serious problems faced by communities as a result of tourism are due to behaviour of individual tourists or particular groups. This can be influenced through:

- Information, provided before and during the visit, on the nature of the host community, their values and any particular sensitivities that should be respected.
- Regulating certain aspects of visitor behaviour, such as noise and littering.
- Mounting or supporting campaigns, backed by legislation as appropriate, to combat sex tourism and the exploitation of children.

- Maintaining an appropriate level of policing.
- Physical control measures to facilitate good behaviour, such as provision of litter bins and information boards in several languages, if necessary.

2.8 Cultural Richness

To respect and enhance the historic heritage, authentic culture, traditions and distinctiveness of host communities

Respect for, and understanding of, cultural diversity between nations and peoples is a key principle of sustainable development. Tourism can be a considerable force for the conservation of historic and cultural heritage and can stimulate arts, crafts and other creative activities within communities. By providing a source of income based around local culture, tourism can encourage communities to value their cultural heritage more highly. However, it is important to guard against the falsification and degradation of culture and heritage in the way they are promoted to tourists.

Policy areas to address:

Ensuring effective management and conservation of cultural and historic heritage sites

Significant historic and cultural sites are a major component of visitor appeal in many countries. Although such sites are often dependent on visitor income for their management and conservation, many are also suffering from visitor pressure that threatens to damage their fabric and devalue the quality of the visitor experience. Policies in this area should focus on:

- Conserving historic and cultural heritage features. The level of designation and protection varies between countries. It may need to be extended in many places. Promoting the inclusion of sites on the World Heritage Convention list is appropriate in certain situations.
- Effective visitor management. This can include a range of techniques such as spreading and deflecting demand, physical site management, etc.[4]
- Avoiding or managing intrusive collateral activities. Some sites suffer from intrusion from neighbouring urban development, unmanaged trading such as informal trinket stalls or street sellers, etc.
- Securing more money from visitors for conservation. This can be achieved through promoting greater use, management of admission income, provision of well managed retail outlets, encouraging voluntary donations, etc.
- Seeking ways to benefit local communities living close to heritage sites. This can in turn help towards conservation as well as improving local livelihoods.

Working with communities on the sensitive presentation and promotion of culture and traditions

Cultural richness can be strengthened and interpreted in a variety of creative ways. Greater respect and understanding for local cultures can be achieved through improved information for guests and hosts and interaction between them. However, in all these activities, sensitivity is required and comodification or devaluing of local culture must be avoided. Policies should focus on:

- Developing interpretative programmes and events based on the heritage and distinctiveness of the area.
- Conceiving creative, sensitive and viable visitor attractions where local culture and traditions can be showcased.
- Incorporating aspects of local cultural heritage and distinctiveness into various elements of visitor experience, such as furnishing in tourism establishments, local cuisine in restaurants, traditional designs in architecture, and art and sculpture in public spaces.
- Capacity building with local communities regarding visitor interpretation and issues of quality and authenticity.
- Capacity building with the private sector to help them and their guests to bridge potential culture gaps.
- Informing tourists about local traditions and local culture before and during the trip.
- Informing local communities about the culture of their potential visitors.
- Guarding against the sale and purchase of items of cultural value as souvenirs.

2.9 Physical Integrity

To maintain and enhance the quality of landscapes, both urban and rural, and avoid physical and visual degradation of the environment

This is about the physical structure of places and their aesthetic quality and appearance. It is an important aim intrinsically from the environmental perspective, as well as affecting the wellbeing of local people. It is also critically important for the long term health of the tourism industry as the physical attractiveness of destinations is a key element of their appeal to visitors.

Land and coastal erosion are particular areas of concern where physical degradation is concerned. They may be caused, for example, by changes in vegetation cover or by marine infrastructure affecting long shore currents. Land degradation can also lead to loss of biodiversity, which is covered more specifically under Aim 2.10.

In relation to visual impacts, most attention in the past has been paid to the quality of rural landscapes and how they affect, and are affected by, tourism. However, there should be equal concern for the integrity and aesthetic quality of built as well as natural environments in rural and urban areas[5].

Policy areas to address:

Ensuring that new tourism development is appropriate to local environmental conditions

Key to the aim of maintaining physical integrity is having policies and instruments in place at a local level that influence the location and nature of new development.

Attention should be paid not only to the building of tourism facilities, such as accommodation, but also to a wide range of associated infrastructure, such as airports, roads, marinas, and ski tows and slopes. Policies should address in particular:

- The scale and density of new development and the extent of urbanization. In many areas, new structures should be avoided in order to keep the place natural. In some situations, policies relating to tourism development may favour the reuse and regeneration of existing buildings and previously used sites rather than new building on greenfield sites. In some situations, clustering of buildings may be more appropriate than sporadic development.
- The siting of new structures with respect to physical landform, vegetation, and the coherence of existing urban structures. Policies should seek an optimum amount of open space and the retention of tree cover. The height of new structures should be sensitive to urban skylines and to the height of trees. In coastal and lakeside settings it may be necessary to establish set back limits for new building (minimum distance from the high water mark).
- Quality of development and attention to detail. The impact of tourism development depends partly on sympathetic and creative designs, effective landscaping using indigenous species, and use of high quality materials. The design of new buildings should be in harmony with the landscape, and where appropriate reflect traditional designs.
- The robustness of structures and their ability to withstand the effects of climate change and natural disasters.
- The long term future and after use of buildings and sites. Consideration should be given to the life cycle of tourism developments and to policies and resources for maintenance and renewal. For some forms of tourism, such as one-off events or seasonal structures, there may be important issues of after use of sites in the short term.

As well as addressing the nature and location of development, policies and control measures may seek to minimize physical degradation caused by the construction process, including care over site preparation, the extraction of building materials, and the removal and treatment of construction waste (see Aim 2.12).

Minimizing the physical impact of tourist activity

Physical degradation of the environment can result from the actions of tourists. This can arise from all types of tourism but is most specifically associated with certain recreational activities. Particular problems to address include:

- Erosion resulting from over-use of sites. This can be a significant issue with popular hiking trails, especially where surfaces are fragile.
- Damage to marine structures, such as coral reefs, from diving or boating activities.
- Environmental degradation caused by dropping of litter.
- Willful damage, such as graffiti.

Policies and actions to minimize such impacts include:

- Visitor management measures to reduce pressures and deflect activities to more robust sites.
- Educational activity to change behaviour.
- Development of codes of conduct, supported by regulation where necessary.

Maintaining high quality rural and urban landscapes as a tourism resource

As well as influencing tourism development and activities per se, policies should seek to maintain the integrity and attractiveness of tourist destinations, including towns and rural areas, by influencing development and maintenance in general, including:

- Controlling intrusive new development, such as unsightly buildings.
- Controlling activities that will damage landscapes, such as mineral extraction or destruction of forests.
- Maintaining the fabric and facades of properties, especially historic buildings.
- Maintaining traditional rural landscapes and features.
- Minimizing the impact of intrusive structures such as power lines.
- Avoiding the proliferation of advertisements and signing.
- Maintaining the quality of public open spaces.

Maintenance of physical integrity and attractive landscapes may partly be achieved through extending and strengthening protected areas and how they relate to tourism. This is covered in more detail under Aim 2.10. However, the overall aim is relevant to all areas and policies and actions should not be restricted to places with protected status.

2.10 Biological Diversity

To support the conservation of natural areas, habitats and wildlife, and minimize damage to them

This is an area where the positive and negative impacts of tourism can be felt most strongly. The very environments which attract visitors can be the most vulnerable. For instance, the development of coastal zones has led to much loss of habitat and dune destruction. Marine environments, such as coral reefs, have been seriously damaged by over use or poor practice linked to diving operations. Boats and shore-based facilities have also caused extensive damage through physical destruction and pollution. All ecosystems, whether mountains, deserts, rainforests, wetlands or inland waters, have their own special sensitivities which need to be considered when planning for tourism activities. On the other hand, income from tourism has proved to be a critically important component of funding for conservation in many national parks, reserves and other protected areas.

Protection of biodiversity is closely related to the maintenance of physical integrity, covered under Aim 2.9. and a number of the policy areas presented below also support that aim. As with physical integrity, preventing destruction of biodiversity not only by tourism itself but also by other activities can be very important in maintaining the visitor appeal of many rural destinations.

Policy areas to address:

Working with national parks and other protected areas

The designation and management of all types of protected area provide an opportunity to strengthen the protection from the negative impacts of tourism, and to focus on sustainable tourism that increases visitor awareness and support for conservation. In many countries, authorities responsible for national parks and protected areas have taken a strong interest in tourism, seeing it as a source of income, an opportunity for a sustainable livelihood for park-based communities and as an activity that needs careful management.[6] Important policy issues include:

- Extending the coverage of terrestrial and marine[7] protected areas, including buffer zones, as appropriate or as needed. This involves identifying areas that need protection and considering their potential to benefit from sustainable tourism.
- Preparing national guidelines on sustainable tourism in protected areas.
- Establishing structures for joint working on tourism with relevant stakeholders, including preparing sustainable tourism strategies that integrate with park management plans and link to regional and national strategies.
- Guaranteeing the availability and use of financial resources for park management.
- Optimizing the level and use of park admissions to support a range of objectives, including biodiversity conservation.
- Developing partnership agreements and concession-based relationships with local communities and private sector operators that offer clear benefits to conservation and habitat management, as well as to communities and users.
- Creating networks of protected areas, and their branding for sustainable tourism.

Promoting development and management of ecotourism

Ecotourism, by definition, is a form of tourism that entails responsible travel to natural areas which conserves the environment and sustains the well-being of local people. It should therefore be encouraged in the interests of conservation. Governments should:

- Bring together tourism and conservation stakeholders to agree priorities and policies for the development and careful management of ecotourism at a national and local level.[8]
- Ensure that products or new projects that are promoted as 'ecotourism' comply with the above definition. This may require application of relevant tools such as certification.
- Encourage well planned and executed ecotourism projects in natural areas, including visitor facilities and interpretation, through technical support, marketing and other appropriate measures.

Using tourism to encourage landholders to practice sustainable land management

In many parts of the world, rural landholders (smallholders, farmers or communities engaged in agriculture on communal lands) can earn additional income from tourism, either directly or indirectly. This may involve providing accommodation or other services on the land, income from the sale of produce into the tourism supply chain, or income from engagement in tourism off the land (e.g. acting as guides). Tourism can stimulate more sustainable land management by providing a new income source (as an alternative to unsustainable practices such as logging or slash and burn agriculture) and can encourage landholders to conserve wildlife or produce organic food, as these are valued by visitors. Policies should seek to develop support, advice and other incentives to encourage landholders to manage their land more sustainably.

Working with private parks and reserves

Private parks and nature reserves have grown significantly in many countries in recent years. Most are actively involved in tourism and there is an opportunity and need to influence their development and management. Priorities include:

- Ensuring that private parks do not siphon away resources, including tourism income, to the detriment of conservation in public parks.
- Ensuring that private parks maintain high conservation and tourism standards. This may involve developing appropriate legal frameworks.
- Integrating the management of private and public parks into a single biodiversity plan.

Minimizing damage to natural heritage from tourism

Careful control of tourism development is particularly important in order to avoid damage in areas of high landscape value or where biodiversity may be especially vulnerable. Guidelines for an agreed development planning process that will deliver such control are set out in the Convention on Biological Diversity.[9]

Policies and actions should also seek to minimize damage to habitats and disturbance of wildlife by visitors. This relates closely to the damage to physical integrity by tourist activity, notably by particular types of recreation, covered under Aim 2.9, and the measures indicated there are relevant.

Policies should also seek to minimize damage and disturbance from visitors. This applies to all tourists, but a particular focus may be required on certain recreational activities such as diving and adventure tourism in sensitive environments. Policy areas include:

- Raising awareness through education and interpretation.
- Visitor management—controlling visitor numbers and behaviour (e.g. physical damage, wildlife disturbance, littering).

Policies should also be put in place that prevent tourism from contributing to the threat to endangered species by either stimulating illegal trade in such species or purchasing of souvenirs made from them.

Raising visitor awareness of biodiversity

Providing tourists with a better appreciation and understanding of the natural heritage of the places they visit should help to prevent adverse impacts and encourage support for conservation, as well as enhancing their enjoyment. Policies and actions should support the provision of:

- Good quality guiding, where possible involving local people.
- Interpretative events.
- Visitor centres, where appropriate, containing creative interpretative facilities.
- Relevant information pre-arrival.
- Educational activity amongst local people and potential domestic markets.
- Better knowledge amongst tourism enterprises that they can pass on to their staff and guests.

Raising support for conservation from visitors and enterprises

Many tourism enterprises recognize the importance of ongoing conservation activity to the visitor experience; others should be encouraged to do so. Polices could be introduced that encourage enterprises to support biodiversity, through maintaining habitats on their own properties and supporting local conservation initiatives, in cash or kind. Financial support for conservation activity can also be raised from tourists and is providing an increasingly important source of income. Tourists can also become engaged in practical ways, for example through participating in conservation holidays.

2.11 Resource Efficiency

To minimize the use of scarce and non-renewable resources in the development and operation of tourism facilities and services

A sustainable future depends on the careful management of resources to ensure their availability for present and future generations. Resources that are non-renewable, in limited supply, or essential for life support are of particular concern. These include land, fresh water, forests, minerals and fossil fuels. Conservation of energy is important, especially where it is derived from non-renewable resources.

Tourism is a significant user of resources in many areas. Ensuring that it uses resources efficiently is important both for the wellbeing of the local environment and host community and in maintaining global resources. Efficient use of resources, notably energy derived from fossil fuels, is also important in the reduction of polluting emissions.

Resource efficiency in tourism will be achieved largely by changing the consumption patterns of tourists and tourism enterprises. Enterprises should be encouraged to establish environmental management systems to minimize impacts and drive a process of continual improvement.

Policy areas to address:

Taking account of resource supply in the planning of tourism development, and vice versa

An integrated planning approach is required to ensure an equitable balance between the needs of local communities and the tourism industry. Growth of tourism in an area may be seriously limited by the availability of land, water, energy or other resources. Equally, predicted growth in demand from the tourism sector must be taken into account when planning provision of water and energy supplies.

Minimizing water consumption by the tourism sector

Fresh water is a vital resource and consumption of water by the tourism sector is high. In developing countries, it has been found that per capita daily use of water by tourists can be as much as 10 to 15 times greater than by local residents. Much tourism demand occurs in places and at times when water is very scarce, such as in summer in arid coastal regions. In many tourist destinations new sources of water, such as desalination plants, would be difficult to establish, costly and bring their own environmental problems. Policies to minimize water consumption are required and should address:

- Restricting water hungry facilities such as swimming pools, golf courses, and artificial snow cannons.
- Reusing and recycling water where possible, (e.g. use of greywater to irrigate parks and gardens).
- Improving infrastructure and maintenance (e.g. reducing leakages).
- Encouraging installation of water efficient technology such as low-flow showers and toilets.
- Persuading visitors to be responsible in their use of water.

Minimizing consumption of energy from non-renewable resources
Policies on energy use should seek to influence both sources of supply and consumption, including:

- Promoting the use of designs and materials for tourism facilities that maximize insulation and the use of natural heat, light and ventilation.
- Providing renewable energy sources in tourist destinations.
- Encouraging individual tourism enterprises to generate their own energy supply, or to supplement it, from renewable sources (such as photovoltaic systems and mini hydro schemes).
- Encouraging use of energy efficient plant and equipment for lighting, water heating, cooking, etc.
- Promoting resource efficient transport options (discussed further under Aim 2.12).
- Persuading visitors to be responsible in their use of energy.

Ensuring the efficient use of land and raw materials in tourism development

In some tourist destinations land may be in short supply. It is therefore important to select sites for tourism development carefully, taking account of alternative uses and the needs of the local community. Although use of local materials can add to quality and distinctiveness, the design and construction of tourism facilities should avoid profligate use of naturally occurring materials such as timber, stone, sand and gravel, and should take account of the capacity of local supply and competing demands.

Promoting a reduce, reuse, recycle mentality

In general, tourism enterprises should be encouraged to be efficient in all their use of materials. This is equally true for their use of resources and generation of waste. These themes are covered under Aim 2.12. Policies should support:

- Purchasing of supplies from sustainable sources. This can be helped by better information on local availability of such sources and ecolabelling schemes for relevant consumer products.
- Minimizing use of unnecessary packaging, for example through economic incentives to return containers such as bottles.

- Encouraging creativity in the reuse of products both within an enterprise or making them available for use in the local community.
- The creation of markets to recycle tourism supplies (paper, glass and plastic in particular).

2.12 Environmental Purity

To minimize the pollution of air, water and land and the generation of waste by tourism enterprises and visitors

Maintaining environmental purity means reducing waste and harmful emissions to the environment in order to preserve the quality of the air, water and land that sustain life, health and biodiversity. Actions should address all aspects of pollution prevention and control throughout the lifecycle of tourism development, during and after the use of facilities, as well as the impacts of tourists themselves.

Although local impacts on the environment, such as local air and water quality, are the most immediately apparent to local communities and to visitors, the tourism industry also has global environmental impacts. Governments need to recognize the responsibilities towards both the global and the local environment that are inherent in maintaining environmental purity. There is a need for a profound change in the way we generate and use energy and in other activities that release greenhouse and other gases into the atmosphere. Global pollution may also impact many local destinations through the consequences of climate change.

As with promoting resource efficiency, waste and pollution control will be achieved largely by changing the consumption patterns of tourists and tourism enterprises. This should be a key component of individual environmental management systems within enterprises.

Policy areas to address:

Promoting the use of more sustainable transport

Transport is one of the most significant sources of environmental pollution resulting from tourism, mainly through air travel and the use of individual private cars. Travel by rail and boat is far less polluting. As well as the global impact of greenhouse gas emissions, emissions and congestion affect the local environment and community. Policies should seek to:

- Favour low-impact forms of transport. This applies both to journeys to and from the destination, and within it. The latter may be easier to influence. Promotion of walking and cycling provides a particular opportunity in many destinations. This can be facilitated by the provision of appropriate infrastructure, including trails and public transport services, more integrated timetabling, and creative marketing.
- Minimize the number and length of journeys made. Although this would reduce environmental impact, it may also have serious economic consequences for the tourism industry and for local communities dependent on visitors. Policies could seek to encourage longer stays, so that the amount of income gained by the

destination per kilometre travelled is increased, and net income is retained.
- Mitigate the consequences of environmental impact from transport. A campaign could be established that invites tourists to offset the impact of their air travel by contributing to carbon sequestration projects.

Reducing the use of environmentally damaging chemicals

The tourism industry uses a variety of environmentally harmful chemicals. Environmental damage may be caused, for instance, by the use or disposal of chemicals present in cleaning products, fuel, paints, fungicides and pesticides, or chlorination products for swimming pools. The industry also contributes to depletion of the ozone layer, by releasing CFCs into the atmosphere from cooling systems and air conditioners, foam packaging and insulation, and through careless disposal of refrigerants in end-of-life fridges. Governments should be vigilant in enforcing high standards for the disposal of hazardous waste. Wherever possible, the use of environmentally damaging chemicals should be eliminated through careful purchasing policies.

Avoiding the discharge of sewage to marine and river environments

Water is an essential resource for both biological and human communities. It is essential for the tourism industry to place a high priority on reducing, managing and treating wastewater and controlling sewage disposal. The impacts of emissions on the environment are not felt solely at the point of disposal or discharge: pollutants disperse and are borne by flowing water or leach through the soil to join watercourses. Wherever possible, connection should be made to mains sewage disposal systems that are designed to treat and discharge to the highest standards. Governments should provide appropriate infrastructure and legislation concerning connection to the sewerage system. In some locations, alternative technologies such as discharge of sewage to reed beds may be appropriate.

Minimizing waste and where necessary disposing of it with care

The tourism industry is a major generator of waste and disposal of non-degradable waste is an important issue, especially in remoter locations. Land can be contaminated through the tipping of waste on landfill sites and landfilled bio-degradable wastes can also release methane into the atmosphere. As well as causing visual intrusion and habitat damage, such wastes can be damaging or life-threatening to wildlife. There should be an emphasis on reducing waste at source and recycling wherever possible. Where disposal is necessary, it should be in accordance with best available practice. This can be helped by governments providing suitable infrastructure and legislation against inappropriate waste disposal.

Influencing the development of new tourism facilities

Choices made prior to the development of a new facility can have a profound effect on environmental impact at the time of development, during operation of the facility, and with respect to the after use and long term future of the site. Policies should seek to influence:

- The location of new development. This includes its general location in terms of the overall environmental sensitivity of the area and its setting, for example in relation to the coast or public transport links.
- Design and materials used. These can influence operational impacts such as emissions, treatment and disposal of waste, etc.
- The construction process. Construction should take place with minimum disturbance to the environment. In many areas, especially coastal sites, it has been found that waste and emissions from the construction phase can be more disruptive to the local environment than the operational phase.

Notes

1 The policy areas identified here reflect a seven point model for addressing poverty through tourism contained in Tourism and Poverty Alleviation – Recommendations for Action. World Tourism Organisation, 2004.

2 The WTO defined guidelines to facilitate tourism for people with disabilities as early as 1991 (see WTO General Assembly resolution 'Creating opportunities for handicapped people: http://www.world-tourism.org/quality/E/main.htm).

3 International Campaign Against Sexual Exploitation of Children in Tourism http:// http://www.ecpat.org/preventing-child-sex-tourism.html.

4 A detailed treatment of management measures can be found in the Handbook on Tourism Congestion Management at Natural and Cultural Sites WTO, 2004. See also the UNEP/UNESCO manual on tourism management in World Heritage Sites, 2002.

5 The participants to the WTO/UNESCO/Sultanate of Oman conference in Muscat, Oman, (February 2005), issued a 'Declaration on Built Environments for Sustainable Tourism' calling on governments to take action in this area.

6 A comprehensive treatment of the relationship between tourism and protected areas can be found in Sustainable Tourism in Protected Areas UNEP, WTO, IUCN, 2002.

7 See recommendations 22 and 23 of the World Parks Congress 2003 held in Durban, South Africa. http://www.iucn.org/themes/wcpa/wpc2003/english/outputs/recommendations.htm.

8 The Quebec Declaration on Ecotourism (2002) provides a framework for sound ecotourism policies. http://www.world-tourism.org/sustainable/IYE/quebec/.

9 Guidelines on Biodiversity and Tourism Development, Convention on Biological Diversity 2003.

Structures and Strategies

This chapter describes structures that help governments to work internally and with other stakeholders to make tourism more sustainable. It also identifies the strategies that are required to develop and drive policies and actions.

Particular attention is paid to the relationship between national and local structures and strategies for sustainable tourism. It is critically important that they are in harmony and that policies and actions at these different levels are complementary.

3.1 Structures for working together

The holistic and equitable principles that underpin sustainable development imply the need to bring together a wide range of stakeholders to develop and manage tourism in a sustainable manner.

In bringing together these different interests, governments must seek to develop structures that have two purposes:

- Engaging stakeholders in the formulation of a strategy and policies for sustainable tourism.
- Ensuring effective coordination of actions and an ongoing dialogue between stakeholders.

In many situations both purposes can be met by the same structures. Permanent structures are required to ensure coordination; additional, temporary, working structures may also be needed in the policy formulation stages.

Structures can be developed in partnership with other stakeholders, to:

- Raise the profile of the sustainable development of tourism, and to ensure that those who can influence it give it their full attention.
- Give a say in the development and management of tourism to those whose interests or areas of responsibility will be affected by its impacts.
- Bring together knowledge and expertise on economic, social and environmental issues that are relevant to tourism.
- Ensure that polices and actions in other sectors or areas of activity that impinge on tourism are coordinated and taken into account, to prevent policy conflicts and enhance synergy.
- Encourage wide commitment of support and resources to a common, agreed programme.

Box 3.1 gives an example of how different stakeholders have been brought together in Honduras.

Relationships and coordination structures within government

Many areas of government have responsibility for policies and actions that have a strong bearing on the sustainability of tourism. These are listed in Table 3.1.

The degree of priority given to different aspects of sustainability will depend on which part of government is responsible for tourism. For example, a separate Ministry of Tourism has the advantage of being able to make relevant connections with and between other ministries, but it may not carry much weight overall. Linking tourism to the Ministry of Environment can underpin awareness of environmental sustainability, and reinforce links with national parks or the promotion of nature based tourism. Location within a Trade or Development Ministry may ensure a higher political and budgetary profile, but may also lead to greater emphasis on foreign exchange earnings and less regard for local impacts.

Box 3.1: Honduras—getting key people together

Honduras has introduced a number of initiatives to develop sustainable tourism based on the country's high quality natural environment and historic heritage attractions. It has recognized the importance of having the right structures for ministries and tourism stakeholders to work together at both a national and local level if it is to achieve its goals.

A special 'tourism cabinet' has been established, involving the President of the Republic and the Secretaries for Tourism, Environment and Natural Resources, Finance, Justice, Security, Transport and Public Utilities, and Arts and Culture.

Within the official Institute of Tourism, there are separate units dedicated to the Environment and to Municipal Development.

At a local level, approximately 60 Municipal Tourism Development Commissions have been established, in each case under the leadership of the Mayor and involving local private sector tourism interests and NGOs. The Institute of Tourism provides technical assistance and training to these Commissions, on issues such as tourism management, the application of environmental legislation and the issuing of guidelines.

Groups of municipalities also work together regionally, for example on a sustainable tourism initiative on the north coast and the area around the World Heritage Site of Copan.

Table 3.1: Areas of government influencing the sustainability of tourism

Tourism	Overall development, coordination and implementation of tourism policy. Support for tourism development, management and marketing.
Prime Ministerial office	Tourism's position within the overall balance of policies and priorities.
Finance	Level of budgetary resources allocated to tourism. Tax policy.
Trade	Terms of trade negotiations. Export and investment promotion.
Economic Development	Sustainable development policies. Support for enterprise.
Environment and Natural Resources	Regulation and control of environmental impact. Conservation of biodiversity. Protected area management. Management of resources for ecotourism.
Transport	Accessibility, traffic management and sustainable transport issues.
Culture	Management and preservation of historic sites and cultural heritage.
Agriculture	Rural development and supply chain issues.
Education	Tourism training.
Health	Safety and social security issues, for visitors and employees.
Sport and Recreation	Promotion of attractions, activities, events, etc. Elements of domestic market.
Internal Affairs	Crime and security. Child protection.
Foreign Affairs	Source country-destination relationships. Visa requirements.

Queensland, Australia adopted a 'whole of government' approach. An inter-ministerial committee was established and senior executives within each relevant ministry were given responsibility for tourism related work (see Case Studies, p 130).

Examples of collaboration include the protocol signed between the Ministries of Economy, Environment and Agriculture in Bulgaria, on implementation of the National Ecotourism Strategy, and the coming together of the Egyptian Environmental Affairs Agency, the Tourism Development Authority and the Red Sea Governorate on planning policies and regulations (see Case Studies, p 135 & p 144).

Irrespective of the location of tourism within government, there are some key requirements if it is to be fully integrated into national sustainable development strategies. These are:

- Tourism should be given a clear, strong voice, with a direct link to top-level cabinet decision makers.
- There should be a formal structure and process for inter-ministerial cooperation on tourism.
- Such relationships should be also reflected within and between lower level public agencies, such as tourist boards and environment agencies.

In addition to these inter-ministerial structures, ministries may collaborate to support or implement specific initiatives. This may take the form of agreements with local government, and can involve collaboration between government agencies. It is helpful if such collaborative structures, agreements and actions are formalized by protocols or memoranda of understanding.

Structures and mechanisms to engage stakeholders

A sustainable approach to tourism development requires structures that enable representatives of local authorities and non-governmental interests to become involved in the formulation and implementation of national tourism strategies and policies. Governments should establish and manage such structures.

Traditionally, this has been achieved through government agencies, such as tourist boards, that have private sector representation on their executive committees. While this should be continued, it is important to find ways to widen the process through additional dedicated structures.

Some countries have permanent tourism councils, which are essentially discussion and advisory bodies. These can be valuable mechanisms for promoting the sustainability of tourism, provided that their membership is well balanced to reflect the different dimensions of sustainability.

Ideally what is required is a permanent forum or standing conference based on a large number of invited stakeholders representing different interests, and a smaller body or council, perhaps elected from the above, dealing with more detailed work.

Such a multi-stakeholder structure should represent the following, amongst others:

- Different government departments and agencies representing the areas of government identified above.
- Regional and local authorities.
- Different segments of the tourism industry—hotel associations, tour operator bodies, etc.
- International travel trade.
- The transport sector (all forms).
- Environmental and community-based NGOs.
- Cultural heritage bodies.
- National parks and other protected areas.
- Tourism/recreation user groups.

- Civil society (not in tourism but affected by it).
- Universities and other bodies involved with tourism education and training.
- Trade (labour) unions.

Such a forum and council should be concerned with all aspects of tourism and should focus on sustainability.

To ensure a focus on sustainability, it may be appropriate in some countries, to set up a dedicated inter-agency communication and working group specifically for this purpose. The challenge would be to ensure that the work of such a separate body relates continually and strongly to the mainstream of tourism and is not marginalized.

Coordination structures at local level

Structures bringing together tourism, environment, community and wider development interests are also required at the local level. Some or all of the areas and functions of national government listed in Table 3.1 may be reflected within local authorities. To strengthen the sustainability of tourism, mechanisms should also be established that encourage joined-up thinking and action within local government.

In a number of countries, 'destination management organizations' have been established at the local level. These are partnerships between local government and the private sector. Their main responsibility is the management and promotion of tourism; they sometimes also address development aspects. Such organizations should take full account of the social and environmental dimensions of sustainability by ensuring sound representation of local community and environmental interests within their governing bodies.

The Scottish Tourism and Environment Forum is a good example of what has become essentially a pressure group for sustainable tourism, checking policy across its members and promoting good practice (see Case Studies, p 172).

3.2 Interrelated national strategies

A strategy determines a goal and outlines the direction and approaches needed to get there. Strategies can address a wide range of issues affecting desired outcomes and may also need to embrace a wide range of stakeholders whose actions will also influence those outcomes. Governments can work with others to develop strategies relating both to broad matters such as sustainable development and poverty reduction in general, and to specific sectors such as tourism. Policies, on the other hand, tend to be more precise statements of position and intent about individual issues and may be more specifically linked to individual stakeholders, notably government. Tourism policies that embrace sustainability should be developed through comprehensive strategies.

Three types of strategy can be identified that have relevance to sustainable tourism:

- An overall tourism strategy embracing sustainability principles.
- Other relevant government strategies recognizing or embracing sustainable tourism (such as a biodiversity strategy).
- Strategies for sub-sectors of tourism that can play a role in making all of tourism more sustainable (such as an ecotourism strategy).

A tourism strategy that embraces sustainability

Every country should have a strategy, contained in a published document, that provides a clear direction and framework for the development and management of tourism, thereby:

- Guiding the policies and actions of the tourism ministry and its agencies, such as the national tourism organization.
- Influencing other government departments and ministries.
- Stimulating and controlling the private sector and potential investors.
- Providing a framework for tourism policies and action at the local level.

Rather than develop a separate strategy for 'sustainable tourism', mainstream tourism strategies should fully embrace the concept of sustainable development.

In the past, tourism strategies (and especially tourism master plans which tend to be more about physical and spatial issues) have often treated sustainability as a separate section of the strategy or plan, being essentially a statement on possible impacts and proposals for their mitigation. This is not sufficient. The whole strategy should be based on principles of sustainable development. It should therefore:

- Emerge from processes that ensure stakeholder participation.
- Promote and respect planning for tourism at the local level, and provide a framework for this.
- Reflect aims and principles for sustainable tourism such as those set out in this Guide, identifying the specific objectives, policies and actions that derive from those aims.

These three requirements are considered in more detail below.

A tourism strategy developed in this way should be able to stand up to external scrutiny with respect to its likely impacts and outcomes. Screening and checking processes for the sustainability of policies are being introduced in some countries. For instance, in the European Union, Strategic Environmental Assessment of all public policies in certain sectors (which explicitly include tourism) is now a requirement. Such processes can also be helpful in moving existing tourism strategies towards more sustainable positions. An example from Fiji is given in Box 3.2.

Effective coverage of tourism in other government agencies

As well as having a separate strategy for tourism that embraces sustainability, governments should ensure that the sustainable development of tourism is fully recognized within other government strategies. There are three reasons why this is particularly important:

- Often it is only through specific and high-profile inclusion within higher level strategies and policies that tourism will be taken seriously by the ministries concerned with sustainable development and the environment. Only then will it be afforded adequate resources.

Box 3.2: Fiji—Assessing the strategy

A Strategic Environmental Assessment (SEA) was undertaken on the Fiji Tourism Development Plan (1998–2005) as part of its mid-term review, as it was felt that the plan had been focusing more on the economic component and less on the social and environmental aspects of sustainable development.

The SEA was undertaken by an external organization, WWF South Pacific Programme, in partnership with government departments, civil society groups and the tourism industry. The Asian Development Bank (ADB) also participated in the preparation of the SEA by providing inputs in the initial concept design and drafting TORs in partnership with WWF and the Ministry of Tourism. ADB provided grant financing for the project with co-financing support from the Government of New Zealand.

The Tourism Development Plan had called for a 'step-change' in the rate of growth of tourism. The SEA involved looking closely at the baseline economic, social and environmental situation and assessing likely changes under the above growth scenario. It concluded that:

- The growth envisaged in the plan could result in large-scale development that would tip the balance towards environmental degradation and social tension. A precautionary approach was needed.
- Although policies and laws enabling such a precautionary approach existed on paper, much more effort was needed to ensure that they were enforced and that good practice guidelines were followed universally.
- There should be greater local involvement in tourism planning, with more local retention of tourism earnings.

The findings of the SEA were exposed to scrutiny by a stakeholder workshop and were adopted and endorsed by the National Tourism Council.

- Legislation and regulations necessary to control the impact of tourism may be initiated by environmental or developmental strategies and policies. These must therefore consider tourism at the outset.
- Sustainable development is holistic in nature. It therefore requires synchronization of policies and coordination of action between sectors.

The following high level strategies (or their equivalent), found in many countries, are especially important for sustainable tourism:

- National Sustainable Development Strategies.
- Poverty Reduction Strategy Papers.
- National Environmental Strategies and Biodiversity Action Plans.

Other important strategies that should include tourism are those covering integrated transport planning, culture and human resource issues such as vocational education.

As well as ensuring that tourism is addressed in these strategies, it is important that tourism strategies should reflect them in the development of their own policies and actions.

In Bulgaria steps were taken to strengthen the chances of work on ecotourism influencing mainstream tourism: e.g. integrating the ecotourism strategy into the work of regional tourism associations and into the preparation by municipalities of regional and local development plans (see Case Studies, p 135).

Costa Rica and Australia have also shown the potential influence of work on ecotourism (see Case Studies, p 130 & 139).

Bulgaria has developed a National Ecotourism Strategy in parallel with 12 regional ecotourism action programmes, with each informing the other in a two-way process (see Case Studies, p 135).

Mexico has an Agenda 21 initiative that is about taking action in a range of local destinations at the same time. This is based on a framework and process established nationally and reflecting one of the principal pillars of the National Tourism Programme (see Case Studies, p 153).

More specific strategies

In addition to general tourism strategies, it may be appropriate to develop strategies or sets of policies for specific aspects of tourism. These could be defined by product or market type: e.g. cultural, rural, health or sport tourism, or the cruise ship sector. They should also reflect sustainability principles.

A number of countries have developed a separate strategy for ecotourism. In some cases this has been stimulated by the Ministry of Environment or by other environmental interests. Such strategies can be very helpful in coordinating and ensuring success of this specific sub-sector. They can also be very helpful in demonstrating processes and formulating policies that can be emulated more widely in tourism in general. On the other hand there is a danger that separate ecotourism strategies may be assumed to be an adequate government response to making tourism sustainable, reflecting a common misapprehension, already mentioned in Chapter 1, that sustainability for tourism refers to a particular type of tourism rather than to a condition for all tourism.

3.3 Integrating national and local level strategies

In order to achieve effective results, policies must be developed and implemented at both national and local levels. Local decision making is an important aspect of sustainable development. All the more so as many countries are in the process of decentralizing their political and administrative structures.

It is increasingly recognized that the most successful route to sustainable tourism is an integrated approach to the development and management of tourism within local destinations. It is at the local level that the tourism industry most readily relates to, and is in turn affected by, environmental and community issues. Box 3.3 gives some useful background information on what is meant by a 'local destination'.

It is critically important that national and local tourism strategies are complementary. Typically, tourism strategies at these two levels may vary in their focus:

- National tourism strategies relate to national tourism vision; overall position and direction for tourism; overall issues of product-market fit; broad spatial issues of tourism development; fiscal issues; setting standards for the industry; controlling legislation, regulations and other mechanisms; support programmes including financial resources; research, and the acquisition and dissemination of knowledge; a marketing and promotion strategy, especially at international level.
- Local tourism strategies relate to a holistic vision for the local destination; local objectives and priorities; local resource opportunities and constraints; the volume and nature of tourism sought; destination identity and branding; product development including location and relationship to land use plans; local networks and supply chains; infrastructure provision; specific tourist sites and attractions; visitor management; visitor information and destination marketing.

Box 3.3: Defining a local destination

According to the WTO's working group on destination management:

'A local tourism destination is a physical space in which a visitor spends at least one overnight. It includes tourism products such as support services and attractions, and tourism resources within one day's return travel time. It has physical and administrative boundaries defining its management, and images and perceptions defining its market competitiveness. Local destinations incorporate various stakeholders often including a host community, and can nest and network to form larger destinations.'

Local destinations may be cities, towns, resorts or rural areas, or groupings of these. A combination of factors determines what may be a functional destination, including:
- Whether the area is coterminous with municipal boundaries or other forms of designation such as a national park.
- Whether it is unified by certain images and intrinsic features and qualities that can contribute to a clearly identifiable brand.
- Whether it is an area towards which local stakeholders feel a natural affinity and within which it is practicable for them to work together.

Put simply, national strategies are more about identifying policies and instruments to create the enabling environment for sustainable tourism, while local strategies are more about determining what happens on the ground. Sustainable tourism requires that both national and local tourism strategies embrace the principles of sustainable development, and that national and local strategies be consistent and mutually reinforcing.

Local Agenda 21 processes and engaging local communities

Many local destinations in different parts of the world have developed strategies and policies for tourism within the context of Local Agenda 21[1]. This is a process for bringing together the broadest possible range of interests in the local area to integrate global environmental concerns into local plans, to decide what sort of future they want and to then work together towards it. Some destinations have pursued Local Agenda 21 processes, where tourism is seen as just one activity alongside many others. Ideally, it is good to take this holistic approach first and to then develop the sustainable tourism strategy out of this process. In some places, where tourism is dominant, a Local Agenda 21 strategy may be tantamount to a sustainable tourism strategy.

It is also important to recognize that a destination may well be made up of a number of clearly identifiable individual communities. A sustainable tourism approach would call for careful consultation within each community to ascertain local concerns and perceived opportunities with respect to tourism. The amount of emphasis to place on this depends very much on the nature of the destination. In many developing countries, the involvement of indigenous communities in determining tourism development in their area is critically important.

In South Africa, a national Tourism White Paper clearly articulates principles of 'responsible tourism' that have provided a direction for tourism policies and strategies throughout the county and have been reflected in the policies, planning frameworks and functions established at a provincial level (see Case Studies, p 162).

Calvia, in Spain, is a major tourism destination that used the participatory process of LA21 to bring all stakeholders together (see Case Studies, p 167).

Notes

1   More information can be found in Tourism and Local Agenda 21, UNEP and ICLEI, 2003.

Shaping Sustainable Tourism

4

This chapter looks at the process of developing a strategy for sustainable tourism, outlining the main steps in the process and relating them to the objective of making tourism more sustainable. It then looks in more detail at the stage, within this process, of making strategic choices about the level and nature of tourism. The focus in the later sections is on how policy can influence the development of tourism and the behaviour of enterprises and consumers (i.e. the tourists) in favour of sustainability. Tools to assist implementation and improve sustainability are also introduced, to be described in detail in the next chapter.

4.1 Developing a sustainable tourism strategy

Developing a strategy for sustainable tourism should be a participatory process that involves a range of stakeholders in order to foster wider adherence to the strategy and commitment to its implementation. The mix of stakeholders involved in developing the strategy should reflect the make up of partnership structures for tourism at a national or local level identified in Chapter 3 (Section 3.1). It is necessary at the outset to secure long term commitment both to the strategy and, crucially, to its implementation.

Three stages can be identified in the formulation of a strategy:

- Analysing conditions, problems and opportunities.
- Identifying objectives and making strategic choices.
- Developing policies and action programmes.

Analysing conditions, problems and opportunities

This first stage involves taking a careful and objective look at the state of tourism in the destination (which may be a country or local area) as well as at the resources on which tourism depends or has impacts, both at present and in the future.

Thought should be given at the outset to aspects and attributes that have a particular bearing on the sustainability of tourism, so that the data gathered and questions asked are appropriate. The 12-point agenda provides guidance on what to include. Initial indicators (discussed further in Chapter 5) should also be determined to allow baseline measurements to be made and future change to be assessed.

The situation should be analysed using surveys, consultation and technical studies. To assist with analysis, Box 4.1 provides a checklist and suggestion of the information that is most relevant to sustainability issues.

The situation analysis is a first step in identifying a number of key issues for the sustainability of tourism in a given destination, and opportunities for the future—for example: the viability of enterprises, capacity issues, market trends, environmental degradation, or community concerns about future development. It can be useful to capture this in an issues paper that is given wide circulation.

Consultation should be undertaken with a wide range of stakeholders to clarify the issues. Priorities will begin to emerge from this process. Various consultation and communication techniques can be used here, including open meetings, stakeholder workshops and web-based consultation, etc. Involving the local media can be helpful in generating interest.

Identifying objectives and making choices

National and local governments should work with stakeholders to agree on a vision and on a broad set of strategic objectives for tourism. These should be based on the analysis set out above and should also reflect closely the 12 aims for sustainable tourism already described.

In Calvia, high level political support (with the mayor playing a key role) added considerable strength, but underlined the need for cross-party commitment to the long term vision and process to ensure that it will last through changes in political climate. Weaknesses in delivering action also pointed, with hindsight, to a need to make stakeholders more accountable for implementation at the outset (see Case Studies, p 167).

Formulation of the Tourism White Paper in Australia made extensive use of consultation through the Internet and email. In Bulgaria, a wide range of promotional activity was used, including numerous press conferences, the use of posters in local communities, etc. (see Case Studies, p 130 & p 135).

The vision and strategic objectives must be appropriate to the country or destination and fully embrace concerns for economic, social and environmental sustainability. Objectives will vary from place to place, but they should always aim to strike a balance in the relative priority given to issues such as alleviating poverty, supporting conservation or reducing negative environmental impact. These broad objectives should be the overarching drivers for tourism policies and actions.

At this stage, a number of strategic choices will need to be made, such as the level and nature of tourism appropriate for the destination, target markets and product selection. This is discussed further in Section 4.2. Other more specific and measurable objectives may be identified reflecting these strategic choices, and may be linked to particular policies and actions.

Developing policies and action programmes

This final stage involves development of specific policies and actions that relate to the aims and strategic objectives and that reflect the strategic choices made. Close attention should be paid here to the policy areas identified in Chapter 2. It can be

Box 4.1: Analysing the situation

Research and data collection should cover the following:
- Analysis of past tourism policies and plans, as well as information and policies relating more widely to sustainable development and the environment.
- Analysis of existing relevant research.
- One to one consultation with key stakeholders and people with particular experience and expertise on relevant topics.
- Visitor survey.
- Survey of tourism enterprises.
- Local residents' opinion—this could be through elected representatives, open meetings, focus groups or household surveys.
- Site inspection, as practical and appropriate.
- Market opinion (e.g. through tour operators) and competitor analysis.

Information of particular relevance to sustainability issues includes:
- The balance of opinion about the level and nature of tourism that is desired and achievable.
- The range of natural and cultural heritage resources, including current state of preservation, level of use, degree of potential tourism interest and sensitivity to future use.
- Economic and social issues in the destination, including contribution of tourism alongside other economic sectors.
- State of the environment, including water and air quality, etc.
- Presence of relevant environmental management processes.
- Employment in tourism and support for this.
- Enterprise performance, outlooks, needs, etc.
- Current visitor flows, market trends and market opportunities.
- Visitor satisfaction, including attitudes to environment and other issues.
- Tourism infrastructure and support services, including transport, water supply, etc., and their capacity.

helpful to consider these policies and actions within a framework of 'influencing development', 'influencing the operation of tourism providers', and 'influencing visitors' (as presented in Sections 4.3–4.5).

Further consultation, including the possibility of establishing technical working groups, may need to be undertaken to develop particular policies and actions.

At this stage the range of instruments that governments can use to implement policies and maximize sustainability should be established or strengthened (see Chapter 5).

An action programme should be established that indicates lead agencies, approximate resources, targets, timescale and associated monitoring. Actions should be implemented by the agencies concerned and progress reported. Results should be measured against the sustainability indicators originally identified, or a modified set of them. Box 4.2 gives an example of good practice.

Box 4.2: Collaborative structures and strategy development for protected areas

EUROPARC, The Federation of National and Nature Parks of Europe, has established a Charter for Sustainable Tourism in Protected Areas.

The first requirement of the Charter is that there should be a permanent forum, or equivalent arrangement, between the protected area authority, local municipalities, conservation and community organizations and representatives of the tourism industry. Links with regional and national bodies should be developed and maintained.

The second requirement is for an agreed sustainable tourism strategy and action plan for the protected area. This must be based on careful consultation and be approved and understood by local stakeholders. It should contain:

- A definition of the area to be influenced by the strategy, which may extend outside the protected area.
- An assessment of the area's natural, historic and cultural heritage, tourism infrastructure, and economic and social circumstances; considering issues of capacity, need and potential opportunity.
- An assessment of current visitors and potential future markets.
- A set of strategic objectives for the development and management of tourism, covering:
  - conservation and enhancement of the environment and heritage;
  - economic and social development;
  - preservation and improvement of the quality of life of local residents;
  - visitor management and enhancement of the quality of tourism offered.
- An action plan to meet these objectives.
- An indication of resources and partners to implement the strategy.
- Proposals for monitoring results.

Twenty-three parks from eight countries have been awarded the Charter so far. In each case, EUROPARC, through the use of external verifiers, has helped the parks to identify ways to strengthen their actions towards sustainability and the Charter has served as a valuable incentive towards good practice.

4.2 Determining the level and nature of tourism

As part of the strategy and policy formulation process, governments, in consultation with partners, should make strategic choices about the general level and shape of tourism that may be appropriate for the country or specific destinations. This includes identifying targets for the volume and value of the sector, and for performance against other indicators relating to sustainability. Many factors will affect decisions on this, including overall strategic objectives and various factors identified in the situation analysis, such as current tourism levels, market trends, and a variety of resource constraints. Decisions can be assisted by the use of indicators and techniques to determine limits to tourism.

Two important issues in determining the appropriate level of tourism activity and the need and potential to accommodate growth are:

- The spatial distribution of tourism. Different locations and communities will be more or less suited to different levels of tourism. Factors influencing decisions on the location of new tourism development are considered below.
- Varying levels of demand across the year. Seasonality is a major issue for the sustainability of tourism. Many destinations experience distinct peaks and troughs. This is welcomed in some places, as communities and environments are able to recover in the off-season, and a seasonal pattern allows tourism to be fitted in alongside other activities and livelihood patterns. However, there are many reasons why tourism would be more sustainable if demand was less seasonal, including:
  - increased enterprise profitability and viability;
  - better quality jobs;
  - more efficient use of resources (such as accommodation capacity) and infrastructure;
  - avoidance of increased congestion at peak periods, which is when most negative impacts on communities and environments occur.

Market selection

Tourism strategies should identify priority markets. This will influence policies on the types of product to favour and also the marketing strategy.

Considerations of sustainability point to the following factors to bear in mind when selecting target markets:

- Seasonality: this is a key factor in market selection for sustainability. Some markets are less restricted than others in terms of when trips can be taken, or are more able and likely to respond to out-of-season products and offers.
- Growth potential: in the interests of economic sustainability, most destinations will seek to compete in markets indicating likely future growth.
- Spend per head in the community: higher spending visitors may contribute more to local prosperity with no greater cost to the community or environment. However, it is also necessary to consider the spending patterns of different market segments, including which types of visitors are most likely to spend money on products and services from which income is retained in the community.
- Length of stay: visitors who stay longer may contribute more in economic terms and become more aware and supportive of local community and conservation

needs, as well as providing more economic benefit (a local gain) per distance travelled (a global environmental cost). However, in many parts of the world, short trips are growing faster than long trips.

- Distance travelled: nearer markets, involving shorter journeys to the destination, will lower global environmental impact from transport emissions.
- Relevance to the offer: some market segments will be more likely than others to respond positively to the type of destination and products on offer.
- Responsibility and impact: destinations with particularly sensitive environments or communities may target particular segments that are likely to be more appreciative and responsible or that will, by the nature of their activities, have less impact on the environment or communities.
- Dependability: there are advantages in selecting markets that are less prone to unpredictable fluctuation, resulting from factors such as world events, exchange rates or the image of the region.
- Offering opportunities for all: aiming to ensure visitor fulfilment implies a need to be inclusive when offering and facilitating tourism experiences, paying specific attention to the needs of people who are physically or economically disadvantaged.
- Ability to reach the market efficiently: markets should only be selected where an efficient and cost-effective communication process can be identified.

Strategic choices based on these factors need to be made between target markets. For example, certain international markets may exhibit strong growth, high spend per head and good affinity with the product, but be more seasonal, less dependable, less inclusive and involve longer journeys. Domestic markets may provide fewer economic returns, but be more dependable, less seasonal and bring needed social benefits to participants. Where appropriate, business tourism and the MICE (meetings, incentives, conferences, and exhibitions) markets can deliver high spend out of season.

Sustainability considerations point to the need for destinations to maintain an appeal to a range of markets, to avoid over-dependency on any one market that may not be consistent in the long term. The importance of sound market research has been strongly underlined as a key factor for sustainability.

Product selection

Tourism strategies should consider the balance of products in a destination. Sustainability considerations may point to gaps in the range of products on offer or types of product to emphasize.

Few tourism products are inherently unsustainable. In almost all cases, impact depends on the nature and location of the development and operation. However, different types of product have different strengths and weaknesses in terms of their relevance to sustainability. This is illustrated by Table 4.1.

Governments, together with the private sector, should aim to reduce the potential disadvantages and reinforce the advantages of the different tourism products.

In general, destinations should seek a diversity of types of product, provided they are in line with market demand, are well planned and developed and are operated to meet the needs of local communities and environments.

Table 4.1: Potential advantages and disadvantages of different types of tourism in terms of sustainability

Tourism type	Potential advantages	Potential disadvantages
Larger resorts and hotels, or similar enterprises	• Generation of significant employment • Resources to support training • Business and marketing skills; financial stability • Ability to invest in environmental management systems and new technology • Potential for market diversification to reduce seasonality • Can absorb large visitor volumes	• Land and resource hungry • Potentially large ecological footprint • May not relate readily to local community • Potentially greater economic leakages, including repatriation of profits • Anonymity and lack of authenticity • Potential for exploitation of community/environment and lack of local influence • Possible lack of long term commitment to the local area
Medium, small and micro enterprises	• Individually owned and potentially responsive to local circumstances • May be located in areas of economic need • Flexible, with potential to grow • Able to deliver authentic experience • Profits may be retained in community	• Moderate to low levels of employment • Variable quality • Lack of resources to make investments in quality and environmental management • Lack of business skills • Difficulty in securing market access
Community-based tourism	• Products owned/operated by community, with sharing of economic and social benefits • Wider community awareness stimulating local support for conservation of culture and nature • Delivery of authentic experiences based on local knowledge • Increased visitor awareness of, and support for, community issues	• Any uncertainty over ownership, and lack of entrepreneurial motivation, may lead to weak economic sustainability • Challenge to ensure fair distribution of benefits • Lack of business skills and difficult access to markets • Can be difficult to break dependency on outside assistance
Ecotourism enterprises	• Growing market interest • All ecotourism products by definition should be specifically designed to minimize environmental impact, and to support conservation and communities • Suited to sensitive/protected areas	• Location in natural areas, and possibly indigenous communities, opens potential for intrusive impact • Potential to abuse term 'ecotourism', with positive impacts not assured • Visitor appeal often seasonal
Activity tourism enterprises	• Growing market interest • Strong recreational benefits • Potential to extend season • Can generate new tourism in remote rural areas • Some environmentally benign activities—walking, cycling	• Can be seriously environmentally damaging if not properly managed/controlled • Potential concerns with visitor safety
Cultural tourism enterprises	• Supporting conservation of heritage and cultural richness • Potential to extend season • Increases visitor awareness	• Term difficult to define • Potential to degrade culture unless well handled

The presence of a significant range of visitor attractions, restaurants, retail outlets (including handicraft sales), and events provided by local enterprises and bodies located within the community, will increase the potential level of visitor spending and the economic value retained locally.

4.3 Influencing tourism development

Government policies that influence the extent and type of new developments are among the most important in terms of making tourism more sustainable. Decisions made at the development stage have a long term effect and are difficult to reverse.

Development of tourism can be influenced when policies are agreed and plans are made for tourism in an area, and by determining the nature and shape of individual development proposals, and deciding whether or not they should happen.

The principles and aims of sustainable tourism, and the policy implications arising from them, point to a number of factors that need to be taken into account when making decisions about tourism development and developing policies that seek to influence it.

These factors are presented, in the following three groups, in Box 4.3:

*   Strategic development factors—relating to the ways in which a development may affect the overall scale and shape of tourism in a destination.
*   Locational factors—relating to choices and decisions about where tourism development may be encouraged or discouraged.
*   Performance and impact factors—concerned with the impacts of specific developments on the economy, society and the environment.

Box 4.3: Factors affecting tourism development policies

Strategic development factors:
*   The effect of new development on the overall level of tourism in the area and the mix of different types of product (as discussed in the previous section).
*   Relevance to target markets.
*   The cumulative effect of individual development projects over time.
*   The effect of associated activities such as traffic flows.
*   The degree of engagement of the local community in determining the level and nature of development.

Locational factors:
*   The relative merits of concentrating development in one place or spreading it geographically, which will depend on the nature of the area and the overall strategic objectives.
*   The environmental conditions and sensitivity of individual sites or wider locations, which should be a critical factor in determining whether any development should occur and the scale, density and nature of development.
*   The potential to cluster development, leading to mutual support and stronger supply chains.
*   Location with respect to population and incidence of poverty and economic need, relating both to avoiding labour supply constraints and to generating benefits... *cont. p 67*

The tools described below may be useful in addressing the different factors explained in Box 4.3. Others tools are presented in similar fashion in subsequent sections; their relevance and use are discussed further in Chapter 5.

Tools

Land use planning and development control is the primary tool for influencing the location and nature of new tourism development. This may also be linked to development regulations. In some circumstances, less formal guidelines can also be useful. The time when new development is being planned or approved can provide an important opportunity to influence future sustainability by introducing obligations for operators—for example introduction of requirements for reporting and auditing of impacts. **Economic instruments** can be used as an incentive for new development to incorporate sustainability aspects. **Capacity building** is important in assisting small enterprises and communities in deciding on, and implementing, new developments. Investment in appropriate **infrastructure** can also affect the sustainability of new tourism development. The application of **sustainability indicators and monitoring** will help to keep a check on the impact of tourism development over time.

Box 4.3 continued

- Ability of the infrastructure (transport, water, other services) to sustain new development without detriment to the community, and potential to support new infrastructure provision if necessary.
- General appeal of the area with respect to different markets, and location with respect to existing and potential visitor flows.
- Accessibility, including accessibility by public transport.

Performance and impact factors:
- Account taken of location issues as identified above.
- The demonstration of need, demand and viability, including a specific market assessment.
- Effect on existing businesses, taking account of the balance of supply and demand and use levels.
- The potential to utilize existing capacity as an alternative, possibly involving improvement or extension to existing enterprises.
- Potential to use existing buildings or previously used sites, as distinct from greenfield sites.
- Proposals for the after-use of sites.
- Proposals for environmental management, minimizing resource use and waste, and reflecting this in the nature and design of development.
- Careful setting of new development with respect to communities, services, landscape features, habitats, etc.
- Design sympathetic to the landscape and local vernacular style.
- Construction processes that minimize negative impact and maximize benefits, such as use of local materials and labour.
- Potential benefits to conservation of natural and cultural heritage, such as utilization of historic buildings, etc.
- Assessment of economic and social benefits accruing, in terms of employment generated (direct and indirect), benefits to other economic sectors, support for services, etc.
- Ensuring that the development and operation will be of sufficient quality and that the personnel have the skills and competence to establish and run a successful business.

4.4 Influencing the operation of tourism enterprises

Although the operation of tourism enterprises is essentially a responsibility of the private sector, there are many ways in which government policies can exert influence in order to encourage sustainability of operation.

Key areas for enterprises

Policies should encourage, support and promote action by enterprises in the following areas:

- Quality and customer care: these are central to issues of economic sustainability and visitor fulfilment.
- Environmental management: establishing more or less elaborate environmental management systems forms part of the actions that enterprises can take. Equitable use of resources, such as water, respecting community needs should also be seen as an aspect of sound environmental management.
- Human resource management: providing good quality, equitable employment opportunities is of fundamental importance. Related issues include providing employment opportunities for local people and for those who are poor or otherwise disadvantaged.
- Supply chain management: different aspects of sustainability point to the need for tourism enterprises to work with suppliers who:
  - are local to the area, thereby benefiting the local economy and reducing transport distances;
  - demonstrate ethical employment and trading policies;
  - are located in poor communities and involve or support the poor;
  - use environmentally sustainable production processes, such as organic agriculture. (It may not always be possible to satisfy all these requirements, and some strategic choices may need to be made).
- Relationships with the local community and environment: enterprises should be encouraged to support local conservation and social causes.
- Influence over guests: enterprises can have a significant impact on the behaviour of their guests. They can exert influence through information, interpretation (e.g. by guides), and facilitation (e.g. helping those who arrive by public transport).

Creating the context for sustainable enterprises

Governments can encourage enterprises to be more sustainable through direct advice and support or through policies and actions to create the conditions for sustainability.

The main conditions for economic viability, are particularly relevant here. They involve market access, a sound labour supply, positive destination images, safety and security and the critical importance of maintaining an attractive environment for the economic sustainability of tourism enterprises.

Other factors for the creation of a suitable context for sustainable enterprises include:

- Provision of the right infrastructure.
- Facilitating networking between enterprises.
- Helping to develop the supply chain through improving contacts and information and assisting with the development of local sources of supply.

Tools

Legislation, regulation and licensing should cover the most fundamental and serious impacts of tourism operation such as the welfare of employees and guests, or avoiding environmental damage. However, much can be achieved by voluntary measures, such as issuing **guidelines** and encouraging **reporting and auditing**. **Voluntary certification** provides a useful method for identifying and thereby stimulating good practice. **Economic instruments** and coverage in **marketing** can also provide an incentive, perhaps linked to **certification** if appropriate. **Capacity building** is important in providing enterprises and communities with the knowledge and skills to improve their management. In some places, the development and management of appropriate **infrastructure** and public services will be necessary to enable enterprises to be more sustainable. Maintaining regular feedback from enterprises that is set against **sustainability indicators** will be important in assessing the impact of policies.

4.5 Influencing visitors—promoting sustainable consumption

The activities of visitors and the decisions that they make have a bearing on the whole sustainability agenda. They affect the flow and retention of income, the benefits and pressures felt by recipient communities and the impact on the global and local environment. Their influence is partly direct and partly through the signals that the market gives to enterprises, which is perhaps in the long term the most sustainable way of affecting industry behaviour.

Consumer awareness of the sustainability of tourism and travel can be raised at any time, through general education, media features, etc. The impact of an individual trip can also be influenced at any stage through images and messages delivered when people are choosing or planning where to go, during the journey, at the destination or afterwards.

Governments can influence visitors directly in a variety of ways, including via marketing and information activities, and indirectly through the effect of their policies on the travel trade.

Sustainable consumption in tourism can be encouraged by influencing travel choices, visitor flows and visitor behaviour. Policy choices should be made about what level and kind of visitor activity should be encouraged or discouraged in the interests of sustainability, and measures introduced that will influence visitors' choices and behaviour accordingly.

Influencing travel choices and visitor flows

Influencing travel choices and visitor flows means influencing the nature of trips taken. Key factors relevant to sustainability include:

- When trips are taken: as already mentioned, travel out of season may often be more sustainable.
- Places visited: strategic decisions should be taken about the level of visitation to be encouraged in different areas. For example, visits to protected areas may be encouraged because of the revenue they bring to conservation or, alternatively, they may need to be discouraged because of the ecological sensitivity of the area.
- Transport used: the significantly greater environmental impact of travel by private car or air compared with other forms of transport has already been mentioned.
- Operators and enterprises selected: encouraging visitors to select operators that follow sustainability principles will make consumption more sustainable.
- Group size: in many places, larger volumes of people arriving at the same time can be more disruptive to environments and communities.
- Length of stay: in general, longer trips may bring more benefits to host communities and be more sustainable than short trips.

Influencing visitor behaviour and awareness

Visitors should be encouraged to:

- Respect host communities and avoid all forms of disruptive behaviour.
- Find out about the natural and historic heritage and culture of the area.
- Purchase local products.
- Reduce personal environmental impact—e.g. using water and energy sparingly, recycling waste and not leaving litter.
- Follow good practice with respect to outdoor activities, including wildlife watching.
- Support conservation and social projects, financially or in other ways.

Tools

Messages delivered through **marketing and information services** constitute the main method of influencing visitor flows and behaviour. These may be backed up as appropriate by the issuing of **guidelines and codes of conduct**. In some circumstances, it may be necessary to control visitor flows and behaviour through regulation, for example where access needs to be restricted or harmful activities prevented. **Voluntary certification** provides a valuable tool for enabling tourists to choose products and enterprises that are more sustainable. **Economic instruments** (e.g. pricing) may influence behaviour and can also be used to raise support from visitors. The provision and management of appropriate **infrastructure** such as public transport is an important enabling tool. Sound management will require processes for monitoring the flow of visitors and obtaining feedback from them, assessed against **sustainability indicators**.

Instruments for More Sustainable Tourism

This chapter presents thirteen instruments that governments can use to influence the sustainability of tourism. Each instrument has a significant role to play, but it is important to realize that they are not mutually exclusive and to consider them as a complete set of tools available to governments. This is backed up by experience and is amply illustrated by the Case Studies which show governments applying ranges of tools in ways that are complementary and mutually reinforcing. However, in the interests of clarity, the following pages present the tools grouped according to their main purpose, as follows:

- **Measurement instruments**—used to determine levels of tourism and impact, and to keep abreast of existing or potential changes.
- **Command and control instruments**—enabling governments to exert strict control over certain aspects of development and operation, backed by legislation.
- **Economic instruments**—influencing behaviour and impact through financial means and sending signals via the market.
- **Voluntary instruments**—providing frameworks or processes that encourage voluntary adherence of stakeholders to sustainable approaches and practices.
- **Supporting instruments**—through which governments can, directly and indirectly, influence and support enterprises and tourists in making their operations and activities more sustainable.

5.1 Measurement instruments

5.1.1 Sustainability indicators and monitoring

Attempting to make progress towards sustainability can be meaningless without some objective way of assessing whether its underlying principles are being respected or of measuring progress. The definition and use of indicators of sustainability is therefore a central component of the planning and management process. This subject has been studied by the WTO for the past 10 years, resulting in the publication of a comprehensive guide.[1]

Why indicators are important

Indicators make it possible to monitor changes over time in a constant and consistent manner. They can help to clarify goals and, most importantly, force them to be more precise. They can be very valuable in fostering greater accountability and in raising awareness of, and support for, actions.

Indicators can be used to show:

- The current state of the industry (e.g. occupancy rates, tourist satisfaction).
- Stresses on the system (e.g. water shortages, crime levels).
- The impact of tourism (e.g. changes in income levels in communities, rate of deforestation).
- Management effort (e.g. funding of cleanups of coastal contamination).
- The effect of management actions (e.g. changed pollution levels, number of returning tourists).

Indicators provide early warning of when a policy change or new action may be needed, as well as providing a basis for the long term planning and review of tourism.

 In Mexico, a set of sustainability indicators agreed at national level was applied in a range of local destinations. Initial measurements taken against these indicators provided a basis for assessing strengths and weaknesses and priorities for local action. As the same indicators were used in the different destinations it was possible to make comparisons between them (see Case Studies, p 153).

Box 5.1: Guiding a strategy with sustainability indicators and targets

In Lanzarote, Canary Islands, Spain, a broad range of indicators were employed to support planning in the context of the Lanzarote Biosphere Strategy addressing tourism alongside wider issues of sustainable development. Six key factors were identified, including the economy and tourism, the terrestrial and marine ecology, key environmental sectors, population changes, urban development and cultural identity. After consultation and discussion, indicators were chosen for each issue and an Island Observatory for Sustainability was established to monitor trends over time.

The strategy, produced in 1997, contained baseline values for each indicator and target values for 2007. This has proved most helpful in keeping abreast of changes and implementing a tourism management system guided by the strategy. In 2003, the indicators were revised, based on the first set but adding new ones according to the island's changing needs.

The use of indicators in policy making and planning

Indicators of sustainability should be defined at an early stage in the process of formulating a tourism strategy for a destination. They can then be used for:

- Baseline assessment of conditions and needs.
- Setting of targets for policies and actions.
- Assessment of actions.
- Evaluation, review and modification of policies.

The selection of sustainability indicators can be built into the process of consultation and participation. This can be most valuable in helping the stakeholders involved to focus their minds on tangible sustainability issues and priorities. Box 5.1 gives an example of use of indicators and the process is described more fully in the WTO guidebook on indicators referred to in Note #1.

Indicators need to be linked to the priority issues identified in the destination. It is normal for a wide range of possible indicators to be identified initially, which may then be refined according to relevance and practicability of use.

In addition to their use in planning and making of tourism policy, indicators can provide a highly effective and flexible tool when applied more widely in the sustainable management of a destination, including to issues such as development control. Regular monitoring of changes in environmental or social conditions using indicators can allow for an adaptive management approach that is more flexible than the heavy use of regulation. Use of indicators in this way can be undertaken by local authorities or be imposed by them on developers. Box 5.15 (page 101) provides a practical example of the use of indicators in development control.

In Calvia, 750 indicators were identified initially by experts. After further consultation and examination, they were reduced to a more manageable quantity (see Case Studies, p 167).

Criteria for selecting and reviewing indicators

Five criteria have been identified for the selection of indicators:

- Relevance of the indicator to the selected issue.
- Feasibility of obtaining and analysing the information required.
- Credibility of the information and reliability for users of the data.
- Clarity and ease of understanding amongst users.
- Comparability over time and across regions.

A regular review of indicators is required to see whether the information is making a difference, to determine whether the issues have changed, to consider any practical issues associated with the usability of specific indicators, and to consider whether new sources of data might permit alternative indicators to be used.

The WTO study has identified many hundreds of different indicators that might be considered by destinations. It is stressed that it is not expected that all of these should be used at any one time. Selection of indicators should be a matter of local determination of priority issues, as identified above. However, 29 'baseline indicators', that correspond to 12 baseline issues of sustainable tourism, are recommended (see Annex 1).

Monitoring sustainability

Monitoring sustainability involves taking measurements of environmental, social and economic conditions using selected indicators. Monitoring against a baseline set of results enables trends to be identified; change to be detected and, if possible, anticipated; and progress to be tracked. To be effective, monitoring should be undertaken regularly and follow a well-defined protocol.

Governments are often well placed to take the lead where monitoring is concerned. Some countries and destinations have established tourism observatories to monitor the volume and impact of tourism. Involving a wide variety of stakeholders in gathering relevant data to be used in monitoring can be beneficial and may also help to bind them into the process of management for sustainability (see Box 5.2). The range can include tourism service providers and visitors themselves.

One form of monitoring of the sustainability of tourism is to make specific, mainly quantified, measurement of:

- Levels of tourism: including both supply (e.g. by audits of the accommodation stock), and demand, (e.g. admission numbers to key sites or recorded bednights).
- The state of the environment and society: this may either be an outcome of tourism or affect its performance—examples include employment levels, crime levels, air and water quality, and species counts in sensitive or heavily visited environments.

Another form of monitoring is keeping abreast of the activities, needs and opinions of key stakeholder groups, notably:

- Visitors: through site surveys, focus groups and feedback via hosts, etc., to check on profiles and levels of satisfaction.
- Enterprises: through surveys, meetings, etc., to check on their economic and environmental performance and their perceptions and needs.
- The local community: through household surveys, focus groups, etc., to check on attitudes to tourism and concerns about its impact.

Certain forms of monitoring, such as the measurement of environmental impacts, may require particular expertise. Provision of relevant guidance and training can help here.

 In Egypt, an Environmental Monitoring Unit was established within the Tourism Development Authority and an operations manual prepared containing guidelines on the monitoring of coral reefs and other natural resources (see Case Studies, p 144).

Box 5.2: Involving users in data gathering

In Argentina, the Iguazu Natural Forest Reserve diversified its economic base, including the development of ecotourism. In order to assist with conservation and to plan the interpretative component of the tourist offer, more information was needed on the location and visibility of different animal species. It was decided to involve the local tour guides and tourists themselves in this process. A form for recording of sightings was provided, together with appropriate training.

Although not scientifically rigorous, the process made it possible to form a good picture of wildlife movement and also of visitor perceptions over a period of time. Involvement of local guides in the process increased the local communities' knowledge and appreciation of the ecological and economic value and importance of fauna. It also added value to the visitors' experience.

Benchmarking

A valuable use of indicators and associated monitoring is to enable a destination to check its sustainability performance against comparable destinations. This can help to show up points of relative weakness that may need to be given priority. Such a benchmarking exercise requires destinations to cooperate in the use of similar indicators and monitoring processes.

Governments are well placed to facilitate benchmarking at international or national level. International benchmarking can take place between countries or between comparable types of destination within different countries.

At national level, benchmarking exercises can be carried out between destinations within one country, perhaps coordinated by national government departments working with a group of local authorities.

5.1.2 Identifying the limits of tourism

One of the principles of the sustainable development of tourism is preparedness to recognize and abide by limits on the development of tourism and visitor flows.

Kaikoura, New Zealand, provides an example of a benchmarking process for a destination against international standards within the global Green Globe 21 system (see Case Studies, p 157).

Why it is important to identify limits

It has been widely demonstrated that where tourism is associated with negative impacts on the environment or society, this is frequently due to the volume of tourists or the extent of development exceeding the capacity of the recipient destination.

It is important to identify limits to tourism development in order to assist planning and policy making, and to respect those limits through action to control what actually happens on the ground.

In Mexico, the use of a standard set of sustainability indicators across a large number of local destinations, within the government coordinated Agenda 21 for Tourism initiative, has provided the right conditions for benchmarking (see Case Studies, p 153).

The concept of carrying capacity

The concept of carrying capacity in tourism has been the subject of much academic debate and discussion over many years. It usually refers to the number of tourists that a place can accommodate without detriment to the environment or host population nor any reduction in tourists' satisfaction. Different kinds of carrying capacity have been identified, including:

- Ecological capacity: based on biological and physical factors such as ability of certain species to withstand disturbance.
- Socio-cultural capacity: determined by unacceptable impacts on the local community or limitations due to the availability of human resources.
- Psychological capacity: the amount of crowding that tourists perceive as acceptable without affecting their quality of experience. This will vary according to types of tourist and types of activity or use.
- Infrastructural capacity: such as number of bedrooms or the capacity of transport systems or water supply. This is perhaps the element that can be most readily changed in the medium to long term.
- Management capacity: the number of tourists that can be realistically managed in an area without bringing economic and administrative problems.

Instruments 5

A realistic approach to carrying capacity assessment

There are many critics of the concept of carrying capacity as applied to tourism. It is felt that it can be meaningless and perhaps misleading to put a precise capacity limit on the number of tourists. The different factors affecting capacities and impacts are both numerous and complex, the concepts are quite subjective, conditions change over time, and there is no clear way of arriving at a figure.

On the other hand there are many circumstances where it can be very useful, and sometimes necessary, to quantify a maximum or optimum level of usage or scale of additional development. Such numbers can be used, for example, as the basis for measures to regulate, or otherwise maintain a control on visitor flows in congested places, or to guide planning decisions about the number of accommodation units that may be acceptable in an area. Rather than reject the idea of quantification on account of the above weaknesses, a realistic approach should be adopted. This might entail:

* Recognizing the inevitable subjectivity of any assessment, therefore using relatively simple approaches to estimate some sensible limits based on the different components of capacity identified above. Estimates can be made through close observation of sites, surveys, consultation, etc.
* Using these estimates to stimulate debate and discussion.
* Avoiding applying measures appropriate to one area to other areas that may not be comparable.
* Identifying ranges rather than precise numbers.
* Being flexible about the capacity limit and being prepared to make adjustments in the light of experience.

It should also be accepted that the overall concept of carrying capacity is important and can be the subject of valuable study to guide policies, even if a quantified capacity limit is not actually identified. Carrying capacity studies, which have looked in detail at economic, social and environmental capacity issues, have proved very useful in a number of countries (see Box 5.3), although they have sometimes not been as clearly reflected in subsequent policies and plans as might be expected.

Limits of Acceptable Change

The problems associated with quantification of carrying capacity have led to the use of alternative approaches to recognizing limits to tourism. The Limits of Acceptable Change (LAC) concept recognizes that it is the level of undesirable impact (or change) that is the problem, rather than the quantity of activity per se, and limits should therefore be described in terms of impact. The process entails:

* Identification of impacts that should limit development or use.
* Identification of usable indicators related to these impacts (see Section 5.1.1).
* Identification of a range of values associated with these indicators that are considered to be acceptable or unacceptable (based on expert evidence, consultation, etc.).
* Maintaining a monitoring process to check that performance remains within the acceptable range.
* Taking management steps to adjust levels of use if limits are exceeded.

The LAC approach has the advantage of being flexible and based on a real assessment of impacts of concern. However, it may sometimes be difficult to rectify problems by making adjustments only after they have occurred.

Box 5.3: Malta's tourism carrying capacity

In Malta, a small island state with 380 000 inhabitants, tourism accounts for a very significant proportion of employment and gross national product. In the late 1990s the government recognized a danger of unplanned tourism development leading to poor quality and a spiral of degradation. It, therefore, instigated a study of tourism carrying capacity.

Comprehensive data gathering and consultation over two years involved surveys of visitors and residents, aerial surveys of beaches, and analysis of existing data on the state of the environment and the economic contribution of tourism. A study group was established, with representatives of different interests.

Possible scenarios for future development were considered: free development; planned intensive development; sustainable development; restricted up-market tourism; or no tourism. The sustainable development approach was agreed upon, maintaining significant levels of tourism but within recognized limits.

A wide range of factors were analysed to identify those most critical in determining future rates of growth. These were found to be: a need to maintain tourism as a critical source of foreign exchange earnings; avoiding excess supply of accommodation leading to poor performance and quality; saturation in summer affecting visitor satisfaction and society's tolerance; scarce land resources; and use of energy.

It was recognized that to establish carrying capacity a quantifiable starting point was needed. This was taken as the supply of bedstock. It was calculated that this should stay at current levels (41 000) in order to achieve viable occupancy rates, rather than the considerable expansion that was then on the table. At the same time, a set of policies was widely agreed to improve the returns from tourism within these volume limits, including increasing per capita expenditure, strengthening the off-season, and promoting resource efficiency. This had implications for selection of relevant target markets and improving the quality of the offer.

The carrying capacity assessment and the clear policy direction that resulted from it has remained the cornerstone of Malta's tourism strategy, and is now used as justification for the application of European Structural Funds to improve the quality rather than the quantity of tourism facilities and the conservation and interpretation of the islands' heritage.

5.2 Command and control instruments

5.2.1 Legislation, regulation and licensing

Legislation, regulation and licensing are inter-related tools that can be used to strengthen sustainability by setting out requirements that are compulsory and enforceable, and which lead to sanctions and penalties if they are not met. Legislation provides the authority to enforce requirements, which are defined and elaborated by regulations. Licensing is a process of checking and signalling compliance with regulations or otherwise identified obligatory standards, conveying permission to operate.

Governments are in a position to apply laws, regulations and penalties to control aspects of business development and operations and to influence people's behaviour. This can be applied to the whole business sector and community or be more specifically targeted.

Legislation and regulations should be applied when governments deem them to be necessary. However, success requires regulations that are relevant, clear, practicable in terms of compliance and capable of being enforced. A sensible approach is to:

- Have the legislation in place that enables and supports the sustainability of tourism and gives authority to act.
- Have clear and enforceable regulations, supported by licensing as appropriate, where this is necessary to ensure important minimum standards.
- Seek to raise sustainability performance above such standards through other means, which also stimulate personal commitment towards continual improvement.

When might obligatory controls be needed for sustainable tourism?

There are a number of aspects of the development, operation and management of tourism that should be controlled through legislation and regulations in order to protect the environment, communities, visitors and the functioning of business. These include:

- The location and nature of development, covered under planning and development regulations.
- Rights and conditions for employees.
- Visitor health and safety, such as food hygiene and risk from fire and accident.
- Trading practices and ability to trade.
- Serious environmental damage (e.g. caused by discharges to air and water).
- Fundamental nuisance to local communities, such as excessive noise.
- Use of water and other scarce resources.
- Serious misconduct and exploitation by visitors of local people and vice versa (e.g. child prostitution).
- Right of access to services, land, etc.

The above aspects are of universal concern and should therefore be covered by a basic legal framework in each country applicable to all types of tourism in all locations. There may also be situations where further specific regulations are needed, relating to particular activities or locations. These are covered below.

'Enabling legislation' in support of tourism sustainability

Existing legislation should be reviewed, and where necessary strengthened, to ensure that it is adequate not only for purposes of control but also to promote sustainable tourism. Important areas to address are:

- The spectrum of legislation that relates to the areas of concern listed above. It is important to determine whether it can be fully applied to tourism and whether there are any gaps that need to be filled.
- The legal basis for positively encouraging sustainable tourism. This can include powers and authority to promote tourism as an activity per se. It also includes the ability to provide incentives and other support and, critically, the freedom and scope to utilize those incentives to favour enterprises and activities deemed more sustainable than others.
- The powers and responsibilities of particular bodies—for example, the authority of protected area bodies to control or promote tourism.
- The ability of particular stakeholders to engage in sustainable tourism. A critical issue in many developing countries concerns land tenure. Legislation that clarifies or strengthens the land rights of individuals or communities can be very important. In appropriate circumstances, this may also allow conditions to be attached that encourage, or possibly require, the land and resources to be used in ways conducive to sustainable tourism (see Box 5.4).

Box 5.4: Legal recognition of rights and responsibilities

In Namibia, the Nature Conservation Amendment Act (1996) made provision for members of rural communities to establish conservancies. This gave them recognized rights and responsibilities over the management of wildlife and natural resources in agreed areas of land. It has enabled the communities to establish their own ecotourism enterprises. It has also given them the authority to negotiate terms of agreement with private sector tourism operators that secure clear environmental and social benefits.

The raft of legislation that may relate to the sustainability of tourism will be considerable and it would be impossible and unnecessary to consolidate all of this in a single law. Moreover, legislation relating to particular issues (e.g. employment) should be attached to those bodies that are ultimately able to enforce it, rather than dividing it along sectoral lines. What is needed is a supportive national tourism law coordinated with a suite of other laws that cover the above requirements.

Reflecting sustainability in national tourism law

National tourism laws set out the responsibilities of governments and their agencies towards tourism. They provide a constitutional basis for tourism policy in the long term, and are more shielded from short term political influence than non-statutory tourism strategies. Laws—in the way that they describe tourism and the purposes of government intervention in the sector—can provide a vehicle for underpinning sustainability. Principles of sustainable tourism could be included in the preamble to new tourism laws and reflected in the balance and wording of different articles. This could include an emphasis on supporting communities, protecting natural resources, etc.

Tourism laws can also provide the basis for enabling the control and licensing of activities specific to the tourism sector (such as hotels) and for the undertaking of certain actions to support tourism development (e.g. provision of financial assistance) (see Box 5.5)

Box 5.5: Drafting a tourism law for Vietnam

In 2003, the Vietnamese government decided that a new tourism law was needed in the face of a rapid growth in the numbers of international and domestic visitors and concerns about the sustainable management of the country's tourism resources. Such a tourism law would raise the standing of tourism amongst all relevant government ministries and other stakeholders, strengthening coordination between them.

Drafting the law involved collaboration between the Vietnam National Administration of Tourism (VNAT), the WTO (which supplied technical expertise), and the Netherlands Development Organization (SNV), which facilitated the process and helped to integrate it with wider sustainable development issues.

Regional study tours and workshops were conducted for the Tourism Law Drafting Committee, including representatives of the VNAT and other important ministries. This enabled them to cement their own working relationship and also to meet local government bodies, participants in community-based tourism initiatives, tourism training institutions, tour operators and tourism service providers. The purpose was to:

- Ensure that the new law reflected the local reality of provision for tourism and management.
- Seek ideas and informed criticism.
- Avoid any allegations of imposed, ill-informed legislation.
- Strengthen the chances of effective implementation and enforcement.

It was found that this opportunity to participate motivated all ministries and stakeholder groups to provide highly constructive input.

The new draft tourism law underpins sustainability in many ways. For example, the general provisions and specific articles clearly recognize:

- The role of tourism in socio-economic restructuring, generating employment, eliminating hunger and reducing poverty.
- The importance of local communities as beneficiaries and stakeholders.
- A responsibility placed on all stakeholders, including local communities and people's committees, to protect the environment and landscapes at tourism sites.
- Specific obligations placed on tourism businesses regarding stewardship of tourism resources, including facilitating research and conservation.
- The role of the state in providing relevant investment incentives for tourism development in disadvantaged regions and for the restoration of natural and cultural sites and for traditional festivals and handicrafts.

Harmonizing and synchronizing legislation

In principle, the legislation needed to control many aspects of the impacts of tourism will be contained in laws relevant to specific fields (e.g. environmental management or employment legislation) rather than in tourism law. However, links should be identified between tourism law and these other areas.

A process of harmonization and synchronization can be valuable. It should:

- Cover the ways in which relevant legislative requirements do, or should, relate to laws specific to tourism.
- Identify other laws that contain legislation relevant to the sustainability of tourism.
- Seek to minimize any conflict between different areas of legislation.
- Ensure that there is no confusing duplication between the powers and responsibilities of different agencies in this matter.
- Assemble information on all relevant legislation so that this can be clearly disseminated to the industry and other affected stakeholders (see below).

The application of specific regulations

In addition to the fundamental aspects of sustainability of tourism listed earlier—which require legislation and regulations applied to all forms of tourism within a country—it may be necessary to apply specific regulations to certain forms of tourism or in particular circumstances. These may relate to:

- Particularly sensitive environments (e.g. protected areas, or particular types of ecosystem such as coral reefs).
- Especially vulnerable communities (e.g. certain indigenous communities).
- Particular types of activity. This could include certain outdoor sports, such as diving, that may be potentially dangerous to participants and/or damaging to the environment.

Regulations may also be needed to control the number and frequency of certain activities which through their concentration in space and time have a high impact on communities. An example is the arrival of cruise ships.

Regulations could cover many issues, but typically might relate to:

- Access to certain areas.
- Frequency and length of tourism use.
- Qualifications of operators.
- Safety standards of equipment and facilities (applying, for example, to activity based tourism).
- Certain seriously damaging activities that should be controlled.

In some cases, it may also be possible to control such situations through voluntary codes or guidelines (see Section 5.4). In others, it may be helpful to issue such guidelines, but to back them up with regulations.

In Calvia, regulations concerning anchoring and mooring were introduced to limit anchor damage and harbour congestion (see Case Studies, p 167).

In Ghana, simple bye-laws were used to control access and activities in heritage sites providing the focal point for community-based tourism (see Case Studies, p 149).

Instruments **5**

Licensing

Licensing of tourism enterprises can be used to:

- Signal compliance with basic legislation on issues such as employment and environmental protection.
- Signal compliance with other more specific regulations, as above.
- Enforce standards above minimum legal requirements.
- Control the number of operators in any one place.

Licensing has been used in many parts of the world to control activity and enforce standards in areas such as accommodation provision, guiding and informal street trading. Some simple sustainability requirements could be added to licensing conditions, but above a certain level this may be better achieved through voluntary processes.

One form of licensing is the issuing of permits to operate in certain areas, such as protected areas. This has proved to be an important tool for strengthening sustainability, as stringent conditions appropriate to a given set of local circumstances may not be suitable in other situations where more general licensing would be appropriate.

Strengthening compliance

A major problem with using legislation and regulations as a way of improving sustainability is the difficulty of enforcement and of overcoming non-compliance. This is a fundamental issue both in developed and developing countries. Ways in which it can be addressed include:

- Linking regulations to licensing, and issuing the licence in the form of a badge that tourists are asked to look out for.
- Stimulating peer pressure amongst operators.
- Setting targets for implementation and getting operators to report against them.
- Streamlining inspection schemes, so that one inspector can cover various legislative requirements.
- Providing simple information to operators about the regulations they have to meet and what compliance means in practice.

Box 5.6 gives an example of the latter two approaches used in England in relation to provision of accommodation.

5.2.2 Land use planning and development control

These inter-related tools can be used to influence the location and type of new tourism activities and to control potentially harmful development.

The importance of land use planning and development control

These are, arguably, the instruments that have provided the primary means of intervention by governments in shaping the nature of development on behalf of society.

In Australia, tourism enterprises need a permit to operate in protected areas. This provides a basis for agreeing conditions with them, and is also linked to other tools such as guidelines and certification to further strengthen the sustainability of operations (see Case Studies, p 130).

In South Africa many tourism enterprises were not meeting the requirements of the Black Economic Empowerment Act, so targets were set for the industry (see Case Studies, p 162).

Box 5.6: Streamlining inspections and clarifying requirements

In England, the tourist authorities have taken a number of steps to address non-compliance with regulations in the accommodation sector and to make it easier for enterprises to understand the legal requirements they have to meet.

The 'Fitness for Purpose' initiative has involved systematic inspection of establishments in six pilot areas to check compliance with respect to food hygiene, health and safety, fire safety and trading standards legislation. Consideration has been given to ways of coordinating inspection processes to make them more efficient both for the industry and for the enforcement bodies.

The national tourist authority has produced a 'Pink Booklet' as a practical guide to legislation for accommodation providers. The booklet identifies the relevant legislation under different subject headings, spelling out in simple language the circumstances under which it applies, what actions are necessary to meet the requirements, and sources of further information and help.

Land use planning and development control are critically important for the sustainability of tourism, influencing not only tourism development itself but also controlling other forms of development that might be detrimental to the economic sustainability of tourism in the short or long term. At the time when local land use plans are being agreed, or more specifically when decisions are being made to approve or refuse controversial developments (such as industrial plant, mining or timber extraction), economic arguments relating to tourism can be used to advocate environmental conservation.

The potential strength of these tools, and the way in which they can be applied, will vary from country to country according to the nature and functionality of the land use planning system that is in place. This partly reflects political circumstances, legislative frameworks, levels of corruption, and administrative efficiency. The nature of landownership is also a critical question. In some countries where there is widespread government ownership of land, development control may be brought about more directly through the issuing of leases, permits and licenses. However, the fundamental principles behind sustainable land use planning for tourism still remain.

The outreach of land use planning is also very important. In some countries planning control is applied to all areas. In other countries, this may, essentially, be restricted to urban settlements or designated protected areas. In general, the greater the coverage of a sound land use planning system and effective development control, the stronger the chances of achieving more sustainable tourism.

Relating tourism strategies to spatial and land use plans

In the past, tourism planning tended to be executed through the preparation of somewhat rigid and top-down master plans, which indicated locations and sites for tourism development based principally on physical attributes of the land and location with respect to potential visitor flows and accessibility. Sustainability principles point to a more strategic, flexible, bottom-up approach, taking account of a wide range of economic, social and environmental factors and based on local consultation and participation.

The approach advocated for tourism is in line with the advent of integrated 'spatial planning' at a regional level and community-based planning at a local level, which is being pursued in many countries, and tourism planning should align with this.

Tourism strategies built on participatory structures and inclusive processes should provide the basis for tourism planning. Planning should also mirror the preparation of tourism strategies at the national, regional and local destination levels emphasized in Chapter 3. This can be achieved by two interrelated processes:

- National or regional spatial planning: in many countries and regions, it is appropriate for national or regional tourism strategies to be interpreted spatially. These might take into account broad factors of natural resources, economic need, market potential, etc. In some cases they could lead to the indication of broad priority areas for tourism development. Spatial planning at this level should also make links between tourism and important related issues that have a spatial dimension such as transport planning.
- Local community-based land use planning: decisions on the level, pace, nature and location of tourism development at the local level should be based on local strategies and plans, involving thorough assessment of economic, social and environmental opportunities and constraints, together with full community engagement. These processes should then determine land use planning policy.

Making land use planning for tourism more sustainable

The location of tourism development should be based on strategic choices reflecting the agenda for sustainable tourism and these choices should be taken into account when considering wider spatial planning and local land use planning for tourism.

Some important points to bear in mind when developing such plans include:

- Positive planning for sustainability. Land use planning should not simply be a controlling process. It can be used creatively to identify space and location for new development that will contribute to sustainable tourism. For example, it can encourage clustering between tourism enterprises and related businesses, and strengthening of the local supply chain, by facilitating co-location.
- The potential to use other tools in association with planning. For example, the national or regional spatial planning process may lead to the identification of priority areas for the development of tourism that meet sustainability criteria. Such areas may then be used to concentrate economic incentives for the development of appropriate sustainable tourism products. The use of regulations or looser development guidelines can also be closely associated with planning.
- Future proofing. Planning should take account of already predictable changes in conditions, and in doing so should apply the precautionary principle. A particular example is taking account of the effects of climate change, for instance with respect to coastal planning, and responding with the appropriate adaptation measures.
- Flexibility and adaptive approaches. Plans should also be open to less predictable change, such as world events that may alter demand patterns or unforeseeable

 In Calvia, the land use planning tool was used effectively to implement a local sustainable development strategy, centred on tourism. This led to the declassification of land scheduled for new accommodation development in the interest of greater amenity for residents and visitors and a more sustainable future (see Case Studies, p 167).

natural phenomena. Adaptive planning can be assisted through the identification of reviewable limits and the use of indicators, regular monitoring and feedback.

- Checking the sustainability of the process. Some of the systematic approaches used within industry, such as environmental management systems, could be applied to the land use planning process. The Bodensee, Germany, provides an example (see Box 5.7).

Box 5.7: Ecological land use planning (ECOLUP)

Four communities around the Bodensee, a popular tourist destination on the border of Germany and Austria, have worked together to improve their land use planning, with funding from the European Union. This involved using the European Eco Management and Audit Scheme (EMAS) as a framework for auditing and assessing all the various components of the land use planning process. The purpose was to ensure that environmental conditions and needs are reflected in a more rigorous, systematic and integrated way.

The exercise indicated the need to:

- Widen the range of environmental impacts covered in land use planning.
- Strengthen community participation in identifying environmental issues.
- Integrate environmental management into municipality administration structures.
- Delegate responsibilities and tasks between many different bodies.
- Strengthen the use of environmental indicators and checking mechanisms.

Integrated area management

Placing land use planning for tourism within the context of more strategic spatial planning and with participatory processes at a local level is in line with certain other directions that have been taken in the sustainable planning and management of resources. There are some types of location that, because of their special circumstances, require an even more closely integrated approach—coastal areas being the most notable example.

Integrated Coastal Zone Management (ICZM) is a process that brings together all those involved in the development, management and use of the coast within a framework that facilitates the integration of their interests and responsibilities. As tourism is often a major activity in coastal areas, it is clearly very important that tourism strategies, polices and plans are incorporated in the ICZM processes. Although this has a bearing on the wider coordination of organizations, strategies and policies in coastal areas, it is a particularly important issue with respect to land use planning, given the impact of new development on marine and coastal environments and communities[2].

Zoning for tourism development

One approach to land use planning at a local level is to identify a series of zones for different types and levels of tourism development. Zoning may be more or less appropriate as a tool according to the nature of the area, the landownership and planning circumstances and whether tourism is an established or newly developing activity. Community engagement should remain an integral part of any process to define zones, and community related issues may determine whether rigid zoning is an appropriate approach.

The identification of zones should be based on very careful assessment of resources as well as being related to strategic spatial issues. The zones can then form the spatial focus for quite precise planning policies and for the issuing of regulations to control use. This zoning and regulatory approach usually implies some application of concepts of carrying capacity in order to indicate appropriate amounts of development.

Development regulations and planning briefs

Development regulations, issued by governments or local authorities, can be used to inform potential developers as to what will be acceptable or unacceptable before they prepare schemes or projects for approval. They can also be used to ensure compliance with certain standards during the construction phase. In order to improve sustainability, regulations could cover such aspects as the density of buildings, location of buildings (e.g. set-back distances from the coastline), building heights, linkage to services and sewage disposal systems, materials used (e.g. efficiency standards), and aspects of design (e.g. with respect to the local vernacular). Social sustainability issues, such as health and safety features and provision of accommodation for staff, could be built into development regulations (see Box 5.8).

Rather than simply issuing regulations for general application, a planning authority may decide to issue a more specific planning or development brief for a particular site, with which any potential developer must comply. This may have the twin purposes of strengthening the chance of that site being utilized for tourism development, and

 The Egypt Red Sea Initiative provides a clear example of the application of zoning, using extensive data gathering and GIS mapping techniques, and dividing a coastal area into five zonal types, primarily based on the sensitivity of the natural resources. The zones stretch from zero use (strict reserves), through use for ecotourism, to areas for moderate intensity development. This process has led to a considerable amount of scaling down of development previously proposed for certain areas, and the issuing of regulations that achieved agreement by both the tourism and environment ministries (see Case Studies, p 144).

Box 5.8: Maldives development regulations

The small size and fragile environment of the islands in the Maldives requires that any tourism development should be very sensitively planned and designed. For many years, a clear development concept for resorts has been pursued, backed up by regulations, requiring for example, that:

- Buildings should take up no more than 20 per cent of the total land area.
- No buildings should appear above the tree tops.
- Coastal vegetation should be maintained, to retain the natural façade of islands and to guard against coastal erosion.
- A minimum of 5 linear metres of beach shall be available for every hotel room.

The regulations have been supported more recently by guidelines which provide more detail on design, construction and management practice, and also spell out the requirements for Environmental Impact Assessment of new development.

The government believes that the success of tourism in the Maldives can be attributed to a great extent to these clear regulations and the fact that they have been strictly enforced.

---

also of ensuring that the resulting development will match a clear pre-determined style and design. Using such a tool allows sustainability related requirements to be incorporated in more specific detail.

Some governments or local authorities have prepared design guidelines for specific types of tourism facility. While these may be less rigorous than regulations, enterprises may be encouraged to follow them because they can assist in the process of obtaining planning permission.

Development control processes

If land use planning is to be effective, it is necessary to have a development control process that ensures compliance with land use planning regulations and prevents illegal development. There are many reasons why development control may be dysfunctional (see Box 5.9), some of which may be deep seated and require significant political change. However, functionality in terms of tourism planning may be facilitated by:

- Greater availability of human resources to handle applications.
- Capacity building with local administrations to increase knowledge of sustainable tourism issues.
- Clear notification requirements for potential developers, including both procedures to adopt and information to deliver.
- Enforcement of penalties for non-compliance, including financial penalties, criminal prosecution and removal of illegal structures.

Development control depends on potential developers being required to apply for planning approval. The notification procedure and the degree of detail required from developers prior to approval are determined by governments or local authorities, who

---

Box 5.9: Practical problems of implementation in Colombia

A pilot project to demonstrate the application of the CBD's Guidelines on Biodiversity and Tourism Development was undertaken in Colombia in 2002. This looked at the context and reality of tourism development in Tayrona National Park, an attractive, protected coastal area with many fine beaches. The study concluded that a general framework of legislation, planning and development control procedures existed and was relevant. However, there were problems in ensuring effective enforcement, including:

- Limitations of the administration and the shortage of human and financial resources.
- Overlap of powers and authority between different institutions, causing duplication of effort or even leading to lack of action by any of the institutions.
- An unclear situation as to land ownership, making it difficult for the park to reach management agreements with land owners and occupiers of land within the park, and to enforce legal controls over tourism development on private land within the park boundaries.
- The continuation of some tourism projects which had failed to comply with legal requirements, consequently undermining the image and position of the institutions in exercising development control.

may choose to include a wide range of information relating to the sustainability of the development. It is important that the level and nature of information required are relevant and realistic and not so onerous as to discourage compliance with the system. An example of information that could be required is contained in the section on notification within the CBD Guidelines on Biodiversity and Tourism[3]. This may be met by a requirement that the developer produces a formal Environmental Impact Assessment (see below).

A further useful mechanism associated with the development control process is the issuing of conditions attached to the granting of individual planning permission. This could be used to:

- Strengthen or improve certain aspects of the impact of the project itself, as proposed (e.g. design factors, landscaping, or access).
- Achieve some external benefits for the community or for environmental conservation through the process of planning gain (planning obligations). This could include, for example, the inclusion of provision of services for community use, replanting schemes, or the creation of trails or other infrastructure.

Any conditions or obligations that are imposed should be fair and realistic, and not be so onerous as to prevent implementation and the achievement of mutual benefit.

Environmental Impact Assessment

The sustainability of tourism development can be further strengthened by more extensive and effective use of Environmental Impact Assessment (EIA) as a requirement placed on developers.

EIA provides an internationally recognized and structured approach to obtaining and evaluating environmental information about the potential impacts of a physical development; the EIA is then used in decision-making in the development process. It is particularly useful as an adjunct to the process of granting planning permission for new development, and may be required of a potential developer in order to aid decision making. A particular strength of EIAs is the requirement to account for all stages and processes of a proposed development, including upstream and downstream impacts. There is also a requirement to consider alternative proposals that may lead to less harmful impact or provide greater opportunity for benefit.

In many countries, use of EIA is required by law in situations where proposed development-related actions are expected to be environmentally damaging, but its application to tourism varies around the world. There is a lack of consistency in the selection of developments for which specific EIA studies are required. Whether or not an EIA is required is likely to depend on the size and nature of the project, the sensitivity of the location in which it is proposed, and the perceived risk to the environment. Small scale projects are not included in most EIA systems although their cumulative impacts may be significant over time.

The close relationship between social and environmental systems makes it imperative that social impacts are identified, predicted and evaluated in conjunction with biophysical impacts. EIAs are increasingly including prediction and evaluation of social, economic and health impacts as well as environmental impacts. Emerging thinking and practice in the application of EIA is likely to focus mainly on adapting and using EIA in conjunction with other tools as a means of testing development proposals against pre-determined sustainability criteria.

Recommendations for improving EIA processes include:

- Clarifying the screening process that determines whether EIAs are required. The provision for EIA should be based on legislation which is clear and explicit as to the nature and scope of application and the type of approach to be taken.
- Reviewing how EIAs are applied to tourism development and whether coverage should be extended. At present it is unlikely that an EIA will be required. generally for all tourism projects, but the kinds of project and location for which they are required should be clear to developers.
- Providing helpful guidelines, relevant to tourism, on what is required in the EIA.
- Avoiding duplication or uncertainty between the agencies involved, and providing a swift response, in order to prevent projects that do not comply from proceeding without a decision.
- Establishing a process to track compliance with any management and mitigation measures proposed in the EIA and, where necessary, providing enforcement action.

Egypt provides an example of how sloppy procedures prevented EIAs from providing an effective control mechanism, and of how this can be rectified through clearer guidance and coordination (see Case Studies, p 144).

5.3 Economic instruments

5.3.1 Taxes and charges

These measures work through factors, namely cost, price and income, which have long proven to be major influences on the choices and decisions made by enterprises and consumers. They can be applied flexibly and adjusted readily. However, they are indirect instruments, and it is therefore difficult to be sure that the net effect will be that which was intended.

Imposing taxes and setting charges can have two important consequences for the sustainability of tourism:

- Changing the behaviour of consumers and enterprises, through their effect on prices, costs and income. Taxes and charges can be constructed so as to penalize unsustainable practice such as pollution, and to change the pattern of demand.
- Raising revenue from consumers and enterprises that can be used to mitigate impacts and support actions such as conservation or community projects that lead to greater sustainability. For this to happen, taxes should be hypothecated—i.e. constructed in such a way that the revenue raised is restricted to specific types of use rather than simply going into the general public purse.

These effects are interrelated and should therefore be considered together. Often one measure can produce both of the effects at the same time. A balance may need to be struck between them.

Taxes and charges are important instruments in the process of internalizing the total costs, including environmental and social costs, of activities like tourism. Depending on the way they are directed, they can support adherence to the 'polluter pays' principle.

The main ways in which governments can use these measures are by:

- Setting charges for the use of resources or services which they control, such as public utilities and amenities.
- Introducing general or more specific taxes on activities that affect the operation of tourism enterprises and the behaviour of tourists.

An individual tax or charge may influence the behaviour of enterprises or tourists or both. This may depend partly on the response of enterprises and whether they absorb the effect or pass it on to consumers through higher prices. Irrespective of who is affected by the tax or charge, good communication about the measure, the reasons for it and the resulting benefits is very important in winning support and maximizing compliance.

Different types of taxes and charges that have a particular bearing on tourism are described below.

General business taxes

One way in which taxation is likely to affect the sustainability of tourism is through the general impact of the fiscal system on the performance of tourism businesses. Governments should ensure that corporate taxation does not discriminate unfairly against small service sector businesses. They should also take account of how taxation policy may affect the full range of economic, social and environmental issues relating to the particular circumstances of the sector, such as impacts on seasonal jobs and opportunities for micro enterprises and employees to engage in a variety of activities.

General tourist taxes

A number of countries have introduced taxes on tourism in the form of a tax paid per visitor, often raised per overnight stay as a 'bed tax'. This is most usually collected from tourism enterprises, and may or may not be passed on by them to tourists. Normally it is not seen as a way of influencing visitor numbers but rather as a process for raising revenue. Significant sums can be raised in this way, but it can lead to industry concerns about the negative effect on demand and on enterprise profitability. A key issue for sustainability is the extent to which the proceeds are retained locally and used to support destination management, environmental conservation and social causes.

 In Bulgaria the law relating to local government financing has been changed so that revenue from tourism taxes remains in the municipality and has to be used for tourism related infrastructure (see Case Studies, p 135).

Taxes of this kind can be introduced specifically for the purpose of benefiting the destination and sustainability. However, even if they are presented in this way they can prove to be controversial, as was well demonstrated by the Balearics ecotax described in Box 5.10

The successful introduction of such taxes may be more difficult if it is seen by business as adding to their existing tax burden. A more successful approach may be to direct

Box 5.10: Lessons from an ecotax

In 2002 the government of the Balearic Islands, Spain, introduced a tax with the clear objective of raising funds from tourists to be invested in environmental protection and improvement in amenity in tourist areas. The purpose for which the proceeds could be used was enshrined in law. The tax was not seen as a controlling measure, but more as a source of additional revenue to support public expenditure. It was considered as one tool in shifting the direction of tourism in the islands towards sustainability and quality. Examples of projects supported include the purchase and improvement of a natural coastal area for public use, removal of unsightly old hotel buildings, and financial assistance to farmers to plant trees.

The tax involved a flat rate charge averaging around 1 euro per night per adult tourist, collected by hoteliers. In the first year approximately €4.5 million were raised. Although many tourists and local residents were in favour of the tax, hoteliers and tour operators were very opposed to it. It was considered to be unfairly applied (it did not reach the many tourists staying in self-catering or unregistered accommodation), and was assumed to be one reason for a downturn in demand for the Balearics in the year it was introduced. There was also some uncertainty about how the money was spent and the transparency of this process. The new incoming government abolished the tax after one and a half years of operation.

There was a fierce debate about the merits of the tax. Some felt that the long term competitiveness of the islands would have gained from the improvements funded by the tax, despite negative short term reactions. Whatever the merits of it, however, the experience pointed to the need to make sure that the industry is fully supportive of such a process, especially if it is engaged in its implementation, that it is seen to be fair, and that it is positively promoted as a measure seeking to bring benefits to all.

such a charge at visitors, as is the case in Belize (see Box 5.11), which is essentially a hypothecated exit tax. Any tax of this kind needs to be fairly and evenly applied, easy to collect, and fully discussed and supported by all those involved, including the travel trade. The utilization of the tax needs to be completely transparent and made widely known to those who are paying it.

Taxes and charges on specific inputs and outputs

A range of taxes and charges can be used to influence the use of resources by the tourism industry and tourists. Examples include:

- Effluent charges to encourage the reduction of emissions through end-of-pipe measures.
- Waste taxes to make final waste disposal more expensive, promoting reduction and recycling.
- Product taxes on items such as energy and packaging that have an environmental impact in production, consumption or disposal (e.g. carbon taxes on the use of certain fuels).
- User charges for use of precious resources such as water.

In most countries taxes and charges of this kind are applied generally in order to influence the activities of all businesses. It is unlikely that the tourism industry will be singled out for special treatment. However, changes in behaviour on account of these measures will affect the impact of the industry, particularly in places where tourism has traditionally contributed to environmental or social impacts.

An issue of particular relevance to tourism is the use of taxation to influence choice of transport. Some countries have high taxes on petrol in order to encourage a switch from private motoring to public transport; this is likely to have a particular effect on discretionary journeys such as leisure trips. The argument for introducing a tax on aircraft fuel is frequently made, and is an important issue for the tourism industry.

Taxes or charges on water consumption can be very important as a way of keeping consumption down in tourist resorts.

Although taxes of this kind are primarily imposed to influence behaviour rather than raise revenue, the proceeds from them can be used to support relevant activity. An example is the Hospitable Climates scheme in the UK, described in Box 5.12.

In Calvia, the adverse reaction to a water tax illustrates how important it is to communicate effectively with enterprises and consumers over the implementation of such measures (see Case Studies, p 167).

In Bulgaria, ecotourism enterprises are supported by a capital fund raised from environmental taxes on pollution and fuel consumption (see Case Studies, p 135)

Charges on the use of amenities and infrastructure

Charging for the use of public amenities can provide a valuable tool in the field of tourism. As visitors perceive that they are getting a direct benefit, there is often little negative reaction to this. A particular example is the setting of an admission price for entry into a national park or heritage site. Charges may be used for management purposes, to control visitor numbers and environmental impact—this may be related to carrying capacity and targeted levels of demand. They may be varied at different times of the year. Social equity considerations would suggest that differential charges should be used that reflect ability to pay, preventing economic discrimination.

Generating revenue for use in conservation and management, or to support local communities, can be an important objective in the setting of charges of this kind. In some circumstances charges may be specifically augmented in order to increase revenue available for local causes. Where possible a structured and transparent approach should be used for the distribution of financial resources raised, involving local communities and informing those paying the charge about how their expenditure is being used, as in the Madagascar example in Box 5.11.

Charges may also be raised for the use of infrastructure. A common example is the use of car parking charges, which can prove to be a sensitive management tool. As well as helping to limit vehicle use and consequent pollution and congestion, they can sometimes provide the only direct source of revenue for the management of sites where no other form of admission charge is possible. This is the case for certain countryside sites. Road tolls can also be employed to discourage private vehicle use.

Charges influencing after use—assurance processes

Charges can be constructed to serve as an assurance payment leading to sustainable outcomes at some future time, for example:

> ### Box 5.11: Examples of charges supporting conservation
>
> **Belize:** In 1996, the Protected Areas Conservation Trust (PACT) was established, to provide funding for the conservation, awareness, sustainable development and management of protected areas. In excess of US$1.75 million have been disbursed (1997–2004) through more than 70 grants to over 30 organizations. Funds are raised by a compulsory US$3.75 conservation fee charged to visitors on their departure from Belize. PACT also receives 20 per cent of the cruise ship passenger head tax and of the recreational licence and concession fees in protected areas. Corporations and individuals also donate voluntarily to PACT.
>
> **Madagascar:** The government national park service has a policy of distributing 50 per cent of the admission revenue from all parks to local conservation and community development projects. The latter, proposed by special committees made up of elders from individual villages, tend to be very practical (such as fruit growing schemes, bee keeping, construction of grain stores) supporting sustainable livelihoods as an alternative to slash and burn agriculture. The funding link with the local park enhances community awareness and support for conservation.

- Performance bonds may be required of developers, in the form of a payment returned to them later providing certain conditions are met. An example most relevant to tourism is the use of a performance bond to ensure that reforestation is carried out following a development project that has required clearance of areas of forest.
- Deposit/refund charges might, typically, be applied to packaging such as glass or plastic bottles to stimulate reuse or enable controlled disposal.

5.3.2 Financial incentives and agreements

These are economic instruments that influence the behaviour of enterprises by providing them with specific financial support or commercial opportunities provided that they act in a certain way.

Government action may involve:

- Providing financial support and opportunities themselves.
- Influencing and working with development assistance agencies whose policies in recipient countries are increasingly influenced through priorities and programmes agreed with governments.
- Influencing the financial decision making policies and actions of commercial sources of finance.

Positive financial incentives

Various forms of financial assistance can be used to influence behaviour and support change. They can be directed at existing tourism enterprises or new projects.

Where positive subsidy is used, principles of economic sustainability suggest that the type and amount of assistance should be such that it encourages and supports self-sufficient enterprise and avoids dependency.

Three ways in which financial assistance can be used to effect change are:

- Leveraging action by placing conditions on financial assistance.
  This can apply to all kinds of projects. A lead is being taken by the World Bank and other development assistance agencies. The jointly agreed Equator Principles lay down a wide range of social and environmental sustainability conditions for large projects which must be the subject of assessment before assistance is approved. Conditions may relate to minimizing impacts or supporting conservation or social projects such as providing clean water. The approach is very relevant for national as well as international assistance schemes and for small as well as large projects. Micro-credit can, for instance, be used to influence sustainable livelihood decisions.

- Assisting specific forms of tourism that relate to sustainability goals.
  Rather than seeking to influence all types of tourism project, well tailored financial assistance can be provided, as required, to particular types of project that are in line with specific sustainable development priorities. Examples might be small scale community-based projects in poor areas, or certain ecotourism projects. The economic instruments might be closely related to capacity building (see Section 5.5.2), with financial assistance given to such aspects as building market access.

- Funding specific, direct investments that will improve sustainability.
  Financial assistance may be provided for actions that will improve sustainability, such as the installation of environmentally efficient new technology. Assistance may also be given with the costs of establishing environmental management schemes. It is important for governments to avoid simply paying for the improvements that are sought, thus diminishing commitment to them. There are therefore advantages in using soft loans or tax credits. Often, such schemes can be most effective if combined with other instruments such as certification and capacity building, as shown by some of the examples in Box 5.12.

Exerting influence through other financial agreements

Governments may also have an opportunity to influence the behaviour of enterprises by reaching other kinds of financial agreement with them. This may entail conveying some form of property or trading right on the enterprise. Conditions can be attached to this process that require compliance with a sustainability agenda. Examples include:

- The granting by governments of concessions or contracts to enterprises. This has proved to be an effective vehicle for imposing conditions on selected enterprises—for example those providing services in national parks.
- Introducing tradable licenses for water extraction, with basic protection of rights for the poorest communities.
- Developing public-private partnerships with selected enterprises for the provision of certain facilities, such as transport infrastructure, public amenities or information services.
- Government procurement policies—for example, only accommodation certified as meeting sustainability criteria could be used for government business.

In one region of Scotland, all tourism projects receiving assistance from the development agency must participate in an environmental certification scheme. (see Case Studies, p 172).

In Ghana, financial assistance is available to community tourism projects that meet specific sustainability criteria. In order to avoid dependency and encourage enterprise efficiency, grants are given only for infrastructure, with enterprise support being in the form of loans (see Case Studies, p 149)

In South Africa, the government has established conditions and guidelines for the operation of public-private partnerships on state land, and has disseminated these in the form of a toolkit (see Case Studies, p 162)

Box 5.12: Examples of financial assistance for sustainability measures

Morocco: UNEP has worked with the state electricity organization to promote the purchase of solar water heating equipment by hotels, by offering subsidized low interest loans from banks. Monthly repayments are collected as supplements to the regular payment of electricity bills, thus reducing the chances of default and therefore reducing the risk to banks, enabling them to offer lower interest rates. This should strengthen the process of commercial lending in the solar energy sector, so enabling the subsidy to be phased out.

Catalonia, Spain: grants are given to enterprises to meet external costs (such as employment of consultants) of implementing the eco-certification scheme. Some municipalities give enterprises in the scheme a 90 per cent reduction on the normal community charge for waste collection, in order to encourage them to stay in the scheme.

Rimini, Italy: following a successful demonstration project on how to run a beach bathing station sustainably, the Province of Rimini has offered grant assistance to other bathing stations on a competition basis and it is anticipated that 100 will take this up. Assistance includes a special grant for installation of photovoltaic cells.

United Kingdom: the government offers interest-free energy loans and 100 per cent capital tax allowances on energy efficient equipment through the 'Carbon Trust' (which receives funding through environmental taxes such as the Climate Change Levy). This assistance is packaged for hotels, together with a comprehensive advice programme, within the government backed 'Hospitable Climates' initiative.

Barbados: The Tourism Development Act (2002) makes specific provision for expenditure on acquiring eco-certification and on community tourism programmes to be offset at a rate of 150 per cent against tax assessable income.

5.4 Voluntary instruments

5.4.1 Guidelines and codes of conduct

The development of guidelines and codes of conduct provides a mechanism for setting out clear expectations or requirements of tourists, enterprises or other stakeholders, without the back up of laws and regulations . In many circumstances, it may be felt that such non-statutory statements are sufficient to bring about the required approaches, standards or changes in behaviour.

Governments may draw up codes and guidelines themselves or may help other stakeholder groups to do so, acting as a broker in this process.

The purpose and advantages of codes and guidelines

Codes and guidelines are written statements that set out clearly the actions that are or are not appropriate or acceptable in particular circumstances. Codes and guidelines can be used to:

- Exercise control, encouraging everyone to abide by a common approach.
- Give helpful guidance and improve performance, providing a checklist of actions to follow to achieve objectives. However, they are different from training manuals, which tend to be more elaborate (see Section 5.5.2).

They may be reproduced or disseminated in the form of short documents, presented on websites, displayed on notices and promoted through relevant media. Awareness of codes and encouragement to use them may be best achieved by word of mouth and direct distribution to intended users.

The term 'code' is usually applied to short lists of 'do's' and 'don'ts', often written as a clear statement which stakeholders can sign up to more or less formally. A 'guideline' is more likely to be a longer and more detailed statement, containing more advice and information on how to take appropriate action. Codes and guidelines can be complementary, with the latter providing detail on how to comply with the former.

Codes can refer to initiatives of more formal frameworks, such as the Global Code of Ethics for Tourism, approved by the General Assembly of WTO and of the United Nations[4].

The advantages of codes and guidelines are that they are direct, simple and may be developed and used at little cost. The disadvantage is that they rely on voluntary action and there may be no in-built process of checking or enforcement.

It may be more appropriate to use codes and guidelines rather than regulations where:

- Regulations are difficult to disseminate and compliance cannot be controlled.
- The consequences of certain actions may be less serious.
- It is important or helpful to communicate positive actions to pursue, as well as negative actions to control.
- There are stakeholder groups with whom guidelines and codes can be developed and who promote compliance.

There are many examples of codes and guidelines relating to tourism sustainability, international, national, local and at site level. They may be aimed at policy makers, tourism enterprises, and visitors, or a combination of them and may be produced by international agencies, governments, management bodies such as national park authorities, and NGOs.

Codes and guidelines may also be produced by associations of enterprises or other stakeholders, as a way of promoting good practice within a group, seeking common standards and demonstrating this to others. In this way, they form a very useful tool for self-regulation within the tourism sector.

Ways of strengthening the success of codes and guidelines include:

• Drawing them up in close consultation with intended users.
• Keeping the wording simple and the meaning clear.
• Using positive language, and suggesting alternative actions.
• Backing up statements by simple explanation.
• Obtaining feedback, reviewing the statements and improving them over time.
• Linking them to marketing and information services (see Section 5.5.3).

Codes may be more or less formal, depending on circumstances. In some cases it may be appropriate for them to be backed up by an agreement of adherence. They can be used as the basis for other instruments, such as reporting and certification (see below) which will make them more effective.

In some circumstances, codes and regulations may be used together. Codes may cover a wider set of desired actions, but with the most important requirements being backed by legislation and regulations, which are then referred to in the codes and guidelines.

Codes relating to certain activities can be strengthened if they are supported and promoted by a range of organizations working together and applied in different countries through international cooperation. An important example is the code relating to combating child sex tourism (see Box 5.13).

The following subsections extend discussion of codes and guidelines and look at ways in which they can be applied.

Policy guidelines

It is important that all stakeholders are aware of policies that relate to the sustainability of tourism, and the implications of those policies for action. The

---

Box 5.13: A clear code with international backing

The Code of Conduct for the Protection of Children from Sexual Exploitation in Travel and Tourism is an example of a short and clearly worded code that was developed by an NGO and now has international backing from UNICEF, the WTO and a range of tourism industry organizations. The code is also supported and promoted by government bodies, such as the Tourism Authority of Thailand. Associated actions have been developed around the code, including training and publicity.

The Code, aimed at suppliers of tourism services, has just six elements:

1. To establish an ethical policy regarding the commercial exploitation of children.
2. To train the personnel in the country of origin and travel destinations.
3. To introduce a clause in contracts with suppliers, stating a common repudiation of commercial sexual exploitation of children.
4. To provide information to travellers by means of catalogues, brochures, in-flight films, ticket-slips, home pages, etc.
5. To provide information to local 'key persons' at the destinations.
6. To report annually.

The Responsible Tourism Guidelines produced in South Africa provide a particularly good example of a guidelines document. Produced in booklet format and circulated widely, they set out statements of principle relating to economic, social and environmental sustainability, around which more detailed policies and actions should be developed. They have subsequently been reflected in the policies of a number of provincial authorities and have been taken up by at least one of the main banks where they have been used as the basis for criteria for funding. The guidelines have also been used to prepare an advisory manual for private enterprises (see Case Studies, p 162).

development of multi-stakeholder structures and the process of formulating a tourism strategy through widespread consultation may go some way to ensure this. However, this may not be enough.

Guidelines can be used to transmit general directions and key aspects of policy to government agencies, local authorities, NGOs, private sector enterprises and supporting bodies such as development assistance agencies and banks.

A single guideline document could be prepared which is generally applicable to all, or a range of different documents could be produced, with the style and contents adjusted to meet the requirements of the audience.

Codes and guidelines on development and management processes

Codes and guidelines relating to tourism enterprises may cover the country as a whole or be specific to particular types of location (including protected areas) or types of product.

Codes and guidelines may be used to influence the nature of product development. They can cover both procedures and processes to adopt and the nature of development. Examples include guidelines on:

* Planning and development control procedures: in protected areas, these might be based on the CBD guidelines for sustainable tourism.
* The development of community-based tourism: a number of international guidelines exist on working with communities on assessing prospects and establishing projects that embrace sustainability principles.
* Design for different types of development.

Codes and guidelines can also relate to how tourism enterprises are managed in different situations in order to benefit environments and communities (see Box 5.14). These may be prepared by, or for, tour operators or tourism service providers. Typically, they will cover aspects such as:

* Procedures for minimizing pollution from operations or environmental damage from recreational activities.

Box 5.14: Code for operating in a sensitive location

For many years the WWF Arctic Programme has maintained a Code of Conduct for Tour Operators in the Arctic. This has covered, amongst other things, the way in which operators use and manage natural resources; choice of accommodation and other suppliers; visitor management and information given to visitors; ways of respecting local cultures; qualification and education of staff; and safety procedures.

The Code has been translated into several languages and distributed widely. It has proved popular. Operators following it have subsequently looked for greater recognition of their good practice, and options for linking this to certification are being considered.

- Good practice in liaising with local communities.
- Handling and controlling visitors, including group size, the nature of information supplied to them, etc.
- Reporting procedures, covering the enterprises' activities and providing feedback to help destination management.

Visitor codes of conduct

Many codes have been produced with the objective of influencing visitor behaviour. Most of these relate to the use of natural environments for different activities. However, they can also cover wider issues such as purchasing local produce, selecting equitable service providers, tipping practices, dress codes to respect cultural sensitivities, etc.

Codes may range from overall tips for responsible travel, to specific codes focused on particular activities, such as do's and don'ts for mountain bikers in a national park or even on an individual trail.

In general, visitor codes will be more effective if backed up by promotional activity (such as media coverage) and also used as the basis around which more personal advice and information are given (see Section 5.5.3). The Leave No Trace programme in the USA (described in Box 5.28) is an example of an educational programme that promotes its own simple visitor code.

In Scotland, the government conservation agency has been charged by law to draw up a Scottish Marine Wildlife Watching Code which must include guidelines on activities that are likely to disturb marine wildlife, circumstances in which marine wildlife may be approached and the manner in which species can best be viewed with minimum disturbance (see Case Studies, p 172).

5.4.2 Reporting and auditing

Reporting allows an enterprise or organization to describe the outcome of its efforts to manage its sustainability impacts, and to share this information with stakeholders. Governments can encourage both the use of reporting within the tourism industry and the widening of the scope of its concerns. The use of an agreed set of indicators is an essential part of any reporting activity.

A sustainability reporting framework enables tourism enterprises and organizations to communicate any actions taken to improve economic, environmental, and social performance; the outcomes of such actions and the future strategies for improvement.

Reporting can be undertaken at different levels:

- At the level of an individual enterprise or company or across a collection of enterprises trading in a particular tourism segment.
- For a single destination or at a regional or national level.

Why is sustainability reporting important?

Measuring and reporting both past and anticipated performance is a critical management tool. It helps to sharpen the ability of managers to assess progress towards stated social and environmental policies and goals, and is a key ingredient in building and sustaining the engagement of stakeholders. For tourism enterprises, reporting can be used to maintain and strengthen their credibility, engage their customers, gain benefit from any successes and promote market advantage.

Instruments 5

Growing interest in reporting in the private and public sectors

Across the world, there is interest in enlarging the scope of conventional corporate financial reporting to include non-financial information. The growth in private sector reporting has been driven by the industry itself, and there are many voluntary reporting initiatives. The Global Reporting Initiative (GRI) provides a set of reporting guidelines and sustainability performance indicators, to be used in an entirely voluntary capacity, that capture an emerging consensus on reporting practices and attempt to bring some consistency to reporting. GRI Guidelines are intended to be applicable to organizations of all sizes and types, operating in any location.

A number of supplements to the GRI have been developed to capture the different sustainability issues faced by various industry sectors. Issues relating to tour operating are contained in a GRI supplement issued by the Tour Operators' Initiative, backed by UNEP and the WTO. Other sector groups, such as representatives of the hotels sector, have also addressed reporting requirements.

Auditing activity for sustainability

Reporting may or may not be linked to an auditing process. An audit can be carried out on any organization or enterprise that has stated policies and a programme for improving sustainable performance. An audit is a systematic evaluation of the organization's systems and actions, in order to see if it is doing what it says it will do. It can be carried out by self assessment, by the use of an independent auditor or by a third party verifier. Once an environmental management system has been established, it can be audited on a periodic basis to ensure that it is working properly and that it is doing what it should.

Auditing can be used as an internal management tool to improve performance in the tourism industry or to verify compliance with legal requirements. 'Due diligence' is essentially a compliance audit to test whether an organization has consistently met its legal obligations. Such an audit should trigger action or corrective measures.

An audit can also be required by a third party, to verify compliance with conditions that may have been attached to financial support or permissions. Annual monitoring reports may cover ongoing performance of project-specific environmental, health and safety and social activities, reflected in the results of periodic and quantitative sampling and measuring programmes.

How governments can promote reporting and auditing

There are a number of ways in which governments can strengthen the use of reporting and auditing as a tool in making tourism more sustainable. These include:

- Governments undertaking auditing and reporting on their own activities, including that of their agencies. This can be valuable not only in the review and adaptation of their own policies and actions, but also by setting an example to others in the tourism sector.
- Reporting more widely on the state of the sector. The performance reporting arrangements of tourism ministries or local government can be developed to

include reporting on progress within the tourism industry on sustainability targets. Feeding this information back to the industry provides an opportunity to review policies and programmes, to take account of success and identify where effort needs to be renewed or redirected.

- Influencing the agenda for reporting. Private sector companies will often report their actions in relation to national or local environmental and social goals.
- Actively encouraging the process of auditing and reporting amongst groups of operators at a national or local level.
- Encouraging the use of auditing by introducing guidance material and offering technical assistance.
- Including an auditing and reporting requirement within recognized environmental management systems and certification processes.
- Rewarding good practice by recognizing and promoting the results.

Governments may also wish to include a requirement to introduce sustainability measures into existing arrangements for corporate reporting in legislation. In France, for example, mandatory sustainability reporting was introduced in 2002 for the largest companies. Investor pressure to obtain a clearer picture of corporate performance may also lead to regulatory processes that require sustainability reporting.

Governments can require enterprises to carry out auditing and to report on the results, as part of the process of checking on compliance with agreements. The basis for approval of the Sydney Quarantine Station project provides an example (see Box 5.15).

Box 5.15: Required auditing and reporting on environmental and social impacts

The North Head Quarantine Station is a site of natural and historic significance within the Sydney Harbour National Park, Australia. In 2000, the government decided that the best way of securing the future of the site would be to lease it to a tourism operator who would introduce a range of complementary economic uses. However, it was also deemed necessary for the operator to meet some serious conservation and management concerns, many of which had been raised by the local community. These latter requirements were to be formulated as conditions of the planning permission and lease criteria, but it became clear that the costs and limitations that they would impose would render the project unviable.

An alternative adaptive management solution was adopted, dependent on a process of regular auditing and reporting. This involved constant, systematic monitoring against agreed indicators, of a range of social and environmental impacts, to check that agreed optimal conditions were being met. Should impacts be found to be greater than this, agreed management responses would come into force. For example, bird breeding sites are counted regularly and their decrease would lead to measures to reduce noise, lighting and visitor movements. This model approach involves an annual Environmental Management Report on the condition of the site and the sustainability of the operation.

5.4.3 Voluntary certification

Certification is a mechanism for ensuring that an activity or product meets certain standards that may be set by government or agreed within an industry sector. In tourism, certification is used primarily to check on the activities and standards of tourism enterprises, such as accommodation operators, to ensure consumer safety and satisfaction. However, it may also be extended to cover sustainability issues. The key components of certification include:

- Voluntary participation by businesses.
- Well defined criteria and standards.
- A process of auditing and assessment.
- Recognition of those who meet the criteria, through a label or logo.
- Follow up, in due course, to check continued compliance.

The advantages and disadvantages of certification

The main advantage of certification in promoting more sustainability in tourism is that it provides a way of encapsulating at least some of the complex set of aims and objectives that comprise sustainability, and of clearly distinguishing those enterprises that are achieving them. It is one of the few objective ways of enabling those who want to promote sustainability in their actions and choices (e.g. individual consumers, tour operators and governments) to know who to support.

For governments[5], the main advantages of certification are that it can help to:

- Raise the market profile and image of a destination in terms of its quality and environmental standards.
- Provide a way of encouraging the industry to raise standards in specifically identified areas.
- Potentially lower regulatory costs.

The main disadvantage of certification is that it can be costly and time consuming to administer. It can also be difficult to persuade businesses to participate, as they often do not see clear advantages that they can set against the costs of participating in the process (e.g. meeting the inspection fee, and, potentially, complying with the requirements). Certification can therefore be perceived as creating a barrier, especially to very small businesses. There is also a problem with comparability between schemes, which can lead to varying standards, confusion amongst the public, and an unlevel playing field for businesses.

The role of governments in certification

Governments have a very important role in supporting the certification process. Often they may be the initiators, and they should also continue to give support as schemes develop.

The agency responsible for running a certification scheme will need to be totally impartial, and to be widely perceived as being so, as well as technically competent and efficient. In some countries, it may be beneficial for governments to be directly involved in the process if these conditions are to be met. In others it may be best to use an external agency recognized by government.

Whether or not governments become directly involved in running certification schemes, their official endorsement and active support will be very important for its success. This may include:

- Financial support, at least initially as the scheme gets under way.
- Promotion of participation to the tourism sector at national and local level.
- Provision of support and incentives to enterprises who join the scheme, such as coverage in marketing activities (see Section 5.5.3).
- Linking certification to other instruments, which may include, for example, the granting of planning permission, the granting of concessions and economic incentives.

Types of certification

Common themes addressed by certification schemes within the tourism sector include:

- Health and safety compliance (often considered as a pre-requisite for the others).
- The quality of the facilities and service. This may be an objective measure of the level of provision, or a more subjective assessment of the experience on offer.
- Quality management, assessing the whole management process (such as the ISO 9000 scheme).
- Social conditions relating to staff, training, etc.
- Environmental management and performance (such as the ISO 14000 or EMAS schemes).
- Comprehensive sustainability, including environmental, social and economic aspects.

A number of the Case Studies include certification schemes for tourism enterprises pursuing sustainability. The Costa Rica scheme, for example, sees advantages from being government led, and government support has been vital in Scotland and Australia. (see Case Studies, p 167, p 172 & p 130).

Historically, certification in tourism has related mainly to the measurement of the quality of a facility, notably hotel accommodation. Many countries have such schemes (often leading to a 'star' rating) which may be implemented by governments or their agencies or by private bodies (with or without official endorsement).

In recent years there has been a considerable growth in schemes relating to environmental management and performance, which convey what might be commonly termed an 'eco-label'. In 2001, a WTO study[6] estimated that there were some 60 such certification schemes in tourism worldwide; this number will have grown subsequently. Most of these schemes concentrate almost exclusively on environmental issues, though some have a few social components. Certification schemes relating more explicitly to social or labour issues are far less common (see Box 5.16, page 104).

Another important distinction is between schemes that measure 'process' and those that measure 'performance':

- 'Process' schemes certify that businesses have established and documented systems for assuring the improvement of quality or environmental performance. They do not determine any specific performance results other than the company's own and those required by law.
- 'Performance' schemes certify that businesses have reached a specific, measurable level of performance against the standards associated with the different elements of the scheme.

Box 5.16: Certification reflecting national policy on social impact

Fair Trade in Tourism South Africa (FTTSA) awards a certification Trademark to tourism businesses that are able to demonstrate commitment to a set of principles and compliance with predetermined criteria. FTTSA concentrates on social issues, although concern for the environment and use of resources is also taken into account. The criteria are: Fair wages; Fair working conditions; Fair operations; Fair purchasing; Fair distribution of benefits; Ethical business practice; and Respect for human rights, culture and environment.

The Trademark is awarded on the basis of self-assessment followed by external verification. It relates closely to the responsible tourism policy and guidelines of the South African government, whose endorsement has been important to its credibility. The main motivation and benefits seen by those awarded the Trademark have been the opportunity for increased awareness, improved access to niche markets, networking, exchange of knowledge, mutual support and benchmarking between them.

Certification can also vary according to the nature and level of the verification process. Some schemes rely primarily on self-assessment, with only occasional external verification, while most make the latter a requirement. Some schemes allocate a graded result according to the level of compliance or amount of actions taken, others just offer a pass or fail.

Take up of schemes and results achieved

 Businesses that have become certified under Costa Rica's Certification for Sustainable Tourism scheme have become fervent supporters of sustainable practices (see Case Studies, p. 139).

The proportion of tourism enterprises participating in quality certification schemes is often quite high. However, environmental certification schemes have so far achieved a very low take up. For example, amongst European schemes, greatest participation was found in Scotland, with a penetration rate of around 10 per cent of accommodation enterprises in the country.

The outlook for the future of environmental or wider sustainability certification is, however, more positive than this figure might suggest, and the results achieved have been quite significant. Most enterprises that have been engaged in such schemes are very positive about their participation.

 Membership of Scotland's Green Tourism Business Scheme has grown by around 30 per cent per year since its establishment in 1998. In 2004, the scheme had 550 members (see Case Studies, p 172).

Businesses that participate in certification often report that the main advantage to them is the educational process it involves, helping them to clearly understand the requirements of sustainability and focusing their attention on the changes they need to make in their business. Compliance with certification also benefits businesses through:

- Cost savings: most enterprises report clear savings, for example energy costs.
- Providing a potential marketing advantage: however, this appears to be still quite limited in terms of the certification of environmental or social sustainability compared to certification of quality.
- Better recognition by supporting bodies: including opportunities for technical assistance and sometimes finance.

A particularly important sign of possible future market advantage is the growing interest by some tour operators in using certification as a basis for selecting the businesses that they will sub-contract and include in their holiday catalogues, reflecting the increasing integration of sustainability into their business ethics and activities.

Strengthening certification for sustainability

There is growing international consensus that sustainable tourism certification systems should incorporate elements of both process and performance, but should emphasize performance. Schemes should also be based on external assessment and ideally include a grading element to recognize different levels and encourage improvement over time.

In order to more closely reflect the components of sustainability, certification schemes might seek to include more social criteria in addition to the more common environmental criteria.

A very important issue and challenge is the way in which certification of sustainability is linked to certification of quality, and whether combining them into one scheme would dilute the focus on sustainability issues. Having a number of associated schemes, linked and backed by government, may be a good approach.

Experience provides a number of pointers to good practice in certification (borne out by the Case Studies) which should be kept in mind when developing new schemes or strengthening existing ones. These underline the great opportunity and need to link the use of certification to other tools, for mutual advantage. They include:

- Linking certification to capacity building, mainly by strengthening the advice and personal help given to applicants and at the time of inspection, and by delivering associated training programmes.
- Including government services in the certification process, in order to strengthen official ties and encourage enterprises by demonstration.
- Making sure that the requirements and processes are as simple and clear as possible, enabling ease of audit and rapid compliance.
- Pursuing more specific ways of giving teeth to the scheme and linking it to other policy areas.

A common standard for certification

There is increasing recognition of a need to ensure compatibility between different sustainability certification schemes. Consumer confidence may increase as tourists become aware that harmonized criteria mean that certification programmes are all measuring more or less the same elements. Harmonization efforts are well under way in Europe (see Box 5.17, page 106) and in the Americas. There has also been some movement towards the development of a programme to accredit the various certification schemes. This programme—which intends to, one day, become a global Sustainable Tourism Stewardship Council—is developing regional networks for cooperation and harmonization of criteria.

The Scottish Green Tourism Business Scheme has clearly shown the advantage of a separate eco-certification scheme but having this promoted closely alongside the national quality grading scheme as an additional option (p 172).

In Australia, consideration is being given to including the ecocertification scheme within a suite of certification programmes accredited and officially supported by government (see Case Studies, p 130).

In Scotland, certifying Tourist Information Centres has generated new interest amongst enterprises (see Case Studies, p 172).

In Australia, Ecocertification has been used by some states as a requirement for enterprises to be given preferential treatment and extended concessions to operate in parks (see Case Studies, p 130).

Certification of destinations and amenities

In addition to the certification of sustainability of tourism enterprises and their products, there are also schemes that certify destinations or particular types of amenity.

The Blue Flag scheme for beaches and marinas (see Box 5.18) is a good example that could be applicable worldwide. It underlines the advantages of clear focus, practicality, relevance and persistence with a scheme over time.

In a few locations across the world, sustainability certification has been awarded to entire destinations. Such schemes take account of the way the whole destination is managed, in terms of sustainability policies, resource efficiency, pollution control, social services, etc., as well as taking account of the environmental management processes of the tourism sector. The merits of certification for entire communities have been the subject of considerable debate, partly due to the difficulties and costs of acquiring meaningful and comprehensive data.

In Kaikoura, New Zealand, a certification programme has helped to stimulate interest and focus attention within the community on better management of resources (see Case Studies, p 157).

5.4.4 Voluntary contributions

There is increasing evidence that tourists and the tourism industry are prepared to provide voluntary support for environmental conservation and the wellbeing of local communities in destinations. A number of studies have identified that tourists are willing to pay for such outcomes, provided that local benefits can be clearly identified.

Box 5.17: VISIT—a family of European ecolabels

The VISIT initiative, funded by the European Union, links 12 separate eco-labelling schemes for tourism enterprises, from Austria, Denmark, France, Italy, Latvia, Luxembourg, the Netherlands, Spain, Switzerland and the Nordic countries. The purpose of the initiative is to improve sustainability of European tourism by raising the profile and performance of the labels and to raise awareness of certified products.

Each of the labels concentrates on the environmental impacts of the establishments (mainly accommodation). A common standard has been agreed for the labels. This includes: external verification at least once every three years; a requirement that all enterprises meet national legislation; the inclusion of a set of basic performance requirements; a requirement that enterprises regularly monitor consumption of energy and water and creation of waste per overnight guest; common management criteria, including relevant staff training; and issues concerning transparency and promotion of the schemes.

Promotional activity has included the creation of a VISIT Holiday Guide, on paper and on the Internet, which features the participating labels and the individually certified products. Links with tour operators have also been developed, encouraging them to feature the products.

A VISIT Association has been established to promote the interests of members and encourage new participants. Services will include market research and performance benchmarking between the labels.

Many tourism enterprises are taking direct supportive action, or are prepared to do so, as part of their corporate social responsibility.

Although this is primarily a matter for individual and private sector response, governments can play a valuable role in encouraging and enabling the provision of voluntary contributions, by:

- Establishing, supporting and promoting relevant schemes. This may entail coordinating the activities of enterprises and tourists, as in the Lake District example in Box 5.19, page 108.
- Providing financial incentives, such as tax credits, to enterprises that make contributions.

Voluntary contributions and actions can centre around providing monetary support or may involve the provision of assistance in kind. Voluntary contributions have the advantage of being based on goodwill, commitment and active participation, although they are unlikely to raise as much revenue as compulsory charges.

Examples of schemes involving tourists directly include:

- Tourists being invited to make cash donations to local projects, which can vary from small sums to substantial amounts.

Box 5.18: Certification for beaches and marinas

The Blue Flag award for beaches and marinas, run by the Foundation for Environmental Education, has been operational since 1985. In 2004, 2 938 beaches and marinas were granted the Blue Flag in 29 countries across Europe, the Caribbean and South Africa. Criteria include:

- Water quality, including compliance with bathing water standards.
- Environmental education and information, including procedures for notifying users about the water quality and the provision of environmental interpretation.
- Environmental management, including a land use and development plan for the coastal zone, as well as beach cleaning and management processes.
- Safety and services, including guards or relevant equipment, access to telephone, etc.

The scheme has been successfully expanded over the years and has led to improvements in the provision of relevant facilities and procedures. Strengths of the scheme include: meaningful and practical requirements that are clearly relevant not only to the environment but also to the quality and safety of the visitor experience; strong branding (the blue flag itself); combination of management and information/ education requirements; requirement for strong practical engagement by local authorities and communities; and integration with coastal management. Destinations have been able to see the advantages both in terms of improved amenity and visitor response, and many have used the award actively to promote a strong environmental image. The flag is re-awarded each season, or not, after the annual assessment.

The role of government (especially local authorities at the destination level) in backing and promoting the scheme has been very important to its success.

- A small charge made by tour operators or service providers as a routine addition to a bill, and which tourists can opt out of if they do not wish to pay. This has the advantage of simplicity and usually leads to very few refusals.
- Tourists providing help in kind. An example of this is provided by the growing number of holiday and educational travel offers involving participation in conservation or community schemes.
- Contributions by tourists to carbon bio-sequestration schemes (e.g. tree planting), as a way of offsetting the effect of greenhouse gas emissions resulting from their travel.

Tourism enterprises can provide finance or help in kind to local conservation and social projects. There are many examples where support has been given to projects such as a local nature reserve, community group, health service or school. As well as being of considerable benefit to the recipients, enterprises can often benefit from the goodwill this generates towards them from their customers. Assistance can be provided by direct involvement or by establishing or contributing to a trust fund. It can be particularly beneficial if tourism enterprises are able to build up a supportive relationship with neighbouring communities that can be maintained over time.

Box 5.19: A structured scheme for raising voluntary contributions

In the Lake District National Park, in England, a public/private partnership involving the National Trust (an NGO), the National Park Authority and the Regional Tourist Board has been established as a vehicle for raising voluntary contributions. The Lake District Tourism and Conservation Partnership includes around 180 tourism businesses in its membership. Members raise money for conservation (e.g. maintenance of paths and landscape features) by inviting voluntary contributions from guests. This may be via a small, optional supplement on bills, or through simply inviting donations. Beneficiary projects are often specific to each member, thus strengthening individual commitment to them. Annual revenue raised is around US$300 000.

5.5 Supporting instruments

5.5.1 Infrastructure provision and management

Whereas most of the tools available to governments relate to influencing the actions of the private sector, the direct provision by government (or its agents, partners or contractors) of a range of infrastructure and public utilities and services should also be seen as an instrument for making tourism more sustainable.

Where investment is required in new infrastructure, it may be appropriate for costs to be shared between the public and private sectors, based on an assessment of the relative importance of public good and private gain.

General sustainability issues relating to infrastructure and services

The availability of transportation, water, energy, sewerage and waste disposal, telecommunications, and basic health and security services is of fundamental importance for the successful functioning of the tourism sector. Provision is crucial to the economic sustainability of tourism. The level and quality of provision is also crucial to issues of social and environmental sustainability. The provision of these services also forms a key part of the enabling environment, created by government, for a more sustainable tourism industry.

Infrastructure and public services should be supplied in such a way that:

- They benefit the local community, tourism enterprises and tourists, with adequate provision to meet everyone's needs.
- Their provision is cost effective and sustainable.
- Best practices and technologies are used, minimizing consumption of resources and ensuring efficient and effective treatment of waste.

Careful, holistic planning and management of infrastructure and services is needed, taking full account of the existing and potential future demand from tourism as well as from the local community and other sectors. A fundamental principle and priority is to seek to minimize wasteful consumption by the tourism sector. In addition to provision of infrastructure and services, emphasis must therefore be placed on working with the industry on its environmental management, using the relevant instruments.

The need for careful monitoring of levels of use by the tourism sector is of paramount importance for future planning and to prevent over use. Mechanisms for monitoring, such as metering and counters, should be built in to the design of new infrastructure and equipment, and indicators and monitoring procedures should be built in to any service agreements with suppliers and providers.

Transport provision

Transport is a very important strategic policy area for sustainable tourism. Tourism should be fully taken into account in all transport plans, based on current visitor flow patterns and forecasts. The potential conflict between improving accessibility to tourism destinations for economic reasons and reducing emissions from air and car transport has already been pointed out. A general policy line is to improve accessibility to and within destinations using less-polluting transport modes, and to manage tourist traffic in ways that will minimize congestion and adverse impacts on local communities and environments.

Many of the other instruments covered in this document can be used for transport management, notably economic instruments and marketing and information delivery (Section 5.5.3). However, the actual provision of transport infrastructure and public transport services is clearly an important area of action in its own right.

Examples of physical infrastructure measures include:

- Improving access to communities where this is needed to ensure the viability of tourism activity.
- Careful assessment of the environmental, social and economic impact of any new transport infrastructure proposal, especially new roads, or port and airport provision/extension.

- Being prepared to limit the capacity of roads and car parks as a control measure to discourage excessive car use.
- Developing park and ride schemes in popular tourist areas.
- Developing dedicated walking and cycling trails for use by tourists.
- Extending pedestrian areas in towns and cities.
- Introducing traffic calming measures and lane systems that favour public transport.
- Measures to reduce noise pollution from roads, airports, etc.
- Careful planning of signposting as an effective tool in traffic and visitor management, while avoiding unsightly and confusing clutter.

Box 5.20 gives an example of integrated transport development.

Public transport can be made more appealing for use by tourists in a number of ways, including:

- Integrated timetabling and ticketing between different transport modes.
- Adjusting timetables to reflect visitor movement patterns.
- Route planning to take account of the location of accommodation and visitor attractions.

Box 5.20: Integrated development of public transport offers

The combination of high levels of holiday and transit traffic produces significant congestion and pollution in narrow Alpine mountain valleys. In 1997, Austria's ministries for tourism, transport and the environment set up the 'sustainable mobility – car free tourism' project, with funding from the European Union, based on two pilot Alpine resort communities. The project was subsequently expanded into the trans-national Alps Mobility Project, with the purpose of demonstrating the potential to promote holidays in the Alps based on environmentally benign transport options.

A whole range of different initiatives has been undertaken by the communities involved in the project, involving considerable joint working between public sector bodies, transport operators, tour operators and other stakeholders. Much of the project has been about coordinated information provision and creative marketing and packaging of public transport access to and within the region. However, the project has also shown the importance of improved transport infrastructure and services. Examples include:

- Provision and leasing out of zero-emission electric cars and motor scooters, together with solar-electric re-charging stations.
- Provision and coordination of bus routes, with improved visibility and design of bus-stops and associated information panels.
- Establishment of booking systems and luggage transfer services.
- Extension of pedestrian areas and car free zones.

The community of Werfenweng, one of the initial pilots, has seen the proportion of tourists arriving by train rise from 9 to 25 per cent. It has also observed an estimated reduction of 375 tonnes per winter season in CO_2 emissions, amounting to a 15 per cent reduction against the trend.

- Provision of luggage handling services.
- Efficient car and taxi sharing schemes.
- Extension of, and support for, public transport services on certain routes relevant to tourists.
- Improved and widespread availability of information and ticketing.
- Improved quality, security and safety against crime on transport services.

Tourist transport can be made more sustainable by the introduction of improved technology. Governments can assist with this by supporting appropriate research and development and by investing in, and procuring, modern transport systems that employ such technologies.

Public utilities and services

The provision of public utilities requires careful planning in tourist destinations, especially where particular natural resources are in short supply.

- Water: the supply and management of water is a key issue in many tourist destinations, in terms of both its quality and quantity. Increasing supply or introducing new sources (e.g. from desalination plants) can often be costly and have environmental consequences. Equitable water management is critical—if water is rationed, the interests of tourism enterprises should not be favoured over local communities.
- Energy: in some destinations energy (for electricity and heat) may be supplied from local sources. Renewable energy sources should be favoured, while paying attention to the impact of related infrastructure on the landscape (e.g. siting of wind turbines, pylons and hydro schemes).
- Solid waste: infrastructure, collection and management systems should enable waste to be separated and recycled. In some countries, tourism businesses are prepared to recycle waste but the municipality does not provide trade access to collection and treatment systems to back this up. Attention should also be paid to litter collection and the cleanness and maintenance of public open spaces such as parks and beaches (see Box 5.21, page 112).
- Sewerage: wherever possible, tourism enterprises will connect to effective sewage treatment systems that have sufficient capacity to handle the flows arising in the peak tourist season. Discharge points should be carefully sited with respect to beaches and other sensitive areas. Governments should also propose solutions for sewage treatment for tourism facilities that cannot be connected to the public sewerage system.
- Telecommunications: effective telecommunications, including information technology linkages, are very important for market access and economic viability. Associated infrastructure should be carefully located to minimize impact on sensitive landscapes.

The innovative waste management programme in Kaikoura, New Zealand, undertaken by the local authority in partnership with a community body, provides a good example of the provision of a conservation minded waste handling service together with the creative reuse of waste (see Case Studies, p 157).

Security and emergency services

Safety and security are increasingly important issues for destination image and performance. Attention should be paid to levels of policing and provision of other emergency services, such as health and fire services. The suppliers of these services should be in regular contact with tourism managers and sector bodies. A key issue is

Instruments

5

their ability to respond to visitors' needs. Some destinations have dedicated tourist assistance schemes and help lines. Specific tourist police units have been established in some countries.

Systems for dealing with emergency situations such as health scares, terrorism and natural and industrial disasters, including response to early warnings, should be well rehearsed. This includes the provision of evacuation plans where necessary.

5.5.2 Capacity building

Capacity building is about developing the potential and ability of stakeholders to make and implement decisions that will lead to more sustainable tourism, by increasing their understanding, knowledge, confidence and skills.

The advantages and role of capacity building

There are many advantages to using capacity building as an instrument to strengthen the sustainability of tourism. Capacity building is direct and precise, and can be targeted at stakeholders or situations where change is needed or where it is felt that particular success may be achieved. It has the advantage of being a process which is likely to spread commitment to sustainability within the tourism sector, and so can secure long term benefit. It is also a flexible instrument that can be altered at any time. Capacity building can, however, be time consuming and require skilled personnel to carry it out. A particular challenge is securing the participation of tourism enterprises in the process.

Capacity building is particularly important in strengthening the effectiveness of the other tools presented in this document, such as economic instruments, certification and planning regulations, by alerting people to them and assisting with compliance.

Box 5.21: Working together on waste

In the coastal resort of Side, Turkey, a workshop organized by the Tour Operators' Initiative and involving the local government, NGOs and private sector representatives, identified waste management as an urgent priority for the sustainability of tourism in the area.

Activities carried out by the municipality in conjunction with the tourism association, assisted by UNEP and others, included the introduction of:

- A waste separation scheme, involving pick-ups from hotels and other companies.
- A collection scheme for used batteries.
- Waste separation bins in the town for use by tourists and residents.
- Training sessions on solid waste management for hotel and restaurant staff and for municipality officers.
- A new, well located landfill area.

Over 100 hotels and all local shops and restaurants participate in the waste separation scheme.

Capacity building for more sustainable tourism will generally target:

- Tourism enterprises: most notably MSMEs, as these are likely to have more limited professional capacity than larger enterprises and may be more likely to seek assistance.
- Local communities or more specific groups of local stakeholders.
- Organizations and institutions, including government bodies and NGOs.

In the past, capacity building for tourism has tended to concentrate on issues of business performance, competitiveness and quality. A sustainable tourism approach would retain these priorities but add others such as management of human resources, supply chains and the environment. In terms of process, it would emphasize an integrated approach, encouraging enterprises and communities to work together.

Box 5.22: A government agency developing sustainable tourism skills

In France, technical services relating to tourism are supplied by Observation, Développement et Ingénierie Touristique (ODIT France), a public sector structure under the Ministry of Tourism. ODIT member organizations include other ministries, chambers of commerce, private sector representative organizations, regional and local offices of tourism and many other bodies engaged in tourism.

The role of ODIT France is to improve the performance of tourism in France, including its competitiveness, accessibility and the sustainability of its development. A primary function is capacity building and the development and exchange of knowledge and technical skill.

Rather than imposing solutions from the centre, ODIT France works with destinations and networks of enterprises at a local level, inputting technical expertise, developing and experimenting with ideas through consultation and observation, and then disseminating the results. It has worked in this way with a particular group of destinations that have piloted an approach to sustainable tourism, including developing a range of sustainability indicators.

ODIT France has produced good practice guides and advisory publications on sustainable transport, the management of natural sites, and ecotourism, amongst others. It has also been active in helping destinations and specific types of enterprises that wish to develop a sustainable approach, to network, learn from one another and engage in joint promotion on several themes—examples include major heritage sites, rural self-catering accommodation and outgoing tour operators.

ODIT France was created in January 2005 by the amalgamation of AFIT (Agence Française de l'Ingénierie Touristique with two other tourism support bodies: ONT (Observatoire Nationale du Tourisme) and SEATM (Service d'Etudes et d'Aménagement Touristique de la Montagne).

The role of government in capacity building

Governments, both national and local, can play a direct role in the delivery of capacity building activity, or they may provide financial, technical or political assistance to others to do this. Capacity building is often a key part of assistance projects for sustainable development, which may involve a range of agencies including government. Support does not necessarily have to be financial, governments are often well placed to play a facilitation role.

Governments have a particularly important role in initiating and supporting research programmes, of which the results can be used in capacity building, in disseminating good practice, and in establishing stakeholder networks.

In many countries, governments may provide or fund institutions that are central to capacity building, such as research bodies, advisory services, and education and training establishments (see Box 5.22, page 113).

Capacity building with enterprises

An important part of the capacity building process involves helping individual businesses to make their operations more sustainable. Techniques used include the following:

- Providing direct advice: a number of governments support small business advisory services, which may also be assisted by donors. Providing technical advice on environmental management and other sustainability issues has proved to be one of the best ways of achieving effective change. Advice can also be integrated with the certification process as indicated earlier. A challenge is often to get enterprises to seek advice on sustainability in the first place. For this reason a wider audience may be reached by integrating sustainability with more mainstream business and marketing advice.

Box 5.23: Capacity building tools linked to business interest

In England, the government agencies responsible for the rural environment and for tourism joined together to produce a 'green audit kit' for tourism businesses. This is a practical advisory manual on environmental management that gives technical advice as well as seeking to stimulate a response from businesses by demonstrating specific benefits (e.g. cost savings) and to relate actions to wider functions and objectives such as marketing and the quality of the customer experience. The kit was distributed on request, so active circulation was a weakness. The impact on those receiving it was nevertheless extremely positive—66 per cent took action as a result.

It was found that this advisory manual was not enough on its own. To back up the kit, the tourist boards established 'The Green Advantage', a one day training course for enterprises, leading to a certificate. This is offered as part of thematic training under the 'Welcome Host' brand, including customer care. There is now pressure from enterprises that have worked with the kit and undertaken training to receive recognition through certification, which is still to be developed in England. Many of the enterprises also found that their local authorities do not give sufficient back up, such as providing recycling schemes.

- Running training courses and workshops: these may cover relevant aspects of business and environmental management. Training sessions, including familiarization excursions, can also be used effectively to raise enterprise awareness of the special qualities and sensitivities of the local natural and cultural heritage, which may be passed on to guests.
- Using advisory manuals: a number of countries and projects have produced written manuals for enterprises on sustainability, which also include contacts for more detailed information (see Box 5.23). These are a good way to reach a relatively wide audience but may be more effective if combined with direct training and other instruments.

Improving the awareness and skills of individual staff, especially in larger establishments, should also be seen as part of the capacity building process. This is relevant to many aspects of the sustainability agenda, including quality of jobs and overall levels of performance. Some specific issues include:

- The need to make sure that training is designed to be accessible to all, irrespective of educational level.
- The potential to train specific staff in aspects of management for sustainability.

Developing networks and learning areas

One of the best ways of securing more participation in capacity building processes, and of increasing the chances of implementation of good practice over time, is to encourage and help businesses to work together in clusters or networks. Networks can in themselves strengthen the ability of enterprises to address sustainability issues. Networks may be geographically or thematically based, and may be related to established structures such as tourist associations. They provide the advantage of fostering common standards, mutual support and peer pressure between members (see Box 5.24, page 116).

A further development of the network approach is the concept of a 'learning area'. Traditionally, tourism training has been seen as a one way process with individuals or enterprises receiving instruction from training bodies. New approaches point to more dynamic, evolving, two-way processes, based on the concept of continuous learning. A 'tourism learning area' links stakeholders in a destination (or thematic area) so that they can work together to improve their individual performance and the quality and sustainability of tourism in the area, through the development and exchange of skills, knowledge and experience. All relevant public bodies and private enterprises would be seen as part of the learning area, including both recipients and deliverers of training. The learning area approach seeks to ensure that capacity building processes are developed with the enterprises themselves and properly tailored to their needs, while also building cooperation and reducing duplication between training providers. A web portal would play a key role in defining the learning area and facilitating communication within it.

Capacity building with local communities

Capacity building with local communities is an important component of sustainable tourism development relating to community empowerment and a number of other key aims. The process takes time. It should be carefully executed, and be based on the

1. Australia's Business Ready Programme for Indigenous Tourism is designed to assist Indigenous Tourism businesses to develop the skills to set up and run commercially viable tourism operations (see Case Studies, p 130).
2. Ecotourism business development and marketing is a key element of Bulgaria's National Ecotourism Strategy (see Case Studies, p 135).
3. In South Africa, emphasis is placed on skills development. A national qualifications framework has been established, intended to trigger increased investment in training by employers (see Case Studies, p 162).

In South Africa, schemes have been devised for staff lacking formal education to benefit from on-the-job training and assessment leading to qualifications, rather than vocational training based on written examination (see Case Studies, p 162).

In Egypt, hotel environmental officers are identified and receive training and certification (see Case Studies, p 144).

115

In Australia, a government programme is supplying a package of support for tourism development within indigenous communities, including help with fostering alliances with the mainstream tourism industry (see Case Studies, p 130).

In Ghana, international agencies and national government bodies have been involved in capacity building with individual communities, assisting them in deciding on the potential viability of communal tourism programmes based on natural and cultural heritage resources and on the ways in which benefits will be distributed (see Case Studies, p 149).

principle of assisting local communities rather than being prescriptive. In a number of areas, particular success has been achieved through partnership arrangements between individual private enterprises and local communities.

A first stage involves the facilitation of a visioning process and assistance with a realistic assessment of opportunities and impacts. The issue of the level of communal, as distinct from individual, activity and ownership (which will vary widely between different types of society) also needs to be addressed at an early stage, as should social equity issues such as gender. There are many projects around the world that have experience of working with local communities on capacity building for sustainable tourism (see Box 5.25).

A second level of capacity building with communities involves assistance with the acquisition of knowledge and skills. Typically, topics will include: customer care, marketing, environmental management, guiding services, business skills, working and negotiating with commercial operators, developing local supply chains, basic language training, and monitoring impacts and performance.

Institutional strengthening

Capacity building for more sustainable tourism should also be directed at government ministries at all levels, and their agencies. Institutional strengthening in terms of

Box 5.24: Capacity building leading to private and public response

In Jamaica, the Environmental Audits for Sustainable Tourism (EAST) project, funded by USAID, has the Jamaica Hotel and Tourist Association (JHTA) as the main partner, and is supported by the Ministry of Industry and Tourism. The focus of the project has been to improve the environmental management of hotels through direct advice and training, leading to audits on energy, water and chemical use, wastewater and solid waste generation and disposal, and management and staff practices. Participating hotels have been able to demonstrate considerable cost savings and environmental benefits. A special environmental assessment protocol has been designed to meet the needs of small hotels.

Working with the JHTA, which has promoted the scheme and its results to its members, has been very important in spreading interest in environmental management across the private sector. The scheme has also influenced government, which has introduced a National Environmental Management Systems Policy to encourage all businesses to implement environmental programmes.

As an example of further integration of the lessons learned from the project, EAST has been working with the government's Tourism Product Development Company to incorporate environmental practices into accommodation standards and the inspections process. It has also worked with educational institutions on including environmental management best practices in hotel and hospitality training curricula.

structures and relationships was covered in Chapter 3. However, in many countries there is also a need to strengthen awareness and knowledge of sustainability issues in tourism. Different needs and approaches include:

- Developing basic capacity (in terms of awareness, competence and resources) at all levels.
- Ensuring political awareness and support.
- Introducing technical competences in institutions.

Institutional strengthening may also be important for other bodies. For example, NGOs working in the fields of environmental management or community

Box 5.25: Using participatory processes with communities

In Nepal, the Tourism for Rural Poverty Alleviation Programme (TRPAP) is a government programme, funded by a number of international agencies and implemented in partnership with the Department of National Parks and Wildlife Conservation and the Nepal Tourism Board. The objectives of the programme include demonstrating models and institutional mechanisms for sustainable tourism development. It has focused on six districts exhibiting need for poverty alleviation and also tourism potential.

A key component of the programme has been capacity building, working at the lowest level within individual communities. Initial Tourism and Environmental Awareness Programmes helped to orientate community members, including adult groups and school children, towards sustainable tourism issues and resulted in some simple activities such as environmental clean ups. From here, a thorough process of assessment and planning was undertaken with each community using various techniques for community engagement, such as Appreciative Participatory Planning and Action. This takes participants through five stages:

- Discover—what you are proud of and appreciate what you have.
- Dream—about what might be and create a positive image of your chosen future.
- Direction—narrow the dream to realizable proportions.
- Design—turn the dream into real action plans.
- Deliver—the dream and sustain the future.

This has led to strong local ownership of the ensuing activities.

Specific skills training has also been delivered, for example for guides and cooks and for the production of different kinds of handicraft.

The programme found that it was necessary to develop structures to take sustainable tourism forward within communities and existing institutions. This involved establishing Sustainable Tourism Development Committees at the village level, Sustainable Tourism Development Sections within the district authorities, and a Sustainable Tourism Development Unit within the Nepal Tourism Board.

In Ghana, it became clear that success depends on alerting all ministries to sustainable tourism opportunities and issues, strengthening the ability of key agencies such as the tourist board to deliver support, and bringing district administrations onboard (see Case Studies, p 149).

In Calvia, the main requirement was not so much a question of technical ability as the need to secure political backing and educate politicians in the Local Agenda 21 process (see Case Studies, p 167).

In Egypt, an environmental monitoring unit was established in the Tourism Development Authority (see Case Studies, p 144).

development can play a very important role in focusing tourism on sustainable development objectives, but may lack practical knowledge of tourism (see Box 5.26).

Extending and sharing knowledge and good practice

In order to fuel the capacity building process, governments should support education and research into sustainable tourism and dissemination of good practice. This could involve:

- Including sustainability issues in tourism education. Academic and vocational courses on tourism for young and mature students should include sustainability issues in their curricula. Courses in related fields, such as environmental management and sustainable development, should address the role of tourism.
- Supporting and disseminating relevant research and information. Acquisition of and access to information to guide sustainable development can be costly to individual enterprises, projects or communities. Support should be given to relevant research that can then be shared. This includes keeping abreast of international research and knowledge. Particularly relevant topics include market research, management processes and the application of technology.
- Recognizing and disseminating good practice. Some countries and international bodies use award schemes for sustainable tourism as a way of highlighting good practice. Different techniques for dissemination can be employed.
- Encouraging study tours and other exchanges. The value gained from learning about the experience of similar destinations or initiatives within the same country or from abroad is frequently emphasized.

5.5.3 Marketing and information services

The marketing of countries or destinations and the provision of visitor information are traditional tourism functions of governments at the national and local level, most commonly performed by a national or regional tourist board or by a local authority.

Scotland's Tourism and Environment Forum has a very practical newsletter and a website which are good examples of attractive and informative communication (see Case Studies, p 172).

The study tours and international conferences organized by Egypt's Red Sea Initiative were very important in influencing the country's new direction (see Case Studies, p 144).

5.26: Regional assistance in building capacity

In Latin America, the International Labour Organization (ILO) has supported a programme called REDTURS to help small and community based tourism enterprises to prosper and grow. It focused initially on Bolivia, Ecuador and Peru, but extended to other countries in the region. At a micro level, it has involved developing and implementing business development services. At an intermediate level, services are offered to community groups and rural municipalities. Assistance is provided in the development of tourism clusters and networks and the technical skills of local government have been developed. At the macro level, indigenous organizations are strengthened to improve their role of representation, negotiation and advocacy with state institutions and other stakeholders.

Considerable use has been made of information technology in this work, which is integrated with the training, and is vital in the dissemination of a wide range of information and examples of good practice. It is also a key to the other half of the programme's work, which is developing tools for marketing.

In recent years, many countries have tended towards a partnership approach between the public and private sector in providing these functions, perhaps using an independent organization funded by both sectors. Even if governments are not engaged directly in destination marketing activity or in the delivery of information services, they are often able to influence them.

The role of marketing and information services in influencing sustainability

Marketing and information services are direct, powerful and flexible tools that can be used to influence the performance of different types of tourism enterprise and the behaviour of tourists, by providing an essential communications link between destinations, products and visitors[7].

These tools can be used on their own. However they are also very useful, and frequently essential, in backing up other tools, such as economic instruments, guidelines and certification.

The primary functions of these tools in making tourism more sustainable are to:

- Facilitate market access: the vital importance of market access for economic sustainability is relevant to all types of tourism, but governments may need to pay particular attention to small enterprises or community-based tourism initiatives in this regard, owing to their limited resources for marketing.
- Promote particular forms of tourism or specific products that are more sustainable than others. This can enhance sustainability in two ways, by:
  - raising the profile and performance of such products and encouraging use of them;
  - providing a practical incentive. The restriction of certain promotional opportunities to enterprises that meet certain criteria can be used as a powerful incentive for all enterprises to become more sustainable.
- Influence visitors' behaviour, by informing them about sustainability issues and encouraging certain types of activity while discouraging others.

Strategic marketing linked to sustainability objectives

The extent and form of marketing activity should reflect strategic decisions about the amount and type of tourism required, and its location. Strategic priorities common to many destinations and that can be directly addressed through marketing and information include:

- Promoting to selected target markets that relate to sustainability objectives.
- Reducing seasonality, by promoting off-season images and opportunities.
- Promoting alternative destinations, spreading benefits and loads.
- Maximizing value retained locally, increasing spend per head and length of stay.
- Promoting the use of more sustainable transport.

Implications of sustainability for tactical marketing and information activity are identified below.

Instruments 5

Conveying accurate images and information

Successful destination marketing depends partly on developing and promoting a clear brand based on the core values of the destination. In the interests of sustainability, the brand and associated images (including pictures and text) should:

- Be sufficiently strong to successfully command attention and generate new interest.
- Be sufficiently distinctive, to differentiate the destination from others.
- Match the values of the destination's target markets.
- Be authentic, i.e. it should relate to what visitors will actually find.
- Avoid stereotypes and images that may demean local communities and their values.

Box 5.27 gives an example of how some community based tourism networks are jointly promoting a common brand.

Some destinations are seeking to convey concepts of sustainability (such as clean environments and engaged communities) in their core branding and images. This can be helpful in terms of drawing visitors' attention to such issues at the outset, but only if the above conditions are met. Using 'sustainability' images in a contrived way can be damaging.

Irrespective of brands and images, all destinations should ensure that visitors are provided with accurate and sufficiently detailed information, before and during their trip, to enable them to make well informed choices and encourage responsible

---

Box 5.27: Promoting community-based tourism networks

A number of developing countries, including Kyrgyzstan, Namibia, Tanzania and Uganda amongst others, have established networks of community-based tourism projects, partly to assist mutual support and capacity building, and partly for joint promotion within a common brand. Consistency of quality, visitor experience and adherence to sustainability principles are important in maintaining brand values, and it is up to the members and network coordinators to address this.

Most networks offer a range of basic accommodation, such as camping sites or homestays, village visits, cultural programmes, guided walks, and local foods and handicrafts. At least some of the income is disbursed to benefit the community as a whole and projects may be based on varying degrees of community ownership.

Many of these networks have been established with the assistance of development agencies. Although they are becoming self-sufficient, marketing support from government can be very valuable to them.

In Tanzania, the Cultural Tourism Programme, which offers visits to tribal villages, was set up by the Netherlands Development Organization SNV, but the custodianship of it has been handed over to the Tanzania Tourist Board, which was a partner in the programme from the beginning. The Board provides marketing assistance and exposure, including housing the enquiry and reservation facility in the Tourist Information Centre in Arusha to provide a gateway to the communities.

behaviour. This should relate to the destination as a whole and to individual locations, communities and sites. It should cover:

- The natural environment, including special qualities and sensitivities to certain activities.
- The history, cultural heritage and traditions of the place, including implications both in terms of visitor interest and visitor behaviour.
- The current economic and social conditions, and implications for how people should be treated.
- Information relevant to visitors' health and safety.

In some circumstances, it may be appropriate to produce and promote specific guidelines or codes for visitors.

Tourist Boards and local authorities can have an important influence through their own promotions, information print, and websites. However, to be effective they should also work with incoming and international tour operators and with travel media (especially guidebook editors) to get this information across.

Promoting specific products and experiences

Promotional activities and information services may seek to give particular exposure to a range of products and services that relate most directly to sustainability objectives. These may include, for example, enterprises pursuing good practice (possibly identified through certification), particular forms of tourism such as cycling or walking that are environmentally friendly, or community-based tourism projects that have been developed specifically with poverty alleviation in mind. Three important approaches, which are not mutually exclusive, are:

- Identification within mainstream promotion. A key principle is that marketing messages relating to sustainability and associated products should not be treated as a separate component of destination marketing but be given a high profile within mainstream promotions. This should involve integrating relevant information, including features on particular types of product or transport alternatives, within the main destination's guide and website. A particular example is the featuring of ecolabels within official accommodation listings.
- Developing specific marketing campaigns. Alongside mainstream promotion, some types of more sustainable product may benefit from separate marketing activity. For example, many destinations offer walking or cycling holidays, promotion of which may be coordinated within separate print and media campaigns. Giving priority to events and products available in the off-season may also benefit sustainability.
- Supporting collaborative marketing within networks. Joint marketing initiatives have proved to be a useful way of facilitating market access for individual MSMEs or community-based tourism initiatives, which may be too small to achieve effective market penetration on their own. This may be linked to additional services such as central reservation, as well as to capacity building. Marketing assistance can include researching markets, contact making with operators, providing presence at fairs, assistance with publicity and exposure in destination print and websites.

In Scotland, membership of the Green Tourism Business Scheme is indicated against entries in the official accommodation guide and enquirers can click on the official website for a list of certified properties (see Case Studies, p 172).

Ensuring effective local information delivery and interpretation

The availability of good quality information to visitors when they arrive and during their stay can be a very valuable tool for making tourism more sustainable. Information that brings out the qualities, distinctiveness and interest of the immediate local area can help to encourage higher spending within the community.

The delivery of local information can also be combined with an element of interpretation, helping to raise visitors' understanding of local environmental issues and the needs of communities. Key delivery outlets include:

- Tourist Information Centres (TIC): face to face information delivery can be particularly effective in getting the right messages across to visitors. TICs are often government supported, though their long term economic sustainability is frequently a challenge.
- Visitor Centres: these may combine visitor information and interpretative displays.
- Panels and signage providing information and interpretation: these need to be robust, well designed, simply worded, and strategically placed yet unobtrusive.
- Holiday company representatives: introductory information provided to visitors by reps, serving to orientate them within the resort and the wider area, can be very influential.
- Accommodation hosts: proprietors and reception staff provide a regular point of contact throughout a visit. Information they deliver (personally or through notices) can relate to the local area or to behaviour within the establishment itself, such as use of water, turning off lights, etc.
- Guides: tour guides and local guides can play a critical role in influencing visitor behaviour as well as providing interpretation.

All the above should be made well acquainted with sustainability issues in the area, through familiarization visits and training.

Box 5.28: Teaching good practice to visitors

In the USA, Leave No Trace is a national programme run by a non-profit organization, which is supported by a number of federal agencies as well as outdoor recreation bodies and commercial companies. It was established originally by the US Forest Service, and later joined by the National Park Service and others.

The programme teaches people how to behave responsibly in the outdoors, with an emphasis on environmental impact focused round a seven point code: Plan ahead and prepare; Travel and camp on durable surfaces; Dispose of waste properly; Leave what you find; Minimize campfire impacts; Respect wildlife; and Be considerate of other visitors. It is delivered through a range of train the trainer courses, workshop sessions with groups (such as youth groups) and public contact at visitor centres and elsewhere. The courses and a wide range of information material are based on scientific research and practical experience obtained over a number of years.

Using educational programmes

More sustainable behaviour by visitors can also be achieved by educational activities, either on site or in the visitors' home, school or social environment. Governments should promote teaching and training about responsible travel and recreation. An example is the Leave No Trace programme described in Box 5.28. Developed in the USA, this is now being established in some Latin American countries and elsewhere.

Local promotional campaigns and information delivery should not be seen only as tools aimed at visitors.

Governments influencing outgoing markets

Governments can further affect the sustainability of tourism by using marketing and information to influence the behaviour of their own citizens as international travellers. In the past this has mainly been motivated by concern for traveller safety, but some governments in developed countries (see Box 5.29) have recently taken an interest in the impact of travel from their countries on the sustainable development of recipient countries. This can involve:

- Being conscious of the impact of official travel advice about certain countries on the wellbeing of the local tourist industry. Statements need to be carefully worded, specific, accurate and up to date.
- Encouraging and influencing tour operators and the travel media in their support for sustainable development and information given to tourists.

In Calvià a number of awareness raising campaigns have been aimed at local people, covering issues varying from behaviour towards visitors to the use of water (see Case Studies, p 167).

Box 5.29: Helping citizens be responsible travellers

In the UK, the government has taken a number of steps to influence the impact of outbound tourism:

- The Sustainable Tourism Initiative, a multi-stakeholder partnership sponsored by the Prime Minister, seeks to introduce sustainable tourism practice in the UK outbound tourism industry. This led to the establishment of The Travel Foundation, an independent charity that supports environmental and social programmes in destination countries, partly funded by money raised from travellers by a group of leading tour operators.
- Adjustment to travel advisories. In 2004, the government announced that it would be more sparing in its travel advice notices, advising its citizens against travel only in situations of extreme and imminent danger.
- A guide to sustainable travel. In 2004, the Government joined with a well known travel guide publisher to produce 2 million free copies of Rough Guide to a Better World, a guide for the public on how to support action towards the Millennium Development Goals, including a section on ethical travelling.

Instruments

Notes

1 *Indicators of Sustainable Development for Tourism Destinations, A Guidebook*, WTO, 2004.
2 UNEP Global Programme of Action for the Protection of the Marine Environment has issued guidelines for tourism development in coastal areas, *Key Principles for Tourism Development*, available at http://www.gpa.unep.org.
3 The CBD Guidelines are available on the Convention on Biological Diversity web site at http://www.biodiv.org.
4 The Global Code of Ethics for Tourism is a comprehensive set of principles whose purpose is to guide the stakeholders in tourism development: central and local governments, local communities, the tourism industry and its professionals, as well as visitors, both international and domestic. Although it is not a legally binding document, its Article 10 provides for a voluntary implementation mechanism through the recognition of the role of the World Committee of Tourism Ethics (http://www.world-tourism.org/code_ethics/eng.html).
5 WTO prepared a set of *Recommendations to Governments for Supporting and/or Establishing National Certification Systems for Sustainable Tourism*. The document emphasizes the role of governments in establishing and coordinating multi-stakeholder processes for certification systems, gives orientations for developing certification criteria, and for operational aspects. (http://www.world-tourism.org/sustainable/doc/certification-gov-recomm.pdf).
6 *Voluntary Initiatives for Sustainable Tourism: Worldwide Inventory and Comparative Analysis of 104 Eco-labels, Awards and Self-Commitments* (WTO, 2002).
7 For an overview of instruments and channels for marketing of sustainable tourism, see UNEP/Regione Toscana report on *Marketing of Sustainable Tourism Products* (2005).

Conclusions:
The way forward

This Guide has presented and examined the wide range of issues and significant challenges involved in making tourism more sustainable. The most effective structures and strategic approaches to policy making and the relevant implementation instruments have been discussed and illustrated.

How can governments respond?

Based on the evidence and recommendations presented here, governments should consider whether they are paying sufficient attention to tourism within the field of sustainable development, and whether their tourism policies and actions adequately embrace concerns about sustainability.

Participatory structures through which governments could work with other stakeholders to plan, develop and manage tourism in a sustainable manner should also be established. Tourism policies should be developed and implemented within a jointly agreed strategy that has the principles and aims of sustainability at its centre. This Guide aims to support and guide these processes.

It is appreciated that many countries will already have tourism strategies and policies. Where this is the case, strengthening the integration of sustainability into them should be part of the process of their revision and review. Gaps and deficiencies should be identified and addressed. Other countries that are developing tourism policies for the first time are encouraged to pursue the aims and approaches identified here from the outset.

One key to more sustainable tourism is to work in effective partnerships within local destinations. It is at this local level that much of the necessary planning, networking, capacity building and information delivery occur, and where tourism needs to be effectively integrated into local sustainable development. It is therefore important that the material in this Guide is disseminated to local authorities and that they use it to review, develop and implement their own tourism policies together with local stakeholders. National governments are well positioned to foster and facilitate this process.

At all levels of government, long term political support, technical competence and a sufficient allocation of resources will be required to ensure that policies are effectively implemented.

How can other stakeholders respond?

A growing interest in sustainability issues within the market and the private sector of tourism has been identified. This should underline the importance and value to governments of responding to sustainability issues.

Although this Guide is not directed at the private sector, tourism enterprises should take note of its contents. They should seek to improve their own performance and actions in line with the aims and principles articulated here and work together to strengthen their collective response. Private sector enterprises are also best placed to influence the awareness and actions of visitors. Moreover, they have a very important role to play in putting pressure on governments to take appropriate action and to work with them on this. Tourism will not become more sustainable without their active commitment and response to the policies and instruments outlined here.

The messages contained in the Guide are also relevant to other types of organization and institution, including the many kinds of government agencies, quasi-governmental bodies, and NGOs working in the fields of sustainable development, environment and tourism. Such organizations are particularly important in building bridges between government, the private sector and local communities. As well as participating in policy formulation, they have a very valuable role to play in the development and execution of many of the instruments identified here, such as certification and capacity building.

Individual countries should not work in isolation on making tourism more sustainable. Many sustainability issues have trans-boundary, regional and global implications. Inter-regional bodies should take note of the Guide and facilitate joint approaches between governments as appropriate. The document also has many implications for multinational and bilateral development assistance agencies and the way they support tourism policies and projects.

A continual communication process

A sustainable approach to tourism development and management is all about planning for the long term, working together, checking on outcomes and adapting to change. Effective communication is fundamental to this. Policies and instruments will not work unless they are put across in the right way.

Governments should make sure that all relevant stakeholders know what is expected of them. The sustainable tourism strategy and policies should be clearly disseminated. Many of the instruments outlined in this document require effective communication but others can facilitate it, such as regular government reporting on their own actions and the issuing of simple guidelines based on the agreed policies. A commitment to regular monitoring and review, and to communicating results between all stakeholders, should become widespread.

A move towards more sustainable tourism should be widely trumpeted and celebrated, amongst tourists, host communities and the participants in the industry. Yet in doing this, the commitment to change and improvement must be genuine and based on well-established policies and actions that can be delivered.

Conclusions

Case Studies

1. Australia: Strategies leading to practical tools
2. Bulgaria: National Ecotourism Strategy and Action Plan
3. Costa Rica: Commitment supported by certification
4. Egypt: Red Sea Sustainable Tourism Initiative
5. Ghana: Community based tourism initiative
6. Mexico: Agenda 21 for tourism in Mexico
7. Kaikoura (New Zealand): Sustainability of a small community
8. South Africa: Tourism White Paper and subsequent initiatives
9. Calvià (Spain): Local Agenda 21 and resort rejuvenation
10. Scotland (UK): Tourism and Environment Forum and Green Tourism Business Scheme

Australia:

Strategies leading to practical tools

Pioneering work on the development of ecotourism and sustainability, with a focus on quality, based on the development of strategies and a practical mechanism to link tourism and conservation

Tourism is big business in Australia, employing around 7 per cent of the workforce. As a long haul destination, it cannot rely on strategies of price or convenience to grow its markets, but rather on offering quality authentic and enriching experiences—currently referred to as 'Platinum Plus'. The country's natural and cultural heritage resources are a key part of that experience.

This case study describes some of the policies and instruments that have been used over time to develop tourism based on these resources and to underpin its sustainability. It looks initially at the pioneering ecotourism strategy at a federal level and some of the actions that stemmed from this, and then takes Queensland as an example of the practical development of policies and actions within one state.

Initial approaches in planning for ecotourism and sustainability

Australia's National Tourism Strategy, in 1992, highlighted the need for sustainable tourism development and a more balanced approach to economic, social and environmental issues. At that time, the government believed that an overall policy framework for the development of ecotourism would contribute significantly to achieving sustainable tourism in natural areas. The National Ecotourism Strategy that followed (1994) provides one of the earliest and most successful examples of planned and supported development of ecotourism, which has been replicated elsewhere.

The strategy was produced after a year-long consultative process that raised awareness of many of the issues of sustainability. The first stage was the development of an Issues Paper, which was used to stimulate discussion at a series of well publicized workshops held around the country. A call for public submissions was also made through advertisements in major newspapers. The workshop outcomes and 149 written submissions helped form the draft Ecotourism Strategy, which was circulated to all participants in the process. A further 103 follow up responses were used to refine the document in conjunction with further consultation with relevant government agencies at both the state and federal level.

The strategy advocated and supported the promotion of commercially viable and sustainable ecotourism, through the use of integrated regional planning and natural resource management tools. Emphasis was placed on sustainable infrastructure, effective monitoring and relevant education. There was a strong call for more ethical and responsible marketing, rigorous professional standards, and the involvement of indigenous Australians in all aspects of development and delivery.

A key to its success was the allocation of significant, dedicated funding (AUS$10 million), largely made available through competitive grants, thereby ensuring action.

The grants were primarily focused on:

- Infrastructure development (innovative design and technologies plus site hardening through signage, boardwalks and wildlife viewing platforms).
- Baseline studies, monitoring and regional ecotourism planning.
- Four central research and education themes—energy and waste minimization, ecotourism education, business development and market research.

Notable tangible outputs from this funding included: an ecotourism certification programme (described below); research publications into ecotourism profiles; a directory of Australian ecotourism educational opportunities; visitor awareness videos for inbound flights; a community ecotourism planning guide; several publications on private sector waste and energy management practices; and integrated regional planning and business development conferences and workshops.

The strategy together with these grants strengthened established collaborative networks and a sophisticated ecotourism industry that continues to position Australia as one of the world's leading ecotourism providers. With the vast majority of parks under the jurisdiction of state governments, the national strategy actively encouraged states to develop their own specific plans and policies (see Queensland example below).

The Australian Government's AUS$235 million Tourism White Paper, launched in December 2003, reconfirms the importance of sustainable development to the ongoing prosperity of the tourism industry, but places it more in the context of broader regional and rural development processes and support. In terms of sustainability, a focus is placed on: strengthening quality and capability through national accreditation and consolidation of tourism certification programmes; developing niche markets and products; supporting tourism development within indigenous communities; and building partnerships between tourism enterprises and protected areas. The White Paper was based on extensive consultation, with creative use made of the Internet and emails to elicit response.

Evolving approaches to certification

Following the National Ecotourism Strategy, seed funding was provided for a certification programme for enterprises (the NEAP or National Ecotourism

Tourism operations on the Great Barrier Reef require careful management
Photo: Tourism Queensland

Australia

Accreditation Programme), a system that has been led and developed by the industry. Rather than covering all types of tourism, it is limited to ecotourism, as it was felt that there was a particular need to ensure that tourism in fragile natural or cultural environments was definitely sustainable, and that the ecotourism could be an exemplar of sustainability that could act as a mentor to the rest of the tourism industry. The criteria include elements essential to sustainability such as: environmental impact, contributions to conservation, working with local communities, cultural sensitivity and returns to local communities.

Some important points about NEAP (now called the EcoCertification Programme), which is administered by Ecotourism Australia, include:

- Awards, given to individual products, such as tour programmes or accommodation units, rather than enterprises. In 2004, the programme included 414 certified products belonging to 179 operators.
- Anecdotal evidence but no proven research that participants have strengthened their environmental and social management because of the programme.
- The application document gives practical recommendations, contacts and details of courses. The process of assessment has often involved assessors or NEAP Panel members providing informal training and advice.
- As there was unwillingness by enterprises to pay for a fledgling programme, costs had to be kept low, so it was based largely on self-checks with limited on-site auditing. As the program has grown and become more successful, it is demanding a higher degree of rigour through introducing more regular on-site auditing.
- The programme is broadly self-sufficient in terms of day-to-day running, but has relied heavily on external funding and support for marketing, promoting to enterprises, and the auditing and judging processes, especially from state governments (notably Queensland).
- Take up of the programme has been considerably strengthened by certification becoming a condition for enterprises to attain, or be favoured for, other benefits, notably preferential access or extended tenure for operating in protected areas (imposed by Western Australia for example).

As result of the White Paper's emphasis on the delivery of quality experiences, Australia has been giving considerable weight to voluntary certification programmes throughout the tourism industry as a way of strengthening quality. There is a focus not just on provision of facilities against standards, but on business fitness and economic sustainability, such as evidence of legal compliance, basic business planning, marketing plans, human resource management, good operational management systems and risk management strategies.

The EcoCertification Programme has been modified to take account of these wider criteria. Other environmental certification programmes, such as the Green Globe 21, are also active in Australia. Green Globe 21 has led initiatives to coordinate environmental standards with the quality 'star' programmes through collaboration with the Australian Automobile Association. The majority of mainstream and sector-specific tourism certification programmes now include basic environmental and sustainability criteria.

Influencing tourism in protected areas and indigenous communities

With much of the tourism industry dependent on Australia's unique natural and cultural heritage, much of the concern about sustainable tourism in federal policy documents has focused on the relationship between tourism interests and protected area and heritage management.

The Australian Government report, *Pursuing Common Goals: Opportunities for Tourism and Conservation*, released in July 2003, examines the relationship between tourism and protected area management and concludes that there is substantial potential to develop ventures that will grow tourism while improving environmental protection.

Many Indigenous communities are located within national parks and world heritage areas or on lands still in a natural state and with high scenic attraction. Accordingly, park management processes and environmental regulations are likely to have a disproportionately higher impact on Indigenous tourism.
The *Pursuing Common Goals* report identified—through case studies and discussions with stakeholders—that there is a lack of small business skills in indigenous communities, as well as limited product development and poor linkages to existing tourism systems. The report indicated that Indigenous Tourism products and businesses are underdeveloped and that even where indigenous culture is a prime reason for the existence of a protected area and where tourism appears to be developed, more indigenous experience could be added.

The Business Ready Programme for Indigenous Tourism is a Tourism White Paper initiative, designed to assist existing and start-up Indigenous Tourism businesses to develop the business skills and knowledge specifically required to establish and run a commercially viable tourism operation.

The Tourism and Conservation Initiative is also a key element of the Tourism White Paper, aimed at facilitating the development of nature-based tourism attractions while increasing Australia's capacity to protect and conserve the environment. The Tourism and Conservation Initiative aims to encourage an integrated approach to planning tourism and conservation developments and increase the range and scope of innovative tourism centres that will significantly improve protection and presentation of eco-systems.

Skyrail - an EcoCertified attraction
Photo: Tourism Queensland

Funding of AUS$4.6 million will be available over three years to:

- Support Tourism and Conservation Partnerships that stimulate regionally significant nature-based tourism and conservation.
- Conduct research aimed at product development and economic evaluation of park tourism.
- Improve park systems and regulations to engender partnerships between protected area managers and tourism operators.
- Develop a tourism and conservation agenda.

Queensland's approach to practical delivery

Queensland is a state that has been particularly active in the development and management of ecotourism, and extending this to concern for the sustainability of tourism as a whole. The Queensland government has introduced practical initiatives that underpin sustainability, some of which are presented below.

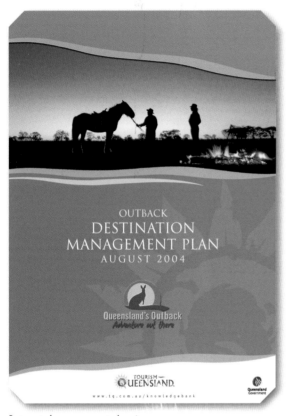

Integrated management planning
at the local level

Effective political and technical structures. The Growing Tourism Strategy has been developed by the State government to provide a 'whole of government approach' to strategic tourism planning, policy and development. The strategy involves key government bodies in its implementation, with coordination facilitated by an across-agency Chief Executive Officer's Committee, and identified tourism contacts in each agency. Industry is involved through a Tourism Industry Consultative Forum. At a technical level, within Tourism Queensland a dedicated unit was established to cover tourism sustainability.

The Queensland Ecotourism Plan. This state level plan, following on from the National Ecotourism Strategy, is seen as a living plan with frequent updates and has been supported by many practical implementation measures, including training workshops and the distribution of a range of self-help manuals.

Support for sustainability certification. The EcoCertification Programme has been strongly supported by Tourism Queensland over the years. This has been through small grants towards the running of the programme, on-site auditing, etc., and also through adding value to participating enterprises by linking them in to major marketing benefits and to the protected area concessions process.

The Tourism in Protected Areas Initiative. Reflecting the issues raised federally, a new participatory relationship has been forged between the Queensland Parks and Wildlife Service and the tourism industry. The initiative has fostered the development of a new and more effective, efficient and equitable system of managing sustainable tourism in Queensland's protected areas. Key elements of the new system, which also provides for greater input from traditional owners, include: collaborative site planning, long term agreements, a market based fee structure and a range of other performance based measures including accreditation.

Local destination planning. Recognizing that effective tourism development and management occurs at the local destination level, Tourism Queensland has established a framework and support for integrated destination management. In each of the twelve tourism regions across the State, Destination Management Plans have been developed which provide a framework for enhancing industry coordination, strengthening partnerships, coordinating stakeholder interests, and providing industry leadership.

Bulgaria:

National Ecotourism Strategy and Action Plan

Influencing national and local thinking on the sustainability of tourism by thorough consultation on a far reaching plan, with associated instruments

Bulgaria is a small country with a considerable natural and cultural heritage. The importance of ecotourism planning was recognized as a result of the development of a National Biological Diversity Conservation Strategy and increasing political support for protected areas and a national ecological network. There was a clear need to create opportunities for economic growth and higher living standards for local communities around protected areas in ways that would also strengthen local support for conservation, and contribute to sustainable development in rural areas in general.

Ecotourism has been defined in Bulgaria as tourism that is based on nature, rural life and associated cultural sites and events. It includes an interpretative experience, benefits conservation and local communities (particularly the rural population), and is based primarily on locally owned, small-scale enterprises.

The 1990s saw numerous attempts to develop ecotourism in local communities across Bulgaria. Most of these initiatives, however, lacked clearly defined relationships with the local and protected area institutions; were not associated with any standards or regulation of tourist use or impact; were often pursued by people with insufficient knowledge skills and resources; and were unprofitable as a result of lack of coordinated marketing effort.

International, national and local partners working together

The development process was initiated by three ministries—Environment and Water; Economy (which includes tourism); and Agriculture and Forests. They formalized their joint support for ecotourism by signing a Cooperation Protocol underpinning their commitment to the implementation of the strategy. The process was supported by four international development assistance agencies—USAID, UNDP, the World Bank and the Swiss Government agency.

Working at both local and national levels was crucial to the process, with each level informing the other. This included:

*   Local pilot initiatives in the Rila and Central Balkans national parks, based on participative planning exercises that led to the formation of two ecotourism partnerships/associations, including the parks, local authorities and local enterprises. This formed a model and also created a groundswell of interest, which spurred the national approach.

Discussing the Regional Ecotourism Action Plan for the Central Balkans

- Establishment of a National Ecotourism Working Group that included the above three ministries, national, regional and local tourism associations, conservation NGOs and the Foundation for Local Government Reform (FLGR).
- Holding of a sizeable National Ecotourism Forum which included input from a range of international bodies and experts.
- Setting up of six thematic working groups at national level covering information technology, product development and marketing, funding and financial mechanisms, enterprise development, institutional development, and regional development.
- Dividing the country into 12 ecotourism-destination regions based on landscape types and clusters of protected areas and cultural sites, and then working at a local level with a range of partners to establish regional associations and prepare 12 regional ecotourism action programmes.

Colourful posters and press coverage encouraged public participation and interest

The whole process, which took two years, was characterized by extensive stakeholder participation and consultation, and national and local interaction. Two consultation drafts of the national strategy were produced before it was finalized. The national strategy provided a basis for the regional action programmes and the regional associations, in turn, provided significant input to the creation of the resulting national ecotourism action plan. In total, over 400 individual and group meetings were held and 800 different institutions and organizations were involved, including 140 municipalities.

Some important elements of the approach included:

- Comprehensive research into the domestic market for ecotourism, including quantitative surveys to measure the percentage of the population with a potential interest in ecotourism, detailed focus groups to find out more about motivations and expectations, and interviews with tour operators.
- Considerable effort to stimulate local interest and support, including posters and widespread dissemination of the summary of the strategic framework and a 'questions and answers' brochure.
- Seeking extensive media coverage through 18 regional and 4 national press conferences which generated 120 features in the press and broadcasting media.

Key elements of the strategy and action plan

The National Ecotourism Strategy spans a 10 year period, with the Action Plan developed to cover the first 5 years. Both the strategy and action plan are very comprehensive and will therefore be challenging to implement. If successful, however, they will make a significant difference to tourism in Bulgaria and to conservation and sustainable rural development.

The following aspects of the strategy and action plan stand out:

- Institutional development. This includes strengthening of the National Ecotourism Working Group as a multi-stakeholder body responsible for

Bulgaria

Mountain landscapes in south-west Bulgaria

overseeing the implementation of the plan and its annual review and update, as well as development of a Federation of Regional Tourism Associations ensuring that local issues are reflected in national policy, providing support and assisting coordination.

- Clustering and networking. The strategy puts a lot of emphasis on gaining strength and impact through networking between enterprises and mutual support between tourism and other sectors at a local level—introducing a concept of competitive clusters.
- Ecotourism business development and marketing. There is considerable emphasis on providing business support through structured advice and training, financial assistance packages, well targeted promotion, quality assurance schemes and branding. The action plan contains some specific product development programmes such as a network of eco-lodges.
- Information management. This includes the development of product databases, regular visitor surveys, and identifying and disseminating best practices.

Developing instruments to support implementation

A number of instruments to support sustainability were developed in parallel with the preparation of the strategy and action plan. These included:

- A guidance manual for ecotourism product development.
- The awarding of prizes for best practice, which also helped to generate interest and publicity.
- A system of indicators to measure the success and impact of ecotourism products, tested in two destinations.

The process also stimulated two important changes to legislation to enable more revenue to be raised from enterprises and visitors to support the environment. The ability to award contracts to small tourism operations in protected areas was established, so that income can be obtained from the contract and management conditions can be enforced. Secondly, the law relating to local government was changed so that revenue from tourism taxes remains in the municipality and has to be used for tourism related infrastructure.

The strategy and action programme provides a vital framework for securing further funding from the European Union and other sources, as well as a dedicated budget from government. In addition, some specific funding mechanisms for ecotourism enterprise development and associated projects include a Trust Fund (the National Trust Eco Fund and associated Protected Areas Fund), which attracts external donor money, and the Ministry of Environment's National Environmental Enterprise Fund. The latter acquires resources from environmental taxes on fuel, pollution, etc. A component (€1 million per year) is specifically earmarked for ecotourism and protected area management.

Other instruments which are to be developed under the National Ecotourism Action Plan include:

- Capacity building structures at a local level, in the form of business growth centres.
- The establishment of guidelines on limits of acceptable change and acceptable use for protected areas and cultural monuments.
- A process of synchronization of relevant legislation to reflect the strategy.

Mainstreaming the approach

Although this is a strategy and action plan for ecotourism, it is widely accepted that tourism in Bulgaria needs to become more sustainable generally. When launching the ecotourism strategy, the Prime Minister said that it pointed the way towards a sustainable tourism strategy for Bulgaria.

Ecotourism in Bulgaria is not seen as something entirely separate from mass tourism and of no interest to larger operators—rather, it is seen as a way of diversifying the tourism product and providing a basis for transforming the image of Bulgarian tourism. Concepts and approaches developed within the ecotourism sector can be used to address tourism more broadly.

Steps that have been taken to strengthen the impact of the ecotourism strategy on tourism and sustainable development generally, include:

- Placing the National Ecotourism Working Group within the National Tourism Council.
- Making it conditional on municipalities that they take the ecotourism strategy into account in preparing regional and local plans. This is particularly important for funding, as decisions on the spending of future EU money will depend on priorities in these local plans.
- Integrating ecotourism into the work of Regional Tourism Associations.
- Involving the influential and respected Foundation for Local Government Reform at key stages in the formulation of the strategy and action plan.
- Seeking to pave the way for ecotourism and sustainable tourism in the wider Balkans region, including close involvement with the Regional Environment Centre.

Costa Rica:

Commitment supported by certification

A country with a longstanding emphasis on ecotourism and sustainability in its approach to tourism markets and products, supported by one of the best established certification programmes and other government led activities

Costa Rica covers just 51 thousand square kilometres but is one of the most richly biodiverse countries in the world. It receives more than one million international tourists per year. The Costa Rica Tourist Board describes the country's strengths as: impressive scenic beauty, a consolidated system of protected areas, social and political stability, high educational levels and an efficient infrastructure and services.

Costa Rica has taken the decision, as a society, to support sustainable development, especially in tourism. General policies articulated in the national tourism development plan (2002–2012) start with the statement that: '*The concept of sustainability will be the fundamental axis of tourism activity and will be considered as the main factor characterizing the national tourism product.*' Moreover, the country is promoted under a slogan which resonates with green sentiment - '*Costa Rica – No Artificial Ingredient*'.

Ecotourism and market awareness lead to a commitment to sustainability

Costa Rica's commitment to sustainable tourism started in the realm of ecotourism. This followed a common pattern—innovation by private individuals followed by strong government support once the benefits for the country become clear.

Red macaws - wildlife is a primary attraction of Costa Rica

Costa Rica

The first ecotourism businesses and private nature reserves were established by biologists and conservationists who had studied Costa Rica's diverse flora and fauna. These businesses were governed from their inception by a strong conservation and social ethic, and they became the models upon which the rest of Costa Rica's ecotourism industry was built. Because of the success of the founders, late-coming businesses often followed the environmental and social lead of the original models.

Another factor that stimulated this approach was the recognition of market opportunity. The tourist board and the traditional business leaders of the tourist industry came to realize the importance of the environment in determining Costa Rica's market position. The country's visitors generally engage in a varied series of experiences that include ecotourism, combined with a visit to a volcano and with conventional beach and city activities. Because the primary motivator for visiting Costa Rica is its reputation as a natural destination, large conventional hotels and tour operators now often implement sound environmental and social practices. Ecotourism and the sustainability of wider forms of tourism have become complementary. It has been good business for the country.

As a younger generation of business leaders developed policy, sustainability criteria became mainstream concepts, in government and industry. Even now, however, promoters of conventional mass tourism exert political influence, although they too have adopted sustainability criteria in their project portfolios.

Tourism strategy and planning

Costa Rica's tourism master plan for 2002–2012 is entirely based on using the principles of sustainable development for the sound expansion of the country's tourist industry. In this plan, preservation, conservation, ecotourism, and conventional yet sustainable tourism to beaches and cities maintain their existing complementarity.

Subsidiary zoning and regulatory plans for several of the larger tourist zones of the country have now been developed down to a 1:20 000 scale, based on sound use (or preservation in other cases) of natural resources for tourism and other activities. These plans are now being integrated into ecotourism management plans for protected areas, and an effort is being made to encourage local governments to convert the plans into binding zoning regulations for private land.

It is too soon to tell whether the sustainable tourism master plan for the country will be fully implemented and enforced. There is a large gap between stated policy and legally binding regulations. In part, this is because Costa Rica's constitution and legislation give wide latitude and freedom to do business in any legitimate form. There is also recognition that it is easy to legislate, but difficult and often impractical to enforce regulations. Finally, there is reluctance, on the part of local governments, to establish legally binding zoning regulations—perhaps because of the high cost of establishing zoning over a large area for the first time, perhaps because of political opposition to establishing limits on permissible construction. Although it is government policy to promote sustainable tourism and ecotourism, there is in fact little government support for sustainable businesses versus conventional ones, because it is in most cases illegal for the government to offer preferential treatment.

Finca Rosa Blanca, a top rated country hotel under the CST certification

Two important tools through which the government can exert influence on business are described below. These may combine with consumer demand for environmental good behaviour to make it easier for businesses to comply with government policy.

Certification for Sustainable Tourism (CST)

One of the few legally permissible instruments for discriminating between sustainable and conventional businesses is certification through the government-sponsored CST programme.

CST was developed by the Costa Rican Tourist Board in response to the perception, in the early 1990s, that it was becoming increasingly necessary to distinguish tourist businesses that were truly conserving natural resources and protecting their cultural milieu from those that claimed to do so, but were actually damaging both the environment and the social fabric of their communities. The businesses that claimed to be 'green', but were not, were perceived to be a direct threat to Costa Rica's enviable market position as one of the world leaders in ecotourism and environmentally sensitive conventional tourism. The certification programme was developed by the Tourist Board, rather than private industry or environmental organizations, because the government was among the first to sense the danger of an erosion of Costa Rica's market position and because of enlightened leadership and advanced technical skills amongst its staff.

The CST programme was designed to reward businesses that are both socially and environmentally responsible, while maintaining a high level of consumer satisfaction. The certification instrument consists of 153 questions covering four basic areas: biological and physical surroundings, physical plant, external client, and socio-

The Certification for Sustainable Tourism emblem

141

economic context. The questions are designed to be self-evident in intent, so that the business owner can do an initial self-evaluation and then improve the characteristics of the business, without the need for outside consultants. The certification standard emphasizes easily measured performance criteria, rather than environmental management systems, although there are a few process-based requirements. This structure allows a business to bring itself into basic compliance rapidly and inexpensively, and auditing is straightforward and also rapid.

Certification is awarded by an independent commission to those businesses that have been shown, upon external audit, to comply with certain minimum mandatory criteria, as well as achieving a minimum score of 20 per cent in **each** of the four basic areas. Further compliance allows the business to achieve up to five levels of CST, indicated by leaves (parallel in concept with one to five stars for quality). However the business is rated by the lowest score in each of the four areas, a strong motivation for added attention to the weakest areas. To reach the fifth level of CST (five leaves), a business must score at least 95 per cent in all four areas. Only two businesses in Costa Rica have accomplished this (out of 49 certified by mid 2004).

The development and continued operation of CST have depended on collaboration between the Tourist Board, the principal business school, the National Institute for Biodiversity, the National Chamber of Tourism, academic institutions, and environmental organizations.

CST has had a salutary effect on Costa Rica's tourist industry, as it establishes a set of credible, objective criteria for sustainability. Those businesses that have been certified and have made an effort to improve their rating, have become fervent promoters of sustainable practices. Because the certification instrument effectively promotes exemplary environmental and social practices, certified businesses have tended to improve their performance in these areas in a noticeable way.

The scheme has been led by government. Strengths, partly as a consequence of this, include:

- Government support enabling certification to be free of charge to businesses.
- High technical and ethical standards, making it one of the best in the world.
- The establishment of an independent accreditation body with wide representation.
- Official recognition and use in marketing Costa Rica.

However, fewer businesses have been certified than might be expected. This may also reflect on government involvement, with some bureaucratic inertia, inconsistency following political changes, and weak promotion to businesses and tourists.

Work with protected areas and private reserves

Another legally permissible mechanism available to the government for supporting sustainable tourism businesses is the payment for the environmental services offered by private nature reserves. More than half of all private reserves in Costa Rica offer some form of ecotourism, and these (along with those that do not) are entitled to receive annual payments for protecting biodiversity, scenic beauty, and water production, as well as reducing the emission of carbon dioxide that would result from deforestation.

The private reserves that are officially registered are also entitled to protection from squatters and exemption from land taxes. Although several studies have shown that the primary motivating factor for the owners of private reserves is the wish to conserve, not monetary considerations, the income and incentives offered by the government, together with modest income from ecotourism, have allowed the landowners to continue to conserve their land in a natural state, most often tropical rainforest. Without the combination of incentives and tourist income, much of this land might be deforested.

Ecotourism is also now seen by the government of Costa Rica as a key tool for financing protected areas independently of the national budget. The most common types of protected areas in Costa Rica are national parks, which are wholly owned by the government. Only non-essential services, such as parking, visitor centres, and souvenir shops can be offered in concession to the private sector. These have been offered by competitive bidding to local conservation or community organizations, which often subcontract the operation to successful businesses. In addition, the Interamerican Development Bank has agreed, in principle, to pay for ecotourism infrastructure in the national parks and some other protected areas, as long as the income is reinvested into the operation and protection of the park.

Furnishings at Lapa Rios ecolodge (CST certified) made from local materials such as cane and bamboo

Certain categories of protected areas, such as wildlife refuges and forest reserves, usually have mixed public and private ownership. In these cases, it is legally permissible to offer aspects of the management of the protected area in concession to an environmental or community organization, but this has been done in only one case. This mechanism is considered too politically sensitive to implement on a wider scale, lest it create the impression that the government is 'privatizing' protected areas.

Egypt:

Red Sea Sustainable Tourism Initiative

A comprehensive approach to coastal planning and management involving zoning of areas and the introduction or strengthening of a range of instruments to encourage developers and operators to embrace sustainability

Tourism is the largest source of foreign exchange earnings for Egypt, contributing almost 12 per cent of GDP including indirect effects, though many sources estimate its share at around 15 per cent. It is one of the most dynamic sectors of the economy, generating large numbers of jobs, with at least 8 per cent of all jobs connected to tourism. Despite erratic tourism trends in the Middle East, due to the region's turbulent affairs, incoming tourists increased in number by over 20 per cent in two years, exceeding an all time record of 6 million visitors in 2004.

Antiquities provided the primary source of visitor attraction to Egypt until the early 1980s. Since then, there has been remarkable growth in tourism on the Red Sea coast, based on the appeal of the abundant marine life in the coral reef systems. The number of hotel rooms has grown from a few hundred in 1980 to almost 45 000 in 2005, attracting 2 million visitors. The Tourism Development Authority (TDA), established under the Ministry of Tourism, in 1991, has initial plans for a four-fold increase in the number of hotel rooms, to 164 000 on the coastal land over which it has jurisdiction (the number of rooms country wide in 2017 will approach 350 000).

Eastern Desert towards Sharm El Loly, a natural deep water bay within the ecotourism development zone
Photo: PA Consulting Group

The TDA allocates large portions of land to private sector investors, who operate under contract with the TDA and who are responsible for the establishment of infrastructure, construction and operation of hotels, and the provision of community utilities for staff.

In the early years, the programme of tourism development was driven by growth targets in terms of visitor numbers and accommodation capacity. However, the TDA has now rethought its approach to embrace concerns for the environment of the destination, its overall quality and long term future. This has been assisted by the Red Sea Sustainable Tourism Initiative (RSSTI), which is based on a bi-lateral agreement between the USA and Egypt. USAID has supported the programme through technical assistance and the provision of cash transfers based on successful adoption of policy measures.

Land Use Management Plan and Zoning Regulations

An important component of the initiative was the preparation of a detailed plan for one of the coastal sectors. The TDA commissioned the South Marsa Alam Sector Strategic Development Plan in June 2001. The strategy considered three development alternatives: high growth (conventional/existing type) tourism development; sustainable tourism development; and low growth/ecotourism development. The study's proposed sustainable tourism alternative suggested around 15 000 rooms for the area, or the equivalent of thirty-eight 400-room hotels along a 30-kilometre coastline of which around 50 per cent consists of fringe reefs and protected areas.

The planning process for the Land Use Management Plan that followed was based on the fact that different resources have different abilities to accommodate various tourism activities. Identifying the key resources of the planning area, and those that are most sensitive, was seen as an initial step in ensuring provision of appropriate types and levels of tourist uses. The following steps for assessing the resource sensitivity and identifying the land use zoning scheme were followed:

1. Collection of data on the existing conditions for each resource as a separate Geographic Information System (GIS) layer.
2. Subdivision of the planning area into homogenous natural sub-zone/habitats by combining all natural resource layers.
3. Classification of the sub-zones/habitats based on ranges of weighted values. Sensitivity to tourism use was graded (based on the professional judgement of experts) as: low, medium, high, or very high.
4. Development of a land use zoning scheme for the different grades of natural sub-zones according to their environmental sensitivity.
5. Development of conservation, management and development regulations for the land use management zones.

All shoreline vegetation is protected
Photo: PA Consulting Group

A Sensitivity Map rates the most sensitive resources in terms of their resilience to the impacts of use. This illustrates an important issue: in general, the resources that the visitors want to see are often those that cannot withstand the impacts of use. The challenge for the zoning scheme was to accommodate use near or in the resources while minimizing or eliminating impacts.

Each of the proposed management zones corresponded to the different grades of sensitivity within the natural sub-zones of the Southern Red Sea Region. The following zoning scheme was proposed for the planning area: Core Zone (Absolute Reserve Areas); Buffer Zone (Restricted Wilderness Areas); Transition Zone (Ecotourism Zone); Low Intensity Development Zone (Coastal Eco-Resort Zone); and Moderate Intensity Development Zone. The Land Use Management plan listed general regulations for the management of zones identified in the zoning scheme to safeguard the area from urban expansion and ensure the best investment of environmental and cultural resources and the preservation of ecological balance.

The result led to radical changes to the regulations applied previously by the TDA, leading to serious modifications and cancellation of development plans in some zones. For example, in the low intensity zone, the new regulations changed the stipulated maximum density from 20 rooms per feddan (0.42ha) to 2 rooms per feddan and maximum heights from three to two or one storeys. In the transition zone, the only type of lodging facilities allowed will be the ecolodges and campsites with a maximum of 50 rooms on specified sites. The regulations also indicate limits on access.

The new regulations govern both development and conservation activities and were approved by a tripartite committee of the TDA, the Egyptian Environmental Affairs Agency (EEAA) and the Red Sea Governorate. For the first time in Egypt, planning regulations are based on sustainability criteria that combine long-term ecological viability, long-term economic viability, ethical use of resources, equity with local communities, and compliance with EEAA guidelines and Environmental Law 4/1994.

Environmental impact assessment (EIA)

The EIA system in Egypt uses a listing approach to screen projects according to the possible severity of environmental impact, dividing them into those with a mandatory requirement for EIA, those where further screening is needed, and those not requiring EIA.

Responsibility for EIAs for tourism projects is divided between the TDA and EEAA, with evaluation by both. The RSSTI identified many weaknesses in the process, including:

- A lack of guidelines for tourism projects (emphasis had previously been on more polluting industries).
- Insufficient coordination between the developer, TDA and EEAA, leading to hold ups in approval and many projects going ahead without it.
- Conflicting information between TDA and EEAA on EIA compliance.
- No systematic review to ensure that mitigation measures and compliance required by the EIA are followed.

The RSSTI introduced improvements, including: a Memorandum of Understanding between the TDA and EEAA; better guidance on initial screening; and establishing an EIA tracking system to verify compliance. At the outset only 20 per cent of tourism projects were approved by EEAA prior to commencing construction. Complete compliance with EIA regulations is expected by 2006-7 as a result of implementation of these changes.

Environmental monitoring and management

The RSSTI has enhanced the TDA's environmental monitoring capabilities, including establishment of an Environmental Monitoring Unit within it. Protocols, procedures and checklists have been established to facilitate monitoring. An operations manual provides guidelines for monitoring of natural resources (such as coral reefs) and tourism facilities (such as marinas). The baseline data collection and recording process, using GIS, has been designed to enable assessment of the cumulative impacts of TDA facilities over time.

The TDA will encourage developers and operators to implement best practices in environmental management, while monitoring progress in order to adjust TDA promotional policies. This process has been assisted by studies, within the RSSTI, of best practices in the field and by the production of best practice manuals for key issues such as solid waste management, landscape architecture, planting, water and sanitation, energy efficiency, and environmental management for resorts. These manuals highlight for developers and consultants the many issues to be considered at each phase of development (planning, design and construction) and operation. A Red Sea Planting Encyclopaedia interactive CD has been produced to allow professionals to select the types of plants to be used according to functional and environmental criteria.

Ababda woman from the Wadi El Gimal Protected Area
Photo: PA Consulting Group

Environmental Management Systems (EMS) have been designed for integrated resorts. The EMS programme includes stakeholder training courses and certification for hotel environmental officers.

A number of hotels and resorts have proceeded to recognition through the Green Globe certification programme.

Economic instruments

Although regulations have been drawn up, the TDA's policy in dealing with developers is to encourage rather than discourage, provide incentives rather than penalize, and guide rather than command. To this end, a set of economic instruments has been developed, including:

- Use of environmental criteria in the competitive land award process.
- Customs duty exemption and preferential financing for clean technologies.
- Promotion of environmental certification and awards of excellence.
- TDA criteria, standards and incentives for solid waste management.

Egypt

Ecotourism development

There is considerable interest in ecotourism in Egypt, as a means of diversifying the tourism offer, attracting a growing market and satisfying conservation objectives. Part of the southern coast, the Wadi El Gemal-Hamata area, was declared as a protected area in 2003. It contains important ancient mining sites, dwindling Bedouin populations and a host of rare and endangered plant and animal species. As part of the RSSTI, careful research and mapping was undertaken of the cultural and natural resources, and a study was produced of the ecotourism potential of the area. Challenges include creating appropriately designed facilities and delivering a safe recreational experience in harsh environmental conditions.

The advantages of good knowledge and communication

Three factors important for the success of the RSSTI are:

- The value of experience from elsewhere. The technical assistance and support programme provided an impetus to consider alternative strategies and adopt a new, more sustainable approach. This was helped by a series of study tours to observe good practice in other countries and international conferences held in Egypt.
- The need for harmonization between plans for tourism development and protected areas. The bringing together of the TDA and EEAA on planning and other measures was vitally important.
- The value of objective information. The concept of sustainable tourism only became a reality after extensive data collection, analysis and concrete recommendations were made. This provided extensive insight into a largely unknown area and was important in order to reach agreement on zoning regulations.

Ghana:

Community based tourism initiative

A project that has created new tourism products based on sustainability principles at the local community level, transforming the country's tourism offer and revealing challenges for government support structures

Ghana has the good fortune of receiving increasing numbers of visitors in a troubled West Africa region. Its attractions include numerous well maintained fortresses along the coast, national parks, beaches and the well documented Ashanti culture. Many visitors are Afro-Americans tracing ancestral links as well as individual travellers looking for an interesting mixture of contemporary African life, history and natural attractions. Critical to Ghana's success are acceptable standards of safety and hygiene, efficient access by air and relative political stability.

In 2002, the Community Based Ecotourism Project was set up, with funding from USAID. The project is government led, through the Ghana Tourist Board (GTB) which chairs the steering committee for the project. Implementing partners are the Nature Conservation Research Centre (NCRC), SNV Netherlands Development Organization and the US Peace Corps, together with local tourism management teams at different locations.

The product created and the role of partners

The main outcome of the project has been the creation of 14 community based enterprises throughout the country. These include five sites where the attraction is based on particular wildlife species, such as hippo, monkey or crocodile sanctuaries; five sites based on village and cultural experiences; and four sites where the attraction is a natural landscape feature. The product provided in each place includes a mixture of access, interpretation, catering and accommodation.

Community Tourism Management Teams at the local level represent the community and control resource utilization. They are supported by the partners, as follows:

- The NCRC has been the recipient of the donor funds and has been the main implementation agency.
- GTB assists with resource planning through its regional offices, and is responsible for the production of promotional materials and marketing. It has also conducted visitor surveys and undertaken pricing reviews.
- The District Assemblies, in whose areas the developments take place, are involved in providing permissions.
- Peace Corps Ghana has placed volunteers at the sites for periods of 12 to 24 months. They have assisted in introducing book keeping principles and standard administration material as well as assisting the community with the production of items such as souvenirs and T-shirts.
- SNV provides specific tourism capacity building support to all partners, including planning and implementation, and placed full time advisors with the NCRC and the GTB during the first phase of the project.

Ghana

The Wechiau hippo sanctuary is linked to facilities provided by the Lobi community

Action at each site has included the provision of an information centre, sanitation facilities, refuse containers, safety equipment, marketing materials and basic training in hospitality skills.

Sustainability objectives and effect on national tourism

This product was developed from the outset around sustainable development objectives. Potential benefits include:

- Community engagement and control.
- Poverty alleviation, including distribution of benefits within the community.
- Conservation of natural and cultural heritage resources, through the efforts of the community supported by visitor income.
- Regional and rural development. Until now, much of the country's tourism focus had been on the capital and coast.
- Product diversification. A variety of different experiences can be placed on tourist itineraries.

Visitor numbers have exceeded initial expectations. Trends are upwards, with almost a doubling in revenue in 2003 over the first year of operation. A number of local and international tour operators are featuring the sites in their itineraries.

The project has had a considerable impact on the national government's outlook on tourism. The Ministry of Tourism has used the experience of the project to make a case in cabinet for the prioritization of ecotourism as a growth sector that contributes to poverty alleviation, and has linked this to Ghana's National Strategy for Poverty Reduction. Partly as a result of the project, the Ministry of Finance has increased its commitment to tourism by increasing the budget for its development. The government has also been able to secure World Bank HIPC funding for tourism projects, now that they are seen as making a contribution to the fight against poverty.

Government capacity at different levels

The project has involved government in the practical issues of tourism development and in the need to adapt policy and approach to incorporate sustainable tourism objectives. However, it has also revealed a number of weaknesses and challenges that need to be addressed, which may also be relevant to other countries seeking more sustainable tourism.

The GTB, as the statutory agency for tourism development and with offices and staff in all regions of Ghana, is hampered by a serious lack of resources and skills. It also suffers from a lack of policy guidelines, meaning that most effort is put into administration rather than development and marketing. There is a tendency to support the development of attractions rather than enterprise, so income generating opportunities may be lost. The distinction between the activities of the GTB and those of the Ministry of Tourism is also insufficiently clear.

A clear commitment to tourism by other relevant ministries is missing. A particular problem rests with the Ministry of Land and Forestry, which is responsible for protected areas. Use of parks for tourism is not a well formulated objective, yet is of critical importance for the wellbeing of sustainable tourism, partly because parks are among the few areas where land tenure has been clarified and guaranteed by government. It is important that the conservation and sustainable tourism use of parks is defended in the face of mining and forestry interests. It is possible that the profile given to sustainable tourism through the project, and the interest generated in the Ministry of Finance, might strengthen the influence that can be exerted over other ministries in this matter.

Canoes at the Nzulezu stilt village
Illustration: Kathryn Buren

At the level of District Assemblies (DA), there are problems with the use of locally obtained income. The DAs can tax economic activities in their areas in order to improve local services and infrastructure such as provision of water, electricity and roads. Such services are in very poor condition in many of the project sites, and their improvement would be one way in which communities could benefit from tourism revenue. However, the DAs that are currently imposing a tax on the income from the community tourism initiatives are not delivering improvements to services. This needs to be resolved.

Instruments used to support sustainable development

The project has made good use of a number of tools in the development of the product and in underpinning sustainability. These include:

Data collection and dissemination.
The regular collection of data on visitor numbers, spending, income, and employment has been very important, not only in the management of the project and tracking progress, but also in providing evidence to ministries. It was only through this data that the government was persuaded of the value of rural tourism in Ghana.

Community consultation
Careful consultation was undertaken through the formal and also the traditional structures of governance—elected district assemblies and traditional authorities.

Project assessment against feasibility and sustainability criteria
A systematic process of assessing proposals was undertaken. Interested communities and individuals may first contact the regional offices of the GTB. At the outset, basic criteria—to do with accessibility, general visitor appeal, ability to deliver local benefits, land tenure and linkages with other attractions—are checked. If these are met, formal consultation with the community is conducted, to investigate the level of community consensus. If consensus is reached, more specific development processes are followed, based on checking against more detailed development criteria, which include sustainability issues such as: community ownership structures, process of distributing benefits, involvement of women and youth, environmental and social carrying capacity, contribution to poverty alleviation and biodiversity conservation.

Funding, reflecting sustainability criteria
The level and nature of funding support to local projects is also assessed against the criteria indicated above. This may be in the form of grants (applied to general attractions and used partly to mitigate negative impacts such as for access control measures and refuse disposal), or loans (applied to enterprise development that has created measurable and significant benefits for the community through a benefit distribution plan). Criteria have also been developed for the termination of support.

By-laws to control use
Most of the projects are related to natural or cultural heritage sites. Although misuse of the site is often prevented through tribal laws, it was felt necessary to establish some official by-laws to add further support to this. These have been aimed mainly at controlling possible damaging activities by the communities and visitors, such as hunting, extraction, vehicle access, etc. Agreement by the communities to these by-laws further underlines their support for the principles of sustainable tourism.

Mexico:

Agenda 21 for tourism in Mexico

A comprehensive initiative to make tourism more sustainable, based on a framework established by central government departments working together, and implemented through a partnership approach at local level using a range of instruments

This large scale initiative in Mexico is founded on principles stemming from the 1992 Earth Summit and its Agenda 21. It also takes account of international and regional policies and declarations made since then such as the establishment of a Caribbean Sustainable Tourism Zone, in 1999, the WTTC and WTO *Agenda 21 for Travel and Tourism*, and the attention given to sustainable tourism at the World Summit on Sustainable Development, in 2002.

It is also a response to fundamental challenges faced by the Mexican tourism industry and to market trends. Tourism is a high priority for the Mexican government. The National Tourism Programme 2001–6 clearly highlights that tourism should provide one of the prime examples of balanced regional development. However, a diagnosis of the sector reveals that Mexican destinations face environmental and social problems, such as disorderly urban growth close to major tourist centres, deterioration of the environment and the loss of cultural identity. Although tourism contributes strongly to GDP, it has not been sufficiently well integrated to local economies to bring maximum benefit to local communities.

The Agenda 21 programme includes established resorts such as Ixtapa-Zihuatanejo

Mexico also recognizes that tourists are becoming more discerning, are using new technology to obtain more information to select their destinations, and will be affected by changes in transportation, geopolitical and security considerations, and social and cultural changes.

All these factors point to the need for tourism planning and development that is more sensitive to visitors needs and to economic, social and environmental impacts.

An integrated policy structure

Agenda 21 for Tourism in Mexico is a joint initiative of SECTUR (Ministry of Tourism) and SEMARNAT (Ministry of the Environment and Natural Resources). It was launched in 2002, with support from the WTO. Essentially, it provides a tool for improving tourism impact at the municipal (local destination) level, supported by state authorities and based on a process developed, coordinated and championed at federal level.

Preserving the historic character of San Miguel de Allende

The initiative is firmly anchored in national policy, stemming from the National Development Plan 2001-6 which set an overall vision for Mexico to 2025, and two policy programmes, the National Programme for the Environment and Natural Resources, and the National Tourism Programme. The latter document identifies the 'maintenance of sustainable tourism destinations' as one of four Principal Axes, under which two objectives call for better, integrated planning at a local level supported by the three levels of government.

The approach was based on extensive consultation, including focus groups and discussion panels with government bodies, private sector, academics and NGOs. Meetings to discuss initial proposals were held with a range of tourism and environment agencies, and consultation was also undertaken via an internet site.

A seven-part framework

The most interesting aspect of the Mexican initiative is the comprehensive, seven-part framework for action that has been established.

1. Implementing Local Agenda 21 within municipalities involved with tourism. Defining an integrated model for destination management focused on sustainability, but sufficiently flexible to take account of local conditions and opinions. Pilot projects were launched in five destinations. The approach has since been extended to 25 principal destinations in Mexico, and will eventually extend to the entire country. The results are disseminated to relevant stakeholders, communities and tourists.

2. Developing a system of sustainable tourism indicators. The use of agreed indicators is recognized as a very potent instrument for strengthening sustainability. Indicators have been developed for different types of destination, tested in the pilot areas and then applied in all destinations.

3. Promoting better environmental practices in businesses and destinations. Developing norms and a programme for water conservation for tourism service providers, and establishing an overall sustainability certification scheme and label for hotels, other tourism enterprises and eventually for destinations.

4. Developing incentives for sustainable tourism activities. Concentrating on establishing financial assistance schemes from a variety of sources, with an emphasis on setting up schemes specifically aimed at improvement of small and medium sized enterprises and disseminating information about these sources.

5. Implementing a training and technology transfer programme. Developing human resources to support sustainability of enterprises and destinations, through training based on needs assessment, careful design and delivery of courses, and benchmarking results. Successful cases are also disseminated and university teaching and research on tourism sustainability updated.

6. Utilizing environmental legislation as a basis for integrated development. Including participation in programmes for the management and protection of coastal zones and studying, applying and developing environmental legislation and its application in the land use planning process in tourist destinations.

7. Establishing ecotourism in protected natural areas. Working with local communities to define a model and methodology for development of ecotourism in protected areas, identifying areas where ecotourism will be successful, investing in appropriate infrastructure such as visitor centres and trails, training businesses and guides, and marketing and dissemination.

Oaxaca, a UNESCO World Heritage Site and participant in Agenda 21

Application of the framework

By mid 2004, the Local Agenda 21 process had been established in 5 pilot areas followed by 15 further destinations. These were selected to span seven types of location: Large integrally planned resorts (Cancun); Beach resorts (Acapulco); Large cities (Tijuana); Medium sized towns (Merida); World Heritage Cities (Oaxaca); Magical towns (a national branding of culturally rich places, e.g. Cuetzalan); and Nature areas (Jalcomulco). The programme is also under way in 12 additional localities.

A Local Agenda 21 Committee for each location is responsible for coordinating and monitoring the programme. The tourism unit within the state government provides leadership at the state level and links with other state authorities and with the federal Tourism Secretariat. The latter is also part of the Committee, as technical advisor, and provides links with other federal bodies.

Each Committee has been developing proposals for action to achieve greater sustainability, in conjunction with the local, state and federal stakeholders and taking account of the diverse and unique circumstances of each place.

A Sustainable Tourism Indicator system has been established, and has been used to make a preliminary diagnosis of the sustainability conditions and possible improvement measures in each of the destinations. This has proved to be very important in identifying and presenting the issues for each committee and in assisting decision making. These initial diagnoses are verified by local stakeholders.

The indicators cover:

- Environmental impact: availability of fresh water; water consumption level; treatment of water/sewage; energy consumption; air quality; generation of waste; handling and recycling of waste; environmental education.
- Socio-economic impact: unemployment level; contribution to local economy; contribution to local income tax; wellbeing and engagement of the local population; demographic pressure; security; access.
- Tourism supply and demand: visitor satisfaction; visitor spending; occupancy and seasonality; offer quality and price; certification; attractiveness of destination; bathing water quality.
- Urban development: planning and environmental legislation programmes; control of urban growth; provision of infrastructure; state of housing; preservation of image (architectural and landscape).

An Environmental Quality certification programme for tourism enterprises has been established and certificates have been awarded, principally to hotels but also to other enterprises such as marinas and attractions.

In the area of technical exchange, workshops on the application of Local Agenda 21 in tourist destinations have been held, in conjunction with the WTO, and on international beach certification, jointly with the World Bank. In addition, regular presentations have been given within commercial, academic and municipal forums, and to the stakeholders in Mexico's principal tourism destinations.

Future challenges include: strengthening the operation of Local Agenda 21 committees; simplifying and rolling out the sustainable tourism indicator system; expanding the number of companies in the environmental certification programme; and strengthening the involvement of federal organizations in the overall initiative.

Kaikoura (New Zealand):

Sustainability of a small community

A small rural town in a fine natural setting, receiving large volumes of nature-based tourists that has taken a number of steps to reduce the impact of tourism on the environment and on the whole community, so genuinely qualifying for recognition as a sustainable tourism destination and achieving certification to back this up

Kaikoura lies on the east coast of New Zealand's South Island. The municipality covers 2 084 square kilometres. With only 12 employees, Kaikoura District Council is the smallest local authority in mainland New Zealand.

Kaikoura is stunningly situated on a peninsular of land between high mountain ranges and the Pacific Ocean. An unusual feature is a deep see trench that comes to within 500 metres of the shore and attracts a richness of marine life, including whales and dolphins, which are easily seen by visitors.

In the 1980s, the town was in economic decline, with downsizing of the public and agricultural sectors bringing a serious loss of jobs. However, since that time tourism has expanded dramatically, spurred by the launch of whale watching activities. Tourism development was largely unplanned and unmanaged during the 1990s, led by the market and with little knowledge of the impact on the environment and local community. By 1998 it was estimated that the town was receiving 873 000 visitors (against a local population of just 3 483), with an annual growth rate of about 14 per cent.

Motivations behind a sustainable tourism approach

There were various reasons why the community of Kaikoura decided that it had to devote more attention to creating the right environment for tourism to be sustainable.

The Kaikoura Peninsula
Photo: Peter Morath

These included:

- The threat of a diminishing visitor experience and income. Visitor surveys showed that the quality of the environment, including the natural setting as well as the marine life, was of fundamental importance to tourists. Moreover, visitors had an image of Kaikoura as an environmentally sound destination, but in fact this was not matched by reality. There was therefore considerable concern that failing to meet visitor expectations could ultimately lead to an economic downturn similar to that previously seen in other sectors.
- Local concern for the environment. Surveys found that the quality of the environment was considered to be equally important by the town's permanent residents as by tourists.
- A local incident underlining tourism's environmental sensitivity. In 2001 a road accident caused a lorry to spill a load of poisonous chemicals into the sea. Although the environmental damage turned out to be slight, Kaikoura received urgent requests for reassurance from visitor markets around the world—the potential for loss of trade was recognized.
- Reaching capacity in accommodating waste. The town's landfill site was forecast to be full by 2004, partly due to the rapid expansion in waste as a result of tourism growth. Constructing a new site would place a considerable financial burden on local ratepayers. Rather than do this, the community decided to pursue active waste minimization (see below). Working together on this provided a catalyst for collaboration on wider environmental management.

Agreeing on a strategy

In order to guide the direction of tourism in Kaikoura, the District Council worked together with representatives of the local community and Lincoln University to produce the Kaikoura Tourism Strategy. This is being implemented through a Tourism and Development Committee, which includes councillors, tourism operators, community and Maori (indigenous) members, fishing industry representatives and the wider business community. Community involvement and buy-in to the strategy was considered to be crucially important.

The tourism strategy focused on the need to address the seasonality of the tourism offer, the length of stay and the economic return to the community, by attracting a more diverse market base and developing more local facilities and land based ecotourism activities. Since the tourism strategy was produced, it has been aligned with a more recent policy statement on environmental and social sustainability which sets out specific commitments by the District Council on environmental management and community support and engagement, and has tourism at its core.

Specific management initiatives

Over the last five years, the District Council, local businesses and the local community have been working together on a number of environmental management initiatives, which are also seen as bringing social and economic benefit. Rather than focusing specifically on tourism, these initiatives are aimed at improving the overall environmental management of Kaikoura, but tourism stakeholders are seen as primary participants and beneficiaries of this.

Waste management

Waste management in Kaikoura demonstrates a sound partnership approach
between community activists, who pioneered some early initiatives, and the
District Council. Action is now carried out by Innovative Waste Kaikoura (IWK),
a non-profit joint venture company between the District Council (49 per cent
shareholding) and a community trust (51 per cent shareholding). This partnership
structure ensures community ownership and the ability to raise funds from
charitable sources, together with the political commitment and financial security
brought by local authority involvement.

Rubbish collection was stopped and replaced by a
recycling service, which quickly led to a 30 per cent
diversion of waste from landfill. This subsequently
rose to over 65 per cent, assisted by a range of
measures including:

- investment in a refuse press and composting
  unit;
- expanding recycling pick-up from businesses;
- introducing a Waste Management Protocol for
  businesses, which outlines ways in which they
  can reduce waste and save money, and is used as
  a requirement when granting consent for new
  development;
- opening a second hand shop and developing marketable products
  from the waste stream.

The community is moving towards a zero waste target in 2015.

An example of promotional innovation in the waste recycling
campaign, linked to sustainable tourism objectives, is the Trash to
Fashion Show (clothing made out of recycled materials), which helps
to attract visitor interest in the low season.

Tree planting—CO_2 offsetting

A study that calculated the amount of greenhouse gas emissions
generated by the community estimated that 2 million trees would
need to be planted to offset the resulting CO_2. This has been
adopted as a target in the Trees for Travellers project, which grows
native species of trees on the compost output from the waste
recycling programme. These trees are sold to tourists, who can track
their progress through the internet. The project also has a social aim,
employing young people who have been in trouble with the police in
tree propagation and planting work.

Waste management - recovery
shed (above) and the refuse press
(below)

Energy efficiency initiatives

A small business energy project was started with the support of the District Council.
This was an advice and capacity building project, focusing on 10 local businesses
over the course of a year, examining energy use and developing and implementing

proposals for its reduction. The Council showed leadership by reducing its own energy consumption as part of the 'energy wise councils programme'.

Biodiversity, land and coastal management
Various projects have been initiated to strengthen biodiversity, including introducing traditional Maori practices of management of marine life and preventing overfishing, and working with private landowners on the management of waterways, wetlands and other habitats. Areas of international, national and local importance to biodiversity have been identified and landowners are encouraged and assisted in their protection through rate relief, private covenants and the establishment of reserves. Conservation working holidays have been introduced, organized by the District Council and IWK in conjunction with the British Trust for Conservation Volunteers, which have assisted the Trees for Travellers project and in the construction of trails used by visitors.

Destination certification

In 2001, the opportunity arose for Kaikoura to be adopted as one of the first pilot communities to work towards certification as a sustainable destination under the international Green Globe 21 scheme. It was felt that this would help to consolidate the various separate initiatives already undertaken and underpin long term commitment.

After signing up to the process, the next stage was comprehensive measurement and benchmarking, covering 10 compulsory topics: presence of a sustainability policy; extent of environmental accreditation of individual tourism enterprises; energy use; greenhouse gas emissions; potable water consumption; resource conservation; waste production; air quality; water quality; and biodiversity. Community wellbeing was

Dusky Dolphins - whale and dolphin watching are the primary attraction
Photo: Dennis Buurman

also included as an optional social topic, measured through a survey of local residents. A final local topic that was added, as it reflects a particular local threat, is the number of road accidents resulting in chemical spills.

To achieve certification, Kaikoura also had to demonstrate that it was meeting a number of standards with respect to the management process, including: the commitment of the lead authority; meeting all legal and regulatory requirements; environmental and social planning; and stakeholder consultation and communication. The community also had to submit to annual external inspection and verification.

Kaikoura was finally certified as a Green Globe destination in 2004. Its experience highlights the hard work and difficulties faced in trying to obtain adequate data to achieve reliable measures of impact at a community level, taking into account both resident and tourist impacts. However, the process has proved valuable in raising the level of awareness and commitment to sustainability management across the whole community. It provides an ongoing framework for monitoring and managing impact. It has also raised the profile of Kaikoura externally in the tourism marketplace, as a destination that can now claim, with justification, not only to offer a supreme nature-based experience for visitors, but also to be taking care of the environment.

Relationship to national policy and action

Kaikoura demonstrates a bottom-up approach towards making tourism more sustainable, at the level of a small local community. It has relied on drive and commitment both within the community and by the local authority, working in partnership.

At a national level, the New Zealand government has recognized the importance of such local initiatives. It has often used Kaikoura as an example of good practice. The approach fits well with the New Zealand Tourism Strategy 2010, which has as one of four key objectives 'Securing and conserving a long term future'. The vision speaks of seeking to conserve and sustain New Zealand's environment and culture in the spirit of 'kaikiakitanga' (Maori word for guardianship). The country's marketing slogan '100% Pure' makes an assertion that needs to be matched by sound environmental management.

The government is now providing tangible support for the approach of working on sustainability with groups of individual tourism businesses and communities at a local level. The ministries of tourism and of the environment have jointly introduced a new fund for six regions, which will implement a sustainable tourism project over a three year period. The regions will be asked to develop a sustainable tourism charter, with local businesses committing to the charter's principles. A sustainable tourism expert will be funded to work within each project to turn the charter into action.

South Africa:

Tourism White Paper and subsequent initiatives

A country that has taken proactive measures to transform tourism, stemming from a forward looking policy document which has led to a variety of initiatives and instruments to influence and support enterprises and communities in pursuing sustainable tourism

In the past ten years South Africa has been one of the fastest growing tourism destinations. In 2004 it received 6.5 million international arrivals.

Since 1994 and the advent of democracy, many areas of policy in South Africa have embraced the concept of sustainable development. Moreover, a fundamental driver of policy has been the process of empowerment and transformation within South African society, which is enshrined in the constitution, and stems from the African National Congress' Reconstruction and Development Programme (RDP).

Tourism has been seen as playing a key role in implementing the RDP, and has become one of the three main sectors promoted by the government for sustainable growth.

In the mid 1990s, the government recognized many weaknesses in South African tourism, largely to do with it being an enclave activity for the privileged. It recognized that a new, integrated approach was needed that stimulated entrepreneurship, opened up opportunities for local communities to engage in tourism and addressed a number of key failings such as poor environmental management.

The Tourism White Paper

Tourism policy for South Africa is based on the White Paper on the Development and Promotion of Tourism, 1996. This document spelt out the above weaknesses and sought to tackle them head on. Principles of sustainable tourism (referred to as 'responsible tourism') are more central to this policy document, and more clearly articulated in it, than in equivalent national tourism policies and strategies in other countries.

The emphasis on sustainability was influenced by the widespread consultation that occurred over the earlier Green Paper, including 10 country-wide workshops and many written submissions. The consultation revealed considerable concerns amongst local communities about their involvement in tourism, which policies have subsequently sought to address.

The responsible tourism principles covered economic, social and environmental elements. The White Paper spelt out 15 ways in which the government would facilitate the implementation of responsible tourism, including: defining it; supporting certification; providing incentives and marketing benefits for responsible enterprises; encouraging creative programmes and linkages; and actively assisting local communities in tourism development. The policy statements in the White Paper reflected this approach.

Disseminating policy through guidelines

The White Paper has had a strong influence on subsequent policy and activity in the tourism sector.

Following on from the White Paper, a set of *Guidelines for Responsible Tourism* was published and distributed in booklet form. The process of developing the guidelines generated a great deal of enthusiasm. The guidelines offer an enabling framework for the public and private, the idea being that trade associations, geographically based groups, etc. should use them to develop their own codes of conduct. Some have done so.

Provinces were all involved in the process of developing the guidelines and have given support to their promotion and implementation. They have, accordingly, created tourism functions and developed provincial policies and planning frameworks sensitive to responsible tourism and in line with the White Paper.

In order to make the guidelines more practically meaningful to individual enterprises, a Responsible Tourism Handbook was published which set out the steps enterprises could take, gave short examples of what others had done, and referred to assistance available.

Encouraging voluntary compliance

The approach in South Africa has been to start by encouraging voluntary commitment to sustainability. Should this not be successful, legal instruments might be considered to underpin the responsible tourism approach.

In order to demonstrate their compliance with responsible tourism, enterprises can apply for relevant certification. The Fair Trade in Tourism trademark scheme focuses on social issues and labour relations. The Hospitality Association also issues awards for responsible tourism, including social and environmental criteria. These are both independent certification schemes, but which receive some indirect support from government.

Drakensberg Park, KwaZulu Natal Province
Photo: Sylvie Blangy

South Africa

Tourism and local communities
benefit from bridge construction
Photo: Great St Lucia Wetlands Park

Setting targets for black empowerment

A key issue in the transformation of South Africa's economy and society, and for its sustainability, is for historically disadvantaged people to have more opportunities to control and benefit from different sectors of the economy. This requires a degree of government intervention to create the conditions to bring it about. Transformation in the tourism sector has been slow—by 2003, it was estimated that only 6 per cent of tourism entities had black ownership and that of people in positions of management and control, only 15 per cent were black males and 2 per cent black women.

The Broad Based Black Economic Empowerment (BEE) Act, 2003, encourages the various economic sectors to develop their own targets and timeframes for BEE. A Tourism BEE Scorecard has been drawn up, based on widespread consultation within the tourism industry. This sets 10 year targets and weightings for the following: Ownership (economic interest and voting rights); Management control; Employment equity (proportions of black people at all skills levels); Skills development; Preferential procurement from BEE compliant suppliers; and Support for community and conservation projects.

Skills and capacity building

Considerable emphasis is placed in South Africa on skills development. A national qualifications framework was initiated under the South African Qualifications Act. Various sectoral education authorities were established, such as the Tourism, Hospitality and Sport Education and Training Authority, with responsibility to promote education and skills development and the establishment of national qualifications for all sub-sectors of the tourism industry. It is felt that the availability of national qualifications will trigger increased investment in training by employers because they have clearly articulated standards of competence against which to measure the impact of training.

Particular features of the approach that are most relevant to the needs of unemployed and historically disadvantaged people, who have practical aptitude but limited formal education, are:

- combining apprenticeships with structured learning (tourism 'learnerships'); and
- national qualifications based on practical assessment on the job rather than through a written or oral examination which can discriminate against people with limited literary or language skills.

Granting concessions and conferring rights

One of the most potent instruments used in South Africa is the process of laying down conditions on developers or operators of tourism facilities, either when granting planning permissions or licences, or when granting concessions to use areas of land over which the government has control. The latter is a tool that government uses to mobilize alternative capacity to develop and manage the country's natural resources for socio-economic development purposes. Conditions imposed often require developers to demonstrate proposals for community involvement and benefit.

An example is the awarding of concessions by South African National Parks to safari operators, caterers and shop managers associated with Kruger National Park. Concessionaires undertook to make sure that 79 per cent of their employees would be recruited from historically disadvantaged communities near the park. They successfully achieved this objective. At the same time, there has been an improvement in the quality of services provided to visitors and more funds have been secured for conservation.

The government recognizes the importance of providing communities with an enabling environment in which they can obtain greater control over private sector operators, and gain more benefit from them. In many situations, communal land rights require clarification. This is important in enabling communities to negotiate concessions with developers.

Trainee chefs participating in a tourism skills development programme
Photo: Great St Lucia Wetlands Park

An initiative of the Treasury has been the introduction of a Tourism Public Private Partnership Toolkit, recognizing that such partnerships offer significant opportunities for job creation, poverty alleviation, infrastructure investment, skills development, environmental protection, black economic empowerment and tourism promotion in especially marginalized parts of the country. The toolkit aims to provide step-by-step guidance to all parties for planning and procuring a range of businesses based on public-private partnership. This initiative's envisaged outcome is to bring certainty and consistency to tourism related commercial investments on state land.

Spatial planning and financial incentives

Over the past 10 years the government has followed a strategic approach to spatial planning for tourism, through the identification of priority locations and corridors to attract tourism investment. Some of these are areas where there is a particular desire to establish more benefits for local communities and to reverse the economic damage of former times. Some of the different types of area designated for development or management purposes have included:

- Spatial Development Initiatives. Broad areas or development corridors, attracting investment incentives and a holistic approach to development, including tourism.
- Priority Areas for Tourism Infrastructure Investment. Small areas seen as offering a new opportunity for spreading the economic benefit of tourism, and providing a focus for tourism investment.
- Tourism nodes. Areas within which tourism enterprises network together, with joint promotions and initiatives coordinated by local Destination Management Organizations.
- Trans-Frontier Parks or Conservation Areas. Large areas of important ecosystems, requiring integrated management, where nature based tourism is seen as one key to conservation by providing sustainable livelihoods for often marginalized communities.

These designations have helped to mobilize economic activity in the area in question.

A range of financial incentives and business advisory services has also been introduced to assist MSMEs, some of which require, or give priority to, enterprises which demonstrate a responsible tourism approach. Some of the incentives have been focused on the development areas mentioned above, others have been more widely available. The Development Bank of Southern Africa has developed its own guidelines, based on the government's Guidelines for Responsible Tourism referred to above, to assist in the evaluation of responsible tourism project proposals.

Transformation and competitiveness

In conclusion, South Africa provides a good example of a consistent approach to sustainable tourism through policies and instruments cascading down from a bold original policy document on tourism that put sustainability to the fore.

The case of South Africa demonstrates the advantage of having a clear government commitment to transforming tourism, with a clear policy focus—widening the base of tourism, making it more equitable and opening opportunities for previously disadvantaged people. The value of such an approach to the performance and standing of tourism as a whole can also be seen. A Global Competitiveness Study, conducted by the government, indicated the potential benefits to the tourism sector arising from transformation, such as introducing innovation, providing a broader range of products, offering an authentic South African experience, stimulating growth and spreading economic benefit across the nation.

Calvià (Spain):

Local Agenda 21 and resort rejuvenation

A major coastal resort area, suffering from degradation of the environment and the visitor experience, that brought the community and tourism stakeholders together to prepare and implement a long-term improvement plan based on sustainability principles

Calvià is an example of a high-volume tourism destination which, in the late 1980s, faced significant economic, social and environmental decline as a result of tourism pressure. However, after adopting an integrated and collaborative approach to the implementation of sustainable tourism policies, using the participatory process of Local Agenda 21(LA21), the municipality has received many international awards in the fields of environmental management and sustainable development.

Background and motivations for adopting a sustainable tourism approach

Calvià, lies on the south coast of the Balearic island of Mallorca, Spain. It is less than a 2-hour flight from most major European cities and is one of the most popular Mediterranean summer resorts. It embraces six tourist zones with 60 kilometres of coastline, 27 beaches and 120 000 tourist units. Each year 1.6 million tourists visit Calvià, mainly between May and September. In 2002, 95 per cent of jobs related to tourism and Calvià's GDP was higher than the European average.

From the 1960s until the late 1980s, Calvià grew rapidly as a tourist destination (from 3 000 inhabitants in 1972 to 50 000 by 2003). This growth was, however, fuelled by short-term economic gain—a model based on high volumes, price competition and a standardized holiday experience focusing on sun, sea and sand. The impacts of this rapid growth adversely affected the attractiveness of Calvià as a tourist destination and as human pressure increased a hundredfold and overloaded the capacity of the coastline, tourism fell by almost 20 per cent between 1988 and 1991. The degradation of the island environment, deterioration of social systems and facilities and the threat of further tourism decline prompted the Municipality of Calvià to look towards a more sustainable approach.

The Local Agenda 21 process

In the early 1990s, the Municipality of Calvià undertook an in-depth and technical diagnosis of the area looking at all three pillars of sustainability (social, environmental and economic).

In May 1995, the diagnosis was made public through an initial document, which contained a vision of a more sustainable tourism model and alternative growth scenarios—maintaining the current level of expansion or adopting an alternative approach based on restoration, contained growth and sustainability.

Interviewing citizens about sustainability at a mobile survey point

Participants in a local forum of industry, government and community representatives reached a unanimous decision that a local action plan was needed to make the area more sustainable. This was to be an integrated action plan for all aspects of the future of Calvià, but with tourism playing a central part in it owing to its dominance in the local economy.

From 1995 to 1997, a great deal of work was undertaken in developing the plan, in collaboration with the university, technical experts and the private sector. This centred around six key thematic areas (population and quality of life; ecology; cultural heritage; economy; town planning; and key environmental sectors) which were the subject of separate study, thematic commissions and reports. Twenty seven fields of reference and more than 750 indicators were identified. The results were then shared with the public in a Citizens' Forum, before being formally accepted and developed into the Calvia Local Agenda 21 Action Plan, which was approved in 1997.

The Action Plan identified 40 initiatives under 10 strategic lines of action, as follows:

1. To contain human pressure, limit growth and foster complete restoration of the territory and its coastal area.
2. To foster the resident population's integration, coexistence and quality of life.
3. To protect the natural and marine heritage and promote the establishment of a regional tourist tax to be used for the environment.
4. To restore the historical, cultural and natural heritage.
5. To promote the complete rehabilitation of residential and tourist areas.
6. To improve Calvià as a tourist destination, replacing growth with sustainable quality, increasing expenditure per visitor and seeking a more balanced tourist season.
7. To improve public transport and encourage people to walk or cycle in town centres or from one centre to another.
8. To introduce sustainable management into the key environmental sectors: water, energy and waste.
9. To invest in human and knowledge resources, to diversify the financial system.
10. To innovate municipal management and increase the capacity of public/private planned investment.

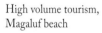

High volume tourism,
Magaluf beach

Key aspects of government involvement

Some important aspects of the approach of the Municipality of Calvià in gaining initial support and involvement in the Action Plan, include:

Increasing understanding of the importance of tourism and its sustainability. This involved lobbying for tourism to be recognized as a core and overarching strategic industry, and educating politicians and technicians about sustainability.

Seeking engagement and endorsement from local people Effective dissemination and communication of the proposed initiatives to local people was deemed imperative. In 1998, signatures were collected from over 25 per cent of the population in support of the Action Plan.

Clearly defining priorities, based on a consensus view The Municipality has worked closely with hoteliers, tour operators and other private sector players such as marinas, trade unions and professional training colleges to achieve consensus on priority actions. Part of the consultation involved voting on the different priorities for action, to help to determine initiatives for immediate action and those for the longer term. Consequently, priorities were clearly defined and public and private budgets allocated for each initiative.

Maintaining a system of monitoring and evaluation Substantial preliminary diagnosis and research (along with the definition of a diverse number of indicators) has enabled Calvià to benchmark, evaluate and monitor progress. This has been fundamental, enabling an adaptive management approach allowing for changing priorities and situations.

Some of the actions implemented since 1997 are considered below.

Planning and regeneration

The Town Planning system has been a major tool supporting the implementation of the new direction and approach. This has been utilized to de-classify land previously allocated for urban development. 1 700 hectares of building land were declassified. Over 30 building clearance action plans were carried out between 1993 and 2002, including actual building demolition and the purchase of urban plots to prevent further construction. By 2004, the entire surface area of demolished buildings was more than 13 500 square metres and urban land saved from construction was over 50 000 square metres. Demolition has included poorly located and unsightly hotel buildings. There was no increase in the number of hotels during this period.

There has also been considerable work on the improvement of amenities. The Magaluf and Palma Nova tourist areas have been upgraded by creating boulevards and pedestrianized zones and planting trees which has improved the overall quality of the area.

Despite these changes, the experience of Calvià suggests that zoning and planning for destinations need to be legislated early on in the development process. Previous lack of planning in Calvià led to over development and critical environmental impacts, which have been too large to fully reverse despite the initiatives undertaken in the Action Plan.

There have been improvements in transport infrastructure. The Paseo de Calvià, a 40 kilometre cycling and walking path, was built linking urban centres, and is now widely used by tourists and residents. However, public transport is still poor, due to factors such as insufficient integration with other territorial plans, lack of consistent political will, limited support from the taxi industry and lack of usage by the local community who favour private cars.

Environmental management

Significant steps forward on protection and restoration of the local environment have included the establishment of a marine park and terrestrial protected areas to protect wildlife and ecosystems. Sea dredging previously used to regenerate beaches has been terminated, and more environmentally friendly measures put in place to minimize erosion. There are new regulations for mooring and anchoring in place and proposals have been made for floating moorings, removable in winter, to limit anchor damage and harbour congestion caused by boats.

Recycling and urban waste reduction plans have been implemented, to ensure that 30 per cent of all urban waste is separated at origin, facilitating and reducing cost of recycling efforts and minimizing landfill.

Efforts have been made to reduce water consumption, including an awareness campaign and tax incentives. However, it has proved difficult to win support for water conservation, with local people not keen to adjust taxes and charges nor to reduce consumption. Demand exceeds supply and water is still being imported from outside of the municipality. Today most of the potable water comes from a desalination plant located in the municipality of Palma.

Actions have been taken to save energy, but targets have not been met. One factor is the expense of renewable energy equipment.

Human resources and socio-cultural integration

A strength of the approach in Calvia has been the integration of actions relating to tourism and to the quality of life of local people. It has been accepted that a successful, sustainable resort needs to address local social concerns. Programmes have been put in place to combat crime and address housing issues. Innovative work has been undertaken to integrate both tourists and immigrants (often working in the tourism industry) into the Mallorquin way of life, including multi-cultural social programmes such as dance, Spanish language classes and other cultural events.

Despite a number of initiatives in the Action Plan, it has proved difficult to make a significant difference to the knowledge base in tourism, through training and education standards. High-volume tourism continues to be regarded as relying on low-skilled, untrained labour and improvement in educational levels has not been seen as a priority by tourism enterprises or local inhabitants.

The need for a consistent, long term approach

Overall, the formulation and adoption of the LA21 process and Action Plan has been successful. Calvià has demonstrated what can be achieved by a careful process of working together at a local level to develop and disseminate a common vision and move towards achieving it. The use of continual monitoring and an adaptive management approach has been an important feature. However, in addition to the points made above, a number of general lessons also emerge from the experience:

Paseo de Calvià, pathway linking urban and rural settlements, lit by solar energy

- Stakeholders should be accountable for implementation on an on-going basis, not simply for engaging in the policy formulation process. This should also apply to the wider population. It has been difficult to maintain widespread commitment and response to some of the necessary measures, such as reducing water consumption.

- Social and environmental concerns must, consistently, be given strong weight alongside economic drivers in all aspects of development. For example, a new highway was constructed in Calvià but public transportation, such as a train from the airport to the major tourist resorts was not put in place, with consequent implications for pollution and congestion.

- There needs to be a source of long-term funding to support sustainability effort. In Calvià, many initiatives have been put on hold or are no longer funded, partially due to the abolishment of the Balearic eco-tax. This will prevent some sustainability targets being achieved.

- Integration and cooperation with all government sectors is key to realizing wider policy objectives (e.g. transportation plans, marine protection and protected parks) which need to be supported at both regional and national levels.

- Sustainability requires long-term political commitment. It is fundamental that a vision for sustainability is developed and subscribed to by as many political parties as possible, to ensure that initiatives continue and are realized over time. Although the municipal government of Calvià changed in May 2003, work on Local Agenda 21 continues towards sustainable tourism. Through working groups open to local stakeholders, NGOs and local citizens, Calvià is now developing a new Plan of Action that will take into account recent methodologies and requirements. It is expected that this new Plan of Action will be completed in summer 2005.

Scotland (UK)

Scotland (UK):

Tourism and Environment Forum and Green Tourism Business Scheme

A longstanding communication structure to pursue the sustainability of Scotland's tourism, together with an effective certification programme

Scotland has a high quality natural environment, which surveys have repeatedly indicated is the main reason why visitors choose the country as a holiday destination. Over 215 000 jobs in Scotland are supported by tourism.

The Scottish Tourism and Environment Forum

Scotland's Tourism and Environment Forum is an innovative and active structure for promoting the sustainability of tourism amongst a wide variety of organizations. When the Forum was formed, in 1994, it was unique in bringing together and being jointly funded by the state agencies responsible for:

The Forum's colourful newsletter promotes examples of good practice

- Tourism development and marketing (VisitScotland);
- Natural heritage conservation and management (Scottish Natural Heritage); and
- Economic development (Scottish Enterprise and Highlands & Islands Enterprise).

Its mission is to: *'Bring long-term business and environmental benefits to the Scottish tourism industry through encouraging sustainable use of our world-class natural and built heritage.'*

The Forum's membership includes 17 other organizations in addition to the agencies mentioned above, representing the government executive, local authorities, the tourism industry, landownership and land management, conservation and education.

This structure enables the Forum to be independent while having a strong voice at the heart of government.

The Forum itself has no legislative base or statutory powers. It works by influencing its members (and others) that have such powers. For example, particular topics may be debated within the forum which then lead to advisory policy statements or to general conclusions which the individual members can build upon within their respective bodies. A key to success has been to have the right people round the table and a healthy balance of interests. In this way, the Forum functions as a kind of internal pressure group for more sustainable tourism.

Agreeing key aims for sustainable tourism

In 2004, the Forum established a new focus for its work in influencing tourism policies and actions in Scotland when it published a statement entitled '*Scotland... Towards Sustainable Tourism*'. This was partly spurred by moves by the UK and Scottish governments towards more sustainable development and by a new European Union requirement that certain development plans be subjected to Strategic Environmental Assessment.

A review of existing policy documents relating to tourism and sustainable development, together with the WTO's definition of sustainable tourism, was used to prepare an initial list of aims. These were debated during a full day event involving a wide range of stakeholders who were divided into workgroups and asked to score each aim in terms of relevance and achievability. Agreement was reached around the following seven aims:

The Trossachs - location for a Tourism Management Programme, now designated as a National Park
Photo: David Warnock

- A more even spread of visitors throughout the year.
- More tourism businesses actively enhancing and protecting the environment, for example by joining the Green Tourism Business Scheme (see below).
- Greater investment in tourism people and skills.
- A better integrated quality tourism product that meets visitors' demands and expectations and encourages them to stay longer and spend more.
- A clearer understanding of tourism's impacts.
- Greater involvement of communities in tourism planning, development and marketing.
- Greater use by visitors of Scotland's public transport system.

These aims were circulated widely throughout Scotland and each policy organization was asked to develop them into specific, measurable objectives and to incorporate them into its business plans. Forum staff facilitate these processes by working with the respective organizations. A particular opportunity to exert influence lies with the forthcoming review of Scotland's national tourism strategy: Tourism Framework for Action.

Practical management and marketing initiatives

As well as influencing policy, the Forum has promoted more sustainable tourism through a whole range of initiatives and the dissemination of good practice. Examples include:

- Tourism Management Programmes. Twelve partnerships were established at local destination level, in towns or rural areas, bringing together local authorities, tourism businesses and conservation and community interests. These established and implemented visitor management actions including promoting alternative transport, environmental improvements, traffic management schemes and information and interpretation initiatives. These were short term programmes (five years) but were successful in demonstrating new approaches and relationships that have now largely been absorbed by individual partners and authorities.

- Wild Scotland. The Forum helped to establish an association of nature and wildlife tourism operators, launched in 2003, with their own charter and establishing best practice guidelines based on sustainability principles.
- Website and newsletter. The Forum's website (www.greentourism.org.uk) and newsletter (Positive Impact) contain a great deal of information and many good practice examples aimed at private sector operators, local authorities, national level departments and agencies, and the media.

The Green Tourism Business Scheme

The Green Tourism Business Scheme (GTBS) is a key instrument in achieving greater sustainability in Scotland's tourism. This is a voluntary environmental certification scheme for tourism enterprises established by VisitScotland in 1998; it is closely linked to the Forum. By 2004, there were 550 establishments in the scheme, including accommodation and visitor attractions. Membership has been growing at around 30 per cent per year.

The scheme is based on a menu of 150 actions that businesses can take in the fields of: energy, waste, water, wildlife, transport, supporting the local economy, management and marketing, and involving and informing customers. Some of the actions are mandatory but most are voluntary. Enterprises obtain a bronze, silver or gold award according to the number of actions taken. All enterprises are required to measure and benchmark their energy and water consumption and waste production. Inspection takes place every two years.

Some important pointers emerging from the scheme include:

- The critical link to quality inspection. All enterprises in the GTBS have to be quality inspected and graded by VisitScotland. Certain basic requirements such as compliance with health, safety and other regulations are therefore already covered. Furthermore, the GTBS is actively promoted as an add-on 'sustainability' option to quality grading, rather than as an entirely separate scheme. The official recognition and credibility that this gives to the scheme is vital to its success.
- Advice to participants. Real change in enterprise performance has been achieved as much through the associated advice and information provided to participants

Gleneagles Hotel (left) and a self-catering croft on the Isle of Skye, contrasting participants in the GTBS
Photos: Jon Proctor

as through the incentive of the label. Personal help is given at the time of initial inspection; a series of data and advisory sheets are provided in a 'green folder'; regular newsletters are sent giving updates on new ideas, regulations, etc.; contacts for more detailed information and assistance are listed; and structured training sessions are offered. Auditors act as green signposts for further advice, financial assistance and as a support team.

- Relating business to government. The scheme provides an excellent communication channel. Each year the criteria are discussed with government agencies (especially Forum members) enabling new concerns to be reflected and feedback from enterprises to be passed on. For example, the Environment Protection Agency's concern about chemical toilet disposal has been translated into a requirement for holiday parks and camp sites.

- Links to financial instruments. Enterprises in the scheme are given up-to-date information about relevant financial assistance such as interest free loans to small businesses for insulation, installation of efficient energy sources, etc. Some government financial assistance schemes to support tourism development or improvement now require enterprises to sign up to the GTBS.

- Involvement of government services. A number of local authorities are having their own services certificated through the scheme. Certification of Tourist Information Centres has been found to be particularly valuable, as their staff have regular contact with small businesses and are able to pass on interest in sustainability through their own experience and example.

- Marketing support. Enterprises in the scheme are clearly identified in VisitScotland's official publications and websites, which display the green label alongside quality rating. In addition, a separate green guide and webpages are dedicated to certificated enterprises only.

- The commercial advantage. Surveys of participants have found that around 30 per cent can point to specific cost savings as a result of their involvement in the scheme and that average bedroom occupancy levels of hotels in the scheme are around 10 per cent higher than for Scotland as a whole. It is these commercial advantages that provide the most persuasive arguments in winning new members.

- The need to keep things simple. Experience has shown that small tourism businesses respond much more positively to simple criteria, clearly expressed.

The GTBS is run by a private sector company on behalf of VisitScotland. Although the scheme is now financially viable in an operational sense, support from VisitScotland and the Forum in promoting the scheme to enterprises and consumers, and maintaining its profile within Scotland, is essential for its survival.

The Forum has found that having a tool like the GTBS is extremely important in influencing government policy. It has demonstrated to politicians that the tourism industry will respond to voluntary initiatives and provides a vehicle for future communication and setting of targets.

Annex 1:
Baseline issues and indicators of sustainable tourism

Baseline issues and indicators of sustainable tourism

The following table is a collection of the most common issues occurring in tourism destinations, selected from among the more than 50 sustainability issues discussed in the WTO *Guidebook on Indicators of Sustainable Development for Tourism Destinations.* Baseline indicators considered most relevant and feasible to measure are suggested for each issue.

Other issues and indicators could arguably be included in the short list—such as health, security, environmental protection, and employment with their corresponding indicators. All these and many other issues and their indicators are covered in the WTO Guide that can be used as a reference. Importantly, the Guidebook also contains a procedure for the development of indicators that correspond to specific issues found at any destination. For this reason, tourism managers need to identify the priority issues at their destinations, in consultation with the main stakeholder groups, and develop indicators that are the most relevant for those priority issues, clear to users and feasible to implement in terms of data availability and the cost to obtain them.

Baseline Issue	Suggested Baseline Indicator(s)
Local Satisfaction with Tourism	• Local satisfaction level with tourism (questionnaire)
Effects of Tourism on Communities	• Ratio of tourists to locals (average and peak period/days) • % who believe that tourism has helped bring new services or infrastructure. (questionnaire-based) • Number and capacity of social services available to the community (% attributable to tourism)
Sustaining Tourist Satisfaction	• Level of satisfaction by visitors (questionnaire-based) • Perception of value for money (questionnaire-based) • Percentage of return visitors
Tourism Seasonality	• Tourist arrivals by month or quarter (distribution throughout the year) • Occupancy rates for licensed (official) accommodation by month (peak periods relative to low season) and % of all occupancy in peak quarter or month • % of business establishments open all year • Number and % of tourist industry jobs which are permanent or full-year (compared to temporary jobs)
Economic Benefits of Tourism	• Number of local people (and ratio of men to women) employed in tourism (also ratio of tourism employment to total employment) • Revenues generated by tourism as % of total revenues generated in the community

Baseline Issue	Suggested Baseline Indicator(s)
Energy Management	• Per capita consumption of energy from all sources (overall, and by tourist sector, per person day) • Percentage of businesses participating in energy conservation programmes or applying energy saving policy and techniques • % of energy consumption from renewable resources (at destinations, establishments)
Water Availability and Consumption	• Water use: (total volume consumed and litres per tourist per day) • Water saving (% reduced, recaptured or recycled)
Drinking Water Quality	• Percentage of tourism establishments with water treated to international potable standards. • Frequency of water-borne diseases: number/percentage of visitors reporting water-borne illnesses during their stay
Sewage Treatment (Wastewater Management)	• Percentage of sewage from site receiving treatment (to primary, secondary, tertiary levels) • Percentage of tourism establishments (or accommodation) on treatment system(s)
Solid Waste Management (Garbage)	• Waste volume produced by the destination (tonnes) (by month) • Volume of waste recycled (m^3) / Total volume of waste (m^3) (specify by different types) • Quantity of waste strewn in public areas (garbage counts)
Development Control	• Existence of a land use or development planning process, including tourism • % of area subject to control (density, design, etc.)
Controlling Use Intensity	• Total number of tourist arrivals (mean, monthly, peak periods) • Number of tourists per square metre of the site (e.g. at beaches, attractions), per square kilometre of the destination, mean number/peak period average

Annex 1

Additional Resources

- General information on sustainable development:
  impacts and principles
- Sustainable development of tourism:
  principles, policies and guidelines
- Structures and strategies to work with other stakeholders
- Measurement instruments
- Command and control instruments
- Economic instruments
- Voluntary instruments
- Supporting instruments

General information on sustainable development: impacts and principles

Global Environment Outlook, 2004, UNEP-GRID
http://www.grid.unep.ch/geo/geo3/

GEO-3 examines environmental trends over the past 30 years to provide an integrated explanation of the developments that have occurred. Continuing the global and regional focus of this series of publications, it complements the detailed assessment of the state of the global environment set out in GEO-2000. GEO-3 not only examines the state of the environment over its reporting period, but also the full range of social, economic, political and cultural drivers that have brought about change. Highlighting human vulnerability to environmental deterioration, it assesses effects of the spectrum of policy measures adopted.

Eco-Efficiency, Regulation and Sustainable Business - Towards a Governance Structure for Sustainable Development, 2004, UNEP
http://www.earthprint.com

This book presents important new research on applied eco-efficiency concepts throughout Europe. The aim of eco-efficiency is to achieve market-based measures of environmental protection, in order to enhance the prospects for sustainable development and achieve positive economic and ecological benefits.

Assessing Human Vulnerability to Environmental Change- Concepts, Issues, Methods and Case Studies, 2003, UNEP-DEWA
http://www.unep.org/dewa/publications/2003/vulnerability.asp

The report presents concepts, issues, methods and case studies relating to human vulnerability to environmental change. Assessment of vulnerability can provide an important guide to the planning process and to decisions on resource allocations at various levels and help to raise public awareness of risks.

Evaluation of Environmental Impacts in Life Cycle Assessment, 2003, UNEP
http://www.uneptie.org/pc/sustain/reports/lcini/UNEP_US%20EPA%20LCIA%20m
tg%20report.pdf

In 1998 and 2000, UNEP joined forces with United States Environmental Protection Agency (EPA) and the Centre of Environmental Science (CML) to facilitate an international discussion forum on two specific issues of scientific development in the field of Life Cycle Assessment. The first issue was the level of sophistication in impact assessment, and the second was the type of environmental indicators to use. In this report, evaluation is meant in its broad sense; here evaluation includes not only the formal step weighting, but also the whole topic of assessing environmental stressors in a life cycle perspective.

Report of the World Summit on Sustainable Development (WSSD), Johannesburg, South Africa, 2002, United Nations
http://www.johannesburgsummit.org/html/documents/summit_docs/131302_wssd_
report_reissued.pdf

The World Summit on Sustainable Development (WSSD), held in 2002 in Johannesburg, South Africa, was a useful step for many issues relating to sustainability. In the field of tourism, substantive progress was made in comparison with Rio, where tourism was not dealt with. The Plan of Implementation which emerged from the Johannesburg conference refers to tourism in relation to energy, biodiversity conservation, Small Island Developing States and African issues. A complete article on tourism (43) was also included.

Agenda 21, 1992, United Nations
http://www.un.org/esa/sustdev/documents/agenda21/index.htm

Agenda 21 is a comprehensive plan of action to be used globally, nationally and locally by organizations of the United Nations System, Governments, and Major Groups in every area in which humans impact on the environment. Agenda 21, the Rio Declaration on Environment and Development, and the Statement of principles for the Sustainable Management of Forests were adopted by more than 178 Governments at the United Nations Conference on Environment and Development (UNCED) held in Rio de Janeiro, Brazil, 3–14 June 1992.

Sustainable development of tourism: principles, policies and guidelines

Sustainable Development of Tourism Department's website, WTO
http://www.world-tourism.org/sustainable

The website presents all the activities undertaken by the Department, announces events related to sustainable tourism and contains reports, recommendations and guidelines in this field.

Sustainable Tourism web site, UNEP DTIE
http://www.uneptie.org/tourism

This site provides information on UNEP DTIE's activities in sustainable tourism as well as providing access to UNEP tourism publications.

Tour Operators' Initiative web site, TOI
http://www.toinitiative.org

The TOI's web site provides an overview of the TOI structure and activities and includes all the TOI publications.

Marketing Sustainable Tourism Products, 2005, UNEP DTIE, Regione Toscana
http://www.uneptie.org/pc/tourism/documents/EUROMEETING/marketing_sustainable_tourism.pdf

This report reviews the strengths and weaknesses of the tools and channels available to promote and distribute sustainable tourism products. The distribution and promotion channels include destination management organizations and tourist boards, tour operators, guidebooks, media, certification schemes, travel fairs, internet retailers and consumer organizations.

A Practical Guide to Good Practice: Managing Environmental Impacts In The Marine Recreation Sector, 2004, TOI/ Center for Environmental Leadership in Business (CELB)
http://www.toinitiative.org/supplychain/supply.htm

This guide provides information, in simple and direct language, on environmental impacts, the rationale for good practice and suggestions on how to reduce impacts

Additional
Resources

related to boat operation and maintenance and during marine excursions (snorkelling, diving and scuba; seafood consumption and souvenir purchasing; recreational fishing; and marine wildlife viewing). A self-assessment checklist is inserted to promote the practice of evaluating environmental performance among marine recreation providers. The guide is available in English and Spanish.

Supply Chain Management for Tour Operators - Three Steps Towards Sustainability, 2004, TOI/ Center for Environmental Leadership in Business (CELB)
http://www.toinitiative.org/supplychain/supply.htm
The Tour Operators' Initiative has developed a methodology for tour operators seeking to integrate economic, environmental and social sustainability criteria in their providers' service agreements. The Guide was developed with a participatory approach, involving from the outset tour operator members of the TOI already working on sustainability with their suppliers. The Guide proposes a three step approach for the integration of sustainability criteria in the selection of suppliers, and is supported by examples and tips.

Tourism and Poverty Alleviation: Recommendations for Action, 2004, WTO
http://www.world-tourism.org/cgi-bin/infoshop.storefront/EN/product/1349-1
This book provides evidence of the contribution that tourism can make to achieving one of the most pressing UN Millennium Development Goals: alleviating poverty. Based on an extensive analysis of successful experiences, it gives clear and practical recommendations—to governments, private tourism companies, international and bilateral development agencies and other stakeholders—on the various ways and means they can utilize to make tourism a poverty alleviation tool.

Sustainable Tourism: The Tour Operator's Contribution, 2003, TOI
http://www.toinitiative.org/good_practices/case_studies.htm
Over 30 case studies, grouped in the key business areas of supply chain management; internal management; product management and development; customer relations; and cooperation with destinations provide an overview of the diverse approaches and tools that tour operators can adopt. The supply chain management examples include the use of 'green' checklists to assess hoteliers, the introduction of environmental clauses into contracts, the provision of technical assistance, and the introduction of a suppliers' food hygiene campaign.

Climate Change and Tourism, 2003, WTO
http://www.world-tourism.org/sustainable/climate/final-report.pdf
This publication was prepared as a result of the First International Conference on Climate Change and Tourism, held on 9-11 April 2003, in Djerba, Tunisia. It includes a basic report and summaries of the discussions and sessions on the consequences, opportunities and risks that the tourism sector is facing as a result of changes in world's climate. The publication includes the Djerba Declaration on Tourism and Climate Change and the Agenda of Action.

A Practical Guide to Good Practice: Managing Environmental and Social Issues in the Accommodations Sector, 2003, TOI/ Center for Environmental Leadership in Business (CELB) http://www.toinitiative.org/supplychain/supply.htm

The guide provides information to managers on key environmental and social issues including: energy and water conservation, waste management, chemical use, purchasing, contributing to community development and biodiversity conservation, staff management and developing environmental management systems. For each issue, the guide offers a brief summary, the business benefits of adopting good practices and a sample of actions that managers can adopt to improve the performance of their facilities. References to additional resources are also provided.

Switched On: Renewable Energy Opportunities in the Tourism Industry, 2003, UNEP-DTIE
http://www.uneptie.org/pc/tourism/library/energy.htm

A handbook exploring how clean and renewable forms of energy can sustainably power the tourism industry. It provides the latest information on solar, wind, hydro, geothermal and biomass resources. Written in simple non-technical language with specific tourism case studies, the handbook can help small and medium-sized tourism business assess which technologies and systems are most cost-effective.

Tourism and Biodiversity: Mapping Tourism's Global Footprint, 2003, UNEP-DTIE / Conservation International
http://www.uneptie.org/tourism/library/mapping_tourism.htm

A publication illustrating the overlap between tourism development (present and forecasted) and biodiversity hotspots, highlighting tourism related threats and opportunities for biodiversity conservation and improved human welfare. To explore the relationship between tourism development, biodiversity conservation and poverty reduction at the global level, a series of maps were produced that plot tourism and socio-economic data against priority biodiversity areas.

Tourism and Local Agenda 21 - The Role of Local Authorities in Sustainable Tourism, 2003, UNEP-DTIE and the International Council for Local Environmental Initiatives (ICLEI)
http://www.uneptie.org/pc/tourism/library/local-agenda21.htm

This study looks at how tourism has been taken into account in local Agenda 21's, as drawn up and implemented by local authorities. The Agenda 21 planning framework is useful to local authorities facing the impacts of tourism development, in defining strategic goals for all stakeholders, and using tourism effectively to achieve a community's main goals. It is based on a study of the hands-on experience gained by five European local communities involved to varying degrees in tourist activity, and having adopted a local Agenda 21 approach.

Sustainable Development of Ecotourism - A Compilation of Good Practices in SMEs, 2003, WTO
http://www.world-tourism.org/cgi-bin/infoshop.storefront/EN/product/1312-1

A compilation containing 65 case studies from 47 countries of exemplary practices in small ecotourism businesses. The studies provide rich details on methodologies and business approaches applied successfully by a wide range of ecotourism companies; they provide a valuable well of information that can serve to generate ideas and adapt sustainable ecotourism practices to specific local conditions elsewhere. The experiences presented in this book come directly from the field, from the people who have developed these initiatives and who are daily in charge of these business ventures. They are a good reflection of the complexity of small businesses, the great challenges and opportunities they face, and the endless creativity that this business allows for.

Tourism and Poverty Alleviation, 2002, WTO
http://www.world-tourism.org/isroot/wto/pdf/1267-1.pdf
This report reflects the WTO's concern that the benefits of tourism should be widely spread in society and that the poor should benefit from tourism development. It reviews current experience of tourism and poverty reduction in order to identify what is known about the contribution which the tourism industry can make to the elimination of poverty. It also makes recommendations for action by government, the industry, development agencies and local communities.

WTO Contributions to WSSD, 2002, WTO
http://www.world-tourism.org/sustainable/wssd/WTO-contributions-eng.pdf
In preparation for the World Summit on Sustainable Development, WTO published a complete document containing, amongst others, the Report of the WTO Secretary General, a Policy Report on sustainable development of tourism and a list of the Actions in Assisting Developing Countries to Implement Agenda 21 undertaken by the WTO since 1992.

Industry as a Partner for Sustainable Development: Tourism, 2002, World Travel and Tourism Council (WTTC), International Federation of Tour Operators (IFTO), International Hotel and Restaurant Association (IH&RA), International Council of Cruise Lines (ICCL), facilitated by UNEP DTIE
http://www.uneptie.org/pc/tourism/library/wssd_report.htm
UNEP, in partnership with various industry organizations, launched a reporting initiative to gauge progress by the private sector towards sustainable development. This effort contributed to the wider review of progress with the implementation of Agenda 21, under the framework of the World Summit on Sustainable Development.

Ecotourism: Principles, Practices and Policies for Sustainability, 2002, UNEP-DTIE / TIES
http://www.uneptie.org/pc/tourism/library/ecotourism.htm
A publication reviewing the current status and trends in ecotourism globally, the challenges ahead and the lessons learned in over 15 years of ecotourism development involving a broad range of stakeholders. It incorporates comments and suggestions from recognized academics, NGO, representative and inter-governmental agencies as WTO, IUCN and UNEP.

Industry and Environment, Vol.25 No.2, Responsible Entrepreneurship for Sustainable Development, 2002, UNEP
http://www.uneptie.org/media/review/vol25no2/I&EVOL25.PDF
This issue of Industry & Environment formed part of UNEP's contribution to the World Summit on Sustainable Development in Johannesburg. It examines the role of business and industry in bringing about the changes urgently needed for sustainable development.

International Year of Ecotourism, Report of Activities, 2002, WTO
http://www.world-tourism.org/sustainable/IYE-Main-Menu.htm
At the request of the United Nations General Assembly, the WTO has prepared a report on the activities undertaken by States and major international organizations

in the framework of the International Year of Ecotourism. The report and archives of IYE 2002 (preparatory conferences reports, etc.), can be found at the above website.

The World Ecotourism Summit - Final Report, 2002, UNEP and WTO
http://www.world-tourism.org/sustainable/IYE/quebec/anglais/index_a.html
This report contains the summaries of the debates held and conclusions reached at the World Ecotourism Summit and its preparatory process, as well as the Quebec Declaration on Ecotourism. The World Ecotourism Summit, was held in Quebec City, Canada from 19 to 22 May, 2002. This was the principal event to mark 2002 as the International Year of Ecotourism. The purpose of the Summit was to bring together governments, international agencies, NGOs, tourism enterprises, representatives of local and indigenous communities, academic institutions and individuals with an interest in ecotourism, and enable them to learn from each other and identify some agreed principles and priorities for the future development and management of ecotourism.

Enhancing the Economic Benefits of Tourism for Local Communities and Poverty Alleviation, 2002, WTO
http://www.world-tourism.org/cgi-bin/infoshop.storefront/EN/product/1280-1
This study is based on the document that was presented in a seminar that took place in Petra, Jordan, on 20 June 2002, within the framework of the 68th session of the WTO Executive Council. The document has been complemented by the addition of ten case studies that were presented by the Council members during the seminar. These case studies highlight either the countries' national policies and approaches to community-based tourism or specific projects that are considered success stories.

Sustainable Development of Ecotourism - A Compilation of Good Practices, 2001, WTO
http://www.world-tourism.org/cgi-bin/infoshop.storefront/EN/product/1214-1
Publication prepared on the occasion of the International Year of Ecotourism 2002. It is the second volume within the series of Good Practices published in the area of Sustainable Development of Tourism. The 55 case studies taken from 39 countries present a wide range of successful ecotourism initiatives. Each of them is presented in a systematic form, describing stakeholders involved, objectives and strategies, funding, sustainability and monitoring aspects, problems encountered and solutions found in each project, etc. The sustainability aspects are further detailed according to specific elements of ecotourism such as: conservation, community involvement, interpretation and education, as well as environmental management practices.

Sustainable Development of Tourism - A Compilation of Good Practices, 2000, WTO
http://www.world-tourism.org/cgi-bin/infoshop.storefront/EN/product/1156-1
The progress towards a more sustainable tourism industry is best demonstrated through success stories. This publication contains around 50 examples of good practices in sustainable development and management of tourism, collected from 31 countries. A great variety of projects are presented, ranging from local to regional and national levels, including activities of the public, private and NGO sectors, covering aspects of eco-, rural- and cultural tourism, accommodation, tour operations, transportation, protected area management, regulatory and voluntary frameworks, among others. Each case is described in a systematic order, including detailed background information, success factors for sustainability, problems and their solutions, lessons learnt, and monitoring activities.

Global Code of Ethics for Tourism, 1999, WTO

In October 1999, the General Assembly of the WTO, held in Santiago, Chile, approved the Global Code of Ethics for Tourism which sets a frame of reference for responsible and sustainable development of world tourism. The code includes nine articles outlining the 'rules of the game' for destinations, governments, tour operators, developers, travel agents, workers and travellers themselves. The tenth article involves the redress of grievances and marks the first time that a code of this type has a mechanism for enforcement. The Global Code of Ethics for Tourism is an essential tool to help minimize the negative impacts of tourism on the environment and cultural heritage while maximizing the benefits for residents of tourism destinations. A resolution in support of WTO's Global Code Ethics for Tourism was accordingly considered by the United Nations General Assembly on 19 November 2001.

Sustainable Development of Tourism - An Annotated Bibliography, 1999, WTO
http://www.world-tourism.org/cgi-bin/infoshop.storefront/EN/product/1129-1
To enhance the understanding of sustainable tourism and its practical applications, the WTO has compiled a list of books and articles on the subject. For the second edition nearly 100 books together with more than 250 articles were reviewed. As a result, WTO offers to the international community what is probably the most complete Annotated Bibliography on Sustainable Tourism and related subjects.

Guide for Local Authorities on Developing Sustainable Tourism, 1998, WTO
http://www.world-tourism.org/cgi-bin/infoshop.storefront/EN/product/1016-1
This enlarged and revised edition of WTO's most popular publication *Sustainable Tourism Development: Guide for Local Planners*, presents concepts, principles and techniques for planning and developing tourism and includes sections on managing environmental and socio-economic impacts at the local level. It also contains numerous examples of sustainable tourism best practices readily adaptable to the particular conditions and level of development of each destination. Three supplementary volumes exist for Asia and the Pacific, Latin America and the Caribbean and Sub-Sahara Africa.

How the Hotel and Tourism Industry can Protect the Ozone Layer, 1998, UNEP-DTIE
http://www.uneptie.org/pc/tourism/library
The guide helps the hotel and tourism industry understand the damage being done to the stratospheric ozone layer by ozone depleting substances (ODS) and why they should be concerned. It outlines the steps to be taken by hotel managers to establish their own ODS management programme to properly manage the transition away from these chemicals.

Handbook on Natural Disaster Reduction in Tourist Areas, 1998, WMO and WTO
http://www.world-tourism.org/cgi-bin/infoshop.storefront/EN/product/1022-1
Tourism developments are quite often located in areas exposed to, or likely to be exposed to, sudden-onset natural disasters, in particular beach and coastal areas, river valleys and mountain regions. If these developments are hit by natural disasters, the image of the tourist destination will suffer. This handbook, produced jointly by WTO and World Meteorological Organization experts, demonstrates how to combat natural disasters in tourist areas and mitigate their impacts. It guides the reader through disaster onset to post-disaster reconstruction and the relaunching of a tourist destination.

Agenda 21 for the Travel and Tourism Industry, 1996, WTO and WTTC

http://www.world-tourism.org/sustainable/publications.htm

A joint WTO, WTTC and Earth Council publication outlining practical steps that
governments and private companies can take to implement the goals of the Rio Earth
Summit and make the tourism sector more sustainable.

Rural Tourism – A Solution for Employment, Local Development, and Environment,
1996, WTO

http://www.world-tourism.org/cgi-bin/infoshop.storefront/EN/product/1054-1

This publication is a result of the CEU-ETC Joint Seminar, held in Israel in 1996.
The purpose of this seminar was to promote an exchange of experience on rural
tourism between member countries, including in particular those for whom tourism
presents a new challenge. The publication includes a selection of presentations
submitted to the seminar, covering subjects such as rural tourism: products, market,
and marketing methods; rural tourism and local development, environmental
protection, and government aid; rural tourism: professions, training, qualifications,
and employment creation; prospects for rural tourism in the future: cooperation to
ensure that this product promotes sustainable tourism at local level.

The Environmental Action Pack for Hotels, Technical Report Series No.31, 1995,
UNEP-DTIE

http://www.uneptie.org/pc/tourism/library/

The Environmental Action Pack for Hotels is a response to Agenda 21
recommendations that business and industry shall be encouraged to 'recognize
environmental management as among the highest corporate priorities and as a key
determinant to sustainable development'. The Environmental Action Pack is an
essential first step guide for hoteliers around the world. It is also of interest to industry
associations, teaching institutions and governments directly involved in promoting and
supporting the tourism industry in its environmental management activities.

Structures and strategies to work with other stakeholders

*Environmental Management and Community Participation: Enhancing Local
Programmes*, 2003, UNEP-IETC

http://www.unep.or.jp/ietc/kms/data/1459.pdf

This brief document outlines the mutually reinforcing benefits of environmental
management and community participation at the level of a city or urban area. The
content is based on work done by UNEP-IETC in the Asia-Pacific region on the
themes of environmental management systems and ISO 14001, community studies,
urban management and the interlinkages of environmental issues.

Co-operation and Partnerships in Tourism - A Global Perspective, 2003, WTO

http://www.world-tourism.org/cgi-bin/infoshop.storefront/EN/product/1327-1

The aim of *Co-operation and Partnerships in Tourism: A Global Perspective* is to
give inspiration and guidance on how to build, implement and further develop

partnerships, focusing on strategic and operational issues in partnering and lessons learned from past partnering experiences. By examining cases from all regions of the world and from several different areas in tourism, the study provides insight that can be applied beyond the specific cultural and economic contexts of each case. As tourism is increasingly becoming a sector successfully built on cooperation and partnerships, this study is a valuable resource for anyone interested in Public-Private Sector Cooperation.

Green and Sustainable Businesses from a Local Government Perspective: Fostering Business Partnerships for Environmental Sustainability, 2003, UNEP- IETC
http://www.unep.or.jp/ietc/kms/data/1471.pdf
Effective business partnerships enable local governments and the private sector to assume initiative and co-responsibility in focusing on sustainability. Through effective and equal partnerships, the advantages of the private sector—dynamism, access to finance, knowledge of technologies, managerial efficiency, entrepreneurial spirit—are combined with the social responsibility, environmental awareness, local knowledge and job generation concerns of local governments.

Waste Management in Agenda 21, 2003, UNEP-IETC
http://www.unep.or.jp/ietc/kms/data/1449.doc
This brief document outlines the criticality assigned to waste management within the various chapters of Agenda 21, and discusses the various dimensions of waste management, from global to local. The publication directly emphasize the need to manage waste, or advocate the institution of measures that reduce generation of waste, or its effective integration into a recycling or reuse scheme that maintains material flow loops. It stresses that there is an urgent need to address the prevention and reduction of man-made disasters and/or disasters caused by industries, unsafe nuclear power generation and/or toxic wastes.

Public - Private Sector Cooperation, 2001, WTO
http://www.world-tourism.org/cgi-bin/infoshop.storefront/EN/product/1160-1
This report investigates the actual overall situation of public-private partnership, its relevance and importance for the competitiveness of tourism destinations. Based on a large number of collected projects, a total of 80 concrete case studies from 50 countries around the world were carefully selected, analysed and evaluated. Among the important findings are the essential principles and practices for public-private partnership as well as the basic conditions under which such cooperation functions. The report also describes strategies and guidelines for carrying out these partnerships best to ensure sustainable development and provides a forecast of the importance of such cooperation in the future.

Technical Workbook on Environmental Management Tools for Decision Analysis, 1999, UNEP-IETC
http://www.unep.or.jp/ietc/Publications/TechPublications/TechPub-14/summary.asp
Designed for developing countries, least developed countries, and countries with economies in transition, this workbook focuses on environmental management (EM) tools that aim to anticipate the environmental impact of decisions at the early stages of planning and decision-making, with respect to selection of environmental

technologies, identification and characterization of risks to the environment, health and safety, and planning environmental programmes for cities and municipalities. It does not include auditing and evaluation tools.

Measurement instruments

Indicators of Sustainable Development for Tourism Destinations, 2004, WTO

http://www.world-tourism.org/cgi-bin/infoshop.storefront/EN/product/1369-1

This guidebook is the most comprehensive resource on this topic, the result of an extensive study on indicator initiatives worldwide, involving 62 experts from more than 20 countries. It describes over 40 major sustainability issues, ranging from the management of natural resources (waste, water, energy, etc.), to development control, satisfaction of tourists and host communities, preservation of cultural heritage, seasonality, economic leakages, or climate change, to mention just a few. For each issue, indicators and measurement techniques are suggested with practical information sources and examples. The publication also contains a procedure to develop destination-specific indicators, their use in tourism policy and planning processes, as well as applications in different destination types (e.g. coastal, urban, ecotourism, small communities). Numerous examples and 25 comprehensive case studies provide a wide range of experiences at the company, destination, national and regional levels from all continents.

Guide to Good Practice in Tourism Carrying Capacity Assessment, 2003, PAP/RAC

http://www.pap-thecoastcentre.org/publications.html

The aim of this Guide is to discuss various practices in Tourism Carrying Capacity Assessment (CCA), including those using methodologies other than that of PAP, and to stimulate new ideas for the future preparation of CCA studies in the Mediterranean and in other parts of the world. The examples presented in the document help to demonstrate in which types of area, in both geographic and economic terms, CCA can be used in a most efficient way.

130 Indicators for sustainable development in the Mediterranean Region, 2000, UNEP/ PAM/ Plan Bleu

http://www.planbleu.org/vfrancaise/3-5b1.htm

The indicators have been adopted by the Contracting Parties in Malta, 1999. They were selected during two-years of work by the Mediterranean Commission of Sustainable Development (MCSD), and were validated by the Contracting Parties.

Command and control instruments

Tourism Congestion Management at Natural and Cultural Sites, 2005, WTO

http://www.world-tourism.org/cgi-bin/infoshop.storefront/EN/product/1370-1

This guidebook is aimed at a variety of professional users, both within the tourism industry and for people who welcome and manage visitors at their destination or site, including public authorities in the tourism, culture and nature fields. It provides recommendations to the different stakeholders in the tourism industry on how they might contribute to the minimization of tourism congestion. Destination and site managers will find a range of recommendations to build a well-informed understanding of their places and their visitors, as well as recommendations for upgrading the operational and physical capacities of their areas, in order to handle high levels of tourism activity. The guidebook is intended to provide very practical recommendations, using illustrations from the case studies. Congestion management practices are explained at different levels, linking actions between demand, destination and site management.

Making Tourism Work for Small Island Developing States, 2005, WTO
http://www.world-tourism.org/cgi-bin/infoshop.storefront/EN/product/1372-1
For most islands, tourism is the main economic activity in terms of income generation, employment creation, and foreign exchange earnings. But due to their small size, islands are vulnerable to the negative environmental and social impacts that tourism can sometimes bring. That is why it is vital to plan, manage and monitor tourism development in small island developing states (SIDS), aiming at sustainability objectives. This WTO report presents a summary of the current status of tourism in SIDS, while providing evidence of the key importance it has for the sustainable development of many islands and for the achievement of the UN Millennium Development Goals. It also addresses the key issues that need to be considered by small island nations and provides policy orientations, guidelines and other tools to the National Tourism Authorities, the tourism industry and other tourism stakeholders in SIDS on how to develop and manage tourism in a sustainable manner for the benefit of their population.

Forging Links Between Protected Areas and the Tourism Sector: How Tourism Can Benefit Conservation, 2005, UNEP DTIE/ UNESCO/RARE and UNF
http://www.uneptie.org/pc/tourism/library/home.htm
This manual, based on interviews with tourism companies, provides practical guidance on better ways of understanding the tourism industry. It also details what can be expected from the tourism industry in terms of support for conservation.

Tourism Legislation Database (LEXTOUR), 2004, WTO
http://www.world-tourism.org/doc/E/lextour.htm
LEXTOUR has been designed to act as a referral system facilitating direct access through links to external websites, databases and information servers on tourism legislative data produced and distributed by authoritative sources such as parliaments, central government bodies (including National Tourism Administrations), universities, professional associations, etc.

Environmental Impact Assessment and Strategic Environmental Assessment: Toward an Integrated Approach, 2004, UNEP- ETB
http://www.unep.ch/etu/publications/textONUBr.pdf
This document annotates and compares the lessons of EIA experience in developing and transitional countries to provide points of reference for EIA practitioners to review or develop EIA guidelines appropriate to countries' specific needs, development priorities and socio-economic and cultural background.

Coastal Zone Management Report: English-Speaking Caribbean, 2003, UNEP-GPA
http://www.gpa.unep.org/documents/PADH-docs.htm
This Study was undertaken to facilitate evaluation of the extent to which commitments have been translated into action on the ground, to point out strengths

and weaknesses of the actions taken to date, and to make recommendations on the way forward. In prosecuting these objectives the Study examines the present status of the legal and institutional framework for coastal zone management in the English speaking Caribbean.

UNEP Environmental Impact Assessment Training Resource Manual, Second Edition and Studies of EIA Practice in Developing Countries, 2003, UNEP
http://www.earthprint.com/

The main objective of this publication is to facilitate the preparation of training courses and materials that are specific to a particular country or region. Resource aids are included to help EIA trainers to identify the needs of participants and to custom-design courses to meet them. The case studies have been prepared by EIA specialists from developing countries to exemplify how the EIA process is implemented in different parts of the developing world and to identify difficulties that are commonly encountered in EIA practice in this context. It is intended that the case studies will be of use in two main ways. Firstly, they can be incorporated into customized training materials to give them added relevance and realism. Secondly, the studies can be used as 'reference points' or 'building blocks' to develop specific cases that reflect experience and issues of EIA practice in a country or region.

Sustainable Tourism in Protected Areas: Guidelines for Planning and Management, 2002, UNEP/IUCN/WTO
http://www.uneptie.org/pc/tourism/library/sust_prot_areas.htm
http://www.world-tourism.org/cgi-bin/infoshop.storefront/EN/product/1259-1

Publication aiming to assist protected area managers and other stakeholders in the planning and management of protected areas based on a wealth of practical case studies and experience. Ensuring that tourism follows a sustainable path requires clear leadership and enhanced partnership at all levels, particularly between the tourism industry and relevant government and non government agencies. This book describes how this can be achieved.

Tourism in the Least Developed Countries, 2001, WTO
http://www.world-tourism.org/cgi-bin/infoshop.storefront/EN/product/1170-1

To draw attention to the valuable economic opportunities which tourism can create, the WTO and UNCTAD organized a High Level Meeting on Tourism and Development in the Least Developed Countries. This publication is a collection of the presentations and discussion papers delivered during this meeting. It provides recommendations on how developing countries can present and enhance their tourism resources in order to compete in the international marketplace.

Integrated Coastal Management Guidelines for the ROMPE Region, 2000, UNEP-ROMPE
http://www.ropme.com/pages/publications.asp#

Guidelines that are applicable in almost any coastal situation, such as a gradual process of ICAM implementation within some or all of the seven steps proposed. Other elements such as the importance of individual natural resources, possibilities of implementation, institutional arrangements, or the application of tools and techniques, must be understood and applied with flexibility and with regard to the conditions prevailing in every particular area.

Tourism at World Heritage Cultural Sites, 1999, WTO
http://www.world-tourism.org/cgi-bin/infoshop.storefront/EN/product/1117-1
World Heritage Sites include many of the world's most outstanding attractions and
grandest monuments of the past. For tourism promoters they act as magnets, while
for the nation in which they are found they serve as icons that continue to influence
current values. This handbook concentrates on human-made sites, the physical
evidence of major historical events. It is devoted to helping the managers of World
Heritage Sites accomplish a dual purpose: to conserve the site in their care and
provide meaningful and considerate access to as many visitors as the site can allow.

*Caribbean Regional Training Manual : Integrated Coastal Area Management (ICAM)
for the Tourism Industry*, 1999, UNEP/USAID/SeaGrant
http://www.cep.unep.org/issues/ICAM%20manual.htm
This manual on general principles of ICAM is geared towards tourism industry
practitioners and developers. Its aim is to strengthen the regional capacity to
implement ICAM strategies in order to mitigate the negative impacts of tourism
activities on the coastal resources.

*The International Conference on Sustainable Tourism in Small Island Developing Sates
(SIDS) and other Islands*, 1998, WTO/UNEP
http://www.world-tourism.org/sustainable/doc/lanzarote.pdf
The conference was convened jointly by WTO and UNEP in Lanzarote, Spain, 1998.
Based on its resolutions, regional meetings were organized in collaboration with UNEP:
-   Sustainable Tourism and Competitiveness in the Islands of the Mediterranean,
    Island of Capri, Italy, May 2000,
    http://www.world-tourism.org/sustainable/doc/capri.pdf
-   International Conference on Sustainable Tourism in the Islands of the Asia-
    Pacific Region, Sanya, Island Of Hainan, China, December 2000,
    http://www.world-tourism.org/cgi-bin/infoshop.storefront/EN/product/1217-1

An Integrated Approach to Resort Development, 1992, WTO
http://www.world-tourism.org/cgi-bin/infoshop.storefront/EN/product/1018-1
This WTO study analyses six resorts, all largely completed and representing various
regions of the world and different types of development. For each case study,
comprehensive details are provided on planning and implementation, including the current
status of development. Economic, environmental and socio-cultural factors in planning
and implementation are also analysed, as well as the development impact of these factors.
The report evaluates the financing of both the infrastructure and tourist accommodation of
the resorts, the respective roles of the public and private sectors in financing, and financial
policies and procedures applied. Finally, it assesses the potential of applying these planning
and implementation procedures in other development projects around the world.

Economic instruments

Tourism Satellite Accounts Project Webpage, WTO
http://www.world-tourism.org/statistics
Satellite accounts are a procedure to measure the size of economic sectors which, like
tourism, are not defined as industries in national accounts. Tourism, for example, is

an amalgam of industries such as transportation, accommodation, food and beverage services, recreation and entertainment and travel agencies, among others. A Tourism Satellite Account (TSA) is a means to calculate tourist consumption of these goods and services supplied within a country using a common method which will permit comparisons over time and with other countries.

Tourism, Microfinance and Poverty Alleviation, 2005, WTO

http://ceres.wtoelibrary.org

Tourism can contribute to the fight against poverty in developing countries, and more specifically in the least developed countries. However, this potential is closely linked to the accessibility of financing sources. With the aim of finding solutions to the numerous problems involved in the financing of tourism development initiatives especially for small enterprises and microbusinesses in developing countries, the WTO in conjunction with PlaNet Finance, a leading microcredit institution, is studying the possibilities of adapting microcredit to the specific needs of the tourism sector. This report presents recommendations for small tourism enterprises and microbusinesses as well as microfinance institutions, with the objective of bringing them together and thus stimulate tourism development that benefits the poor. This report encourages governments and MFIs to adapt lending terms to the specific characteristics of tourism activity and poor populations.

The Use of Economic Instruments in Environmental Policy: Opportunities and Challenges, 2004, UNEP-ETP

http://www.unep.ch/etu/Publication/EconInst/econInstruOppChnaFin.pdf

This report seeks to help policy makers, especially in the developing world, to identify, evaluate and apply economic instruments to address a country's environmental problems within its national and local circumstances. It presents an innovative approach by offering tools for comprehensive assessment of the country context and conditions, and by tailoring solutions to the specific country needs.

Leakages and Linkages in the Tourism Sector: Using Cluster-Based Economic Strategy To Minimize Tourism Leakages, 2003, WTO

http://www.world-tourism.org/quality/E/trade2.htm

Leakages are broadly defined as the loss of foreign exchange and other hidden costs deriving from tourism related activities. Leakage avoidance can be undertaken proactively through processes that maximize the ability of the national and particularly the regional economy of countries to build and improve their tourism value-chain. A process for accomplishing this, at least in part, has taken shape in the form of regional cluster-based economic development.

Financing for Sustainable Development, 2002, UNEP DTIE / International Monetary Fund (IMF) / World Bank

http://www.unepfi.org/fileadmin/documents/financing_sustainable_devt_2002.pdf

This paper discusses how developing countries can generate some of the resources they need for sustainable development, and how the private sector, developing countries, donors, and local communities can contribute to this effort. In particular, the paper identifies innovative ways of encouraging more effective sustainability financing though public, private, or public-private approaches. It focuses on the issue of generating additional resources to finance sustainable development and does not discuss how these resources are to be employed.

Financing Sustainable Energy Directory: A Listing of Lenders and Investors, 2002, UNEP-FI
http://www.fse-directory.net/

The Financing Sustainable Energy Directory is an inventory of lenders and investors
who provide finance to the renewable energy and energy efficiency sectors. It is
designed to help project developers and entrepreneurs seeking capital, as well as
investors looking for financing vehicles.

Tourism Taxation, 1998, WTO
http://www.world-tourism.org/cgi-bin/infoshop.storefront/EN/product/1025-1

This study presents a comprehensive analysis of the effects of taxation on the tourism
industry and offers a series of recommendations aimed at assisting governments
in finding the right tourism taxation structure. Building on and complementing
previous reports on this subject, it is the result of detailed research and the input of
six regional seminars held around the world. It provides an analysis and discussion
of tourism taxation concepts and issues, a tourism taxation typology, and examines
future trends. The findings and conclusions are illustrated with an analysis of six
country case studies and a further selection of other geographic examples.

Voluntary instruments

Reports of the Regional Conferences on Sustainability Certification of Tourism,
2003/2004, WTO
Europe— http://www.world-tourism.org/sustainable/conf/cert-czech/eng.htm
Americas— http://www.world-tourism.org/sustainable/conf/cert-brasil/esp.htm
Asia-Pacific— http://www.world-tourism.org/sustainable/conf/cert-malaysia/finalrep.htm

The need for greater sustainability in tourism services and activities is already
widely recognized at all levels. Moreover, there are many and varied planning and
development methodologies, as well as tourism management techniques that make
it possible to attain higher levels of sustainability and to increase them gradually.
Such methodologies and techniques can be complemented by voluntary certification
systems for tourism services. The companies and organizations that provide them
began appearing on the international tourism market in 1990 and have proliferated
over the past few years.

*WTO recommendations to governments for supporting and /or establishing national
certification systems for sustainable tourism*, 2003, WTO
http://www.world-tourism.org/sustainable/doc/certification-gov-recomm.pdf

This document emphasizes the role of governments in establishing and coordinating
multi-stakeholder processes for certification systems, gives orientations for
developing certification criteria, and on the following operational aspects (application,
verification, awarding of certification, consulting, advisory and technical assistance
services, marketing and communication, fees and funding, etc.)

*Voluntary Initiatives for Sustainable Tourism - Worldwide Inventory and Comparative
Analysis of 104 Eco-labels*, Awards and Self-Commitments, 2002, WTO
http://www.world-tourism.org/cgi-bin/infoshop.storefront/EN/product/1232-1

This study, based on the analysis of 104 voluntary initiatives worldwide, provides
an evaluation of the effectiveness of existing schemes. It identifies similarities and

differences among voluntary initiatives and outlines the factors that make them successful in terms of sustainable tourism development. Based on the results, guidelines are made available to tourism companies wishing to adopt any of these voluntary schemes; organizations that run these initiatives, in order to improve existing schemes or create new ones; as well as for governments and NGOs, to provide them with technical criteria and guidelines for the support and supervision they may wish to give to these initiatives.

Sustainability Reporting Guidelines, 2002, Global Reporting Initiative (GRI)
http://www.globalreporting.org/guidelines/2002/GRI_guidelines_print.pdf
The Guidelines represent the foundation upon which all other GRI reporting documents are based, and outline core content that is broadly relevant to all organizations regardless of size, sector, or location. All organizations seeking to report using the GRI framework should use the Guidelines as the basis for their report, supported by other GRI documents as applicable.

Sustainability Reporting Guidelines- Tour Operators Sector Supplement, 2002, Global Reporting Initiative (GRI)
http://www.toinitiative.org/reporting/documents/TourOperatorsSupplementNovember2002.pdf
This book offer performance indicators specific to the sector, developed in multi-stakeholder fashion. The indicators can support tour operators in producing a detailed report on their sustainability performance, for public disclosure as well as to monitor internally their performance and benchmark progress.

Trust Us: The Global Reporters 2002 Survey of Corporate Sustainability Reporting, 2002, SustainAbility
http://www.sustainability.com/online/
Trust Us is the second report in the Global Reporters series to put corporate sustainability reporting under the microscope and focus on the emerging trends and hot topics that are bubbling under—or boiling over—in this increasingly important area of corporate accountability.

Child prostitution in tourism watch - International Campaign Against Sexual Exploitation of Children in Tourism, WTO
http://www.world-tourism.org/protect_children/index.htm
In recognition of the need to engage both governments and the private sector in the international campaign against child sex tourism the WTO child prostitution in tourism watch and partners (ECPAT, International Federation of Journalists and Terre des Hommes, Germany) have implemented a series of interrelated projects. The main activities include the implementation of guidelines for focal points at national tourism administrations and local tourism destinations, the application of the Code of Conduct for the Protection of Children from Sexual Exploitation in Travel and Tourism and its six criteria for tour operators, the incorporation of training modules on SECT in curricula of tourism education centres, the improvement of knowledge about SECT among journalists and young people in Europe. The project also acknowledges the diversity of tourism stakeholders and encourages all sectors to participate, including tour operators, hotels, airlines and government tourism ministries.

Encouraging Voluntary Initiatives for Corporate Greening, 2000, UNEP-DTIE
http://www.uneptie.org/outreach/vi/reports/encouraging_voluntary_initiatives.pdf
This paper maintains that none of the usual options—the market, conventional
regulatory authority and customary propriety—can meet the challenge of moving
toward sustainability in a dynamic, globalizing political economy. At least they cannot
do so as usually applied and haphazardly associated. Efforts to build a coherent
and well-integrated set of motivations for 'voluntary initiatives' are unlikely to be
sufficient by themselves either. Thus, the paper argues, the exercise of building such a
set of motivations along with appropriate individual initiatives is necessary, globally as
well as nationally.

Voluntary Initiatives: Current Status, Lessons Learnt and Next Steps, 2000, UNEP
http://www.uneptie.org/outreach/vi/reports/voluntary_initiatives.pdf
This paper is organized around the five major types of voluntary initiatives and
draws on the presentations and discussions from the UNEP Voluntary Initiatives
Workshop (Sept 2000). It summarizes the key messages and outlines possible next
steps to improve the efficacy and credibility of voluntary initiatives in today's context
of globalization.

Awards for Improving the Coastal Environment: The Example of the Blue Flag, 1997,
FEEE/ UNEP and WTO
http://www.world-tourism.org/cgi-bin/infoshop.storefront/EN/product/1019-1
A joint publication of the WTO, the Foundation for Environmental Education
in Europe (FEEE), and UNEP, this book outlines Europe's Blue Flag campaign.
It explains how Blue Flag assists the tourism sector and at the same time helps to
improve the coastal environment. The book includes chapters on the history of the
Blue Flag campaign, how the campaign is financed and monitored, and criteria
and lessons that can be learned from the European experience. It also looks at the
differences between European beaches and those in other parts of the world and
explains how the Blue Flag programme can be adapted to regions outside of Europe.

Ecolabels in the Tourism Industry, 1996, UNEP
http://www.uneptie.org/pc/tourism/library/ecolabels.htm
This publication examines the role of ecolabels within the context of voluntary
self-regulation in the tourism industry. It aims to help those applying for ecolabels
to better understand the nature of ecolabel schemes (the tourism industry, local and
national government, local communities and non-governmental organization).

Environmental Codes of Conduct for Tourism, UNEP Technical Report No. 29, 1995, UNEP
http://www.uneptie.org/pc/tourism/library/codes_of_conduct.htm
A technical report based on the results of a survey and analysis of existing codes
developed by countries, industry associations and NGOs. It offers not only examples
of environmental codes for the tourism industry, for host communities and for
tourists, but also essential elements common to successful codes and some of the
most common pitfalls; implementation and monitoring tools and programmes
currently in use to activate codes and monitor and report on performance; references
and useful addresses.

Supporting instruments

Guidelines on Municipal Wastewater Management, 2004, UNEP

http://www.gpa.unep.org/documents/wastewater/Guidelines_Municipal_Wastewater_Mgnt%20version3.pdf

These guidelines provide practical guidance on how to plan appropriate and environmentally sound municipal wastewater management systems. They are meant for decision-makers, operational professionals in government institutions and in the private sector, development banks and related organizations.

UNEP Programmes and Resources for Environmental Education and Training: An Introductory Guide, 2004, UNEP

http://www.earthprint.com

This guide showcases some of UNEP's many programmes and resources that support the important work of environmental education and training. It contains details of courses in the UNEP Environmental Leadership Programme, UNEP networks for environmental training, its commitment to supporting environmental action learning activities that link schools with their communities, training programmes for women as managers of natural resources, and examples of its public education programmes in newspapers and television.

Evaluating NTO Marketing Activities, 2003, WTO

http://www.world-tourism.org/cgi-bin/infoshop.storefront/EN/product/1331-1

This report examines the ways in which tourism destinations and NTOs evaluate the effectiveness of their promotional activities. The study takes account of the extensive analysis of the research carried out on the subject. Based on the results of a survey into current evaluation practices among NTOs, the study compares different evaluation methodologies in terms of best practices. As a result, a guide for the evaluation of the marketing activities of NTOs is developed setting out a number of practical steps.

A Manual for Water and Waste Management: What Tourism can do to Improve its Performance, 2003, UNEP-DTIE

http://www.uneptie.org/tourism/library/waste_manual.htm

This manual looks at solid waste and water management and provides guidelines and examples of how tourism operations can achieve positive results and minimize harm to a community's ecological and physical systems. Specific case studies highlight larger hotel chains that have already implemented environmental management systems but the main focus is on SME in developing countries, Small Island Developing States and developing tourism destinations.

Managing Urban Sewage An Introductory Guide for Decision-makers, Freshwater Management Series No. 10, 2003, UNEP-IETC

http://www.unep.or.jp/ietc/Publications/Freshwater/FMS10/index.asp

This document is part of the IETC series of Introductory Guides for Decision-makers. These guides are intended to assist decision-makers at the local level in understanding the issues and making informed decisions for the benefit of all citizens and stakeholders.

Capacity Building for Sustainable Development: An Overview of UNEP Environmental Capacity Development Initiatives, 2002, UNEP
http://www.unep.org/Pdf/Capacity_building.pdf
A UNEP guide highlighting how capacity building is a central element of its activities particularly in its approach to assisting the sustainable development of developing countries and countries with economies in transition. The guide gives selected examples of capacity development taken from ten years since Rio and tries to project into the next decade, after Jo'burg.

Human Resources in Tourism: Towards a New Paradigm, 2002, WTO
http://www.world-tourism.org/cgi-bin/infoshop.storefront/EN/product/1258-1
Human resource development occupies a central role in achieving efficiency in tourism. In this context, the II International Conference on Tourism Professions, which took as its theme 'Tourism Employment: Towards a New Paradigm' was held in Madrid, Spain on 26–27 January 1998, with the participation of more than 30 speakers and 350 people from 28 countries. This publication is a collection of the papers presented during the Conference on topics relating to the present situation of human resources in the tourism industry and the advisability of creating an alternative conceptual framework for the quality and efficiency of human capital in tourism.

E-Business for Tourism - Practical Guidelines for Destinations and Businesses, 2001, WTO
http://www.world-tourism.org/cgi-bin/infoshop.storefront/EN/product/1210-1
A report prepared as guidance for those who are prepared to embrace the E-Business. After explaining the concepts of E-Business and Customer Relationship Management, it provides an overview of the changing value chains and the evolving role of DMOs. It continues with practical guidelines on how DMOs should respond to the challenges by developing E-Business systems, and more specifically, how to go about developing websites for consumers, intermediaries, travel media and tourism businesses. The report also focuses on E-Business for tourism suppliers, particularly Small and Medium Sized Enterprises (SMEs). E-tools can help SMEs to get market access, and ensure economic viability, contribution to local economies, poverty reduction, etc.

Urban Environmental Management: Environmental Management System Training Resource Kit, 2001, UNEP / FIDIC / ICLEI
http://www.earthprint.com
The majority of Environmental Management Systems (EMS) have been designed to improve the environmental performance of private organizations, especially business enterprises. More recently, local authorities have also shown interest in EMS as a systematic tool to achieve urban sustainability, and improve their liveability. They are, in fact, consumers and producers of goods and services (electricity, food, water, infrastructures, etc.) and their activities and policy choices have a significant impact on the local economy, the environment, human health and people's quality of life.

Sowing the Seeds of Change: Environmental Teaching Pack for the Hospitality, 2001, UNEP-DTIE
http://www.uneptie.org/pc/tourism/library/training-hotel.htm
The Teaching Pack enables education professionals to develop tailor-made environmental curricula to suit the needs and objectives of each school and education

system (covering a minimum of 45 minutes teaching time) while for students of hospitality management, it will serve as an environmental information and resource handbook. The pack can also be used by hospitality professionals to support awareness raising programmes and the development and implementation of Environmental Management Systems.

Caribbean Regional Training Manual: Environmentally Sound Tourist Facility Design and Development for the Tourism Industry, 1999, UNEP / USAID / CAST
http://www.cep.unep.org/issues/design-siting%20manual.htm

This manual aims to improve the technical capabilities of coastal developers and planners in the countries of the Wider Caribbean Region in addressing the problems arising from the traditional construction and design of tourism facilities, and to introduce concepts and guidance for the construction and environmental sustainability of new facilities.

Caribbean Regional Training Manual: Solid Waste and Wastewater Management for the Tourism Industry, 1999, UNEP / USAID / CEHI
http://www.cep.unep.org/issues/solid%20waste%20manual.htm

This manual is geared towards improving the tourism sector's technical capabilities in the area of prevention and control of land-based sources of pollution caused by tourism, in implementing strategies that improve water, wastewater and solid waste management in tourist facilities and in promoting best practices for the reduction, recycling and reuse of most solid wastes generated by and impacting on tourism.

Transport and the Global Environment: Accounting for GHG Reductions in Policy Analysis, 1999, UNEP / RISØ
http://www.earthprint.com

This book offers a consistent analytical structure for examining the environmental aspects of transport choices; defines the key economic and environmental concepts used in good policy analysis; and gives information on technologies, environmental impacts and cost effectiveness of various policy options. The book also describes international financial mechanisms that can be used to support sustainable transportation policies and programmes.

Improving Training and Public Awareness on Caribbean Coastal Tourism, 1997, USAID / UNEP-CEP
http://www.cep.unep.org/issues/panos.PDF

This study is a component of a regional project started in late 1995 to promote corrective actions regarding land-based sources of pollution caused by tourism that have a negative impact on coastal and marine resources. It draws on findings and conclusions to propose a set of public awareness and training activities for the project.

Contacts for Further Information

10. Contacts for Further Information

Publication author: Richard Denman, The Tourism Company, UK rdenman@thetourismcompany.com

Further information relating to the Case Studies and to the examples in boxes may be obtained from the following sources.

Case Studies

Case study	Contact name	Organization	Email	Website
Bulgaria	Kamelia Georgieva	Biodiversity Conservation and Economic Growth Project	kgeorgieva@hrc-bg.com	www.ecotourism.bulgariatravel.org
Scotland	Sandy Dear	Scottish Tourism and Environment Forum	sandy.dear@visitscotland.com	www.greentourism.org.uk
Mexico	Juan Carlos Arnau Avila Leonel Uriarte García	Secretaría de Turismo de México	jcarnau@sectur.gob.mx luriate@sectur.gob.mx	www.sectur.gob.mx
Egypt	Ahmed Hassan	Red Sea Sustainable Tourism Initiative	ahassan1@rssti.com	www.rssti.com
Costa Rica	Amos Bien	The International Ecotourism Society	amos@ecotourism.org	www.visitcostarica.com www.turismo-sostenible.co.cr
Australia	Alice Crabtree	The International Ecotourism Society	alice@ecotourism.org	www.atc.net.au
	David Morgans	Tourism Queensland	david.morgans@tq.com.au	www.tq.com.au
Ghana	Wouter Schalken	SNV Ghana	wschalken@snvghana.org	www.snvworld.org
South Africa	Johann Kotze	Department of Environmental Affairs and Tourism	Jkotze@deat.gov.za	www.environment.gov.za
Calvia	Maxi Lange Eduardo Cozar Pablo de la Peña	Ajuntament de Calvià	mlange@calvia.com ecozar@calvia.com	www.calvia.com
Kaikoura	Ian Challenger	Kaikoura District Council	ian.challenger@kaikoura.govt.nz	www.kaikoura.co.nz

Boxed Examples

Boxed example	Box #	Contact name	Organization	Email	Website
Honduras structures	3.1	Yara Zuñiga	Honduras Institute of Tourism	yzuniga@iht.hn	www.letsgohonduras.com
Fiji SEA	3.2	Daniele Ponzi	Asian Development Bank	dponzi@adb.org	www.wwf.org.uk/filelibrary/pdf/fijitourism.pdf
Europarc Charter	4.2	Richard Blackman	EUROPARC Federation	r.blackman@europarc.org	www.europarc.org
Lanzarote Observatory	5.1	-	Cabildo de Lanzarote	-	www.cabildodelanzarote.com/areas/presidencia/biosfera
Iguazu data	5.2	-	Iguazu Forest Natural Reserve	-	www.iguazuforest.com
Malta carrying capacity	5.3	Marie Louise Mangion	Malta Tourism Authority	marielouise.mangion@visitmalta.com	www.mta.com.mt

Boxed example	Box #	Contact name	Organization	Email	Website
Namibia conservancies	5.4	-	Namibia Ministry of Environment and Tourism	-	www.dea.met.gov.na
Vietnam law	5.5	Pham Quang Hung Douglas Hainsworth	Vietnam National Administration of Tourism SNV Vietnam	douglas@snv.org.vn	www.vietnam-tourism.com
England regulations	5.6	-	VisitBritain	-	www.tourismtrade.org.uk/uktrade/advisory
ECOLUP planning	5.7	Marion Hammerl	-	marion.hammerl@bodensee-stiftung.org	www.ecolup.info
Maldives regulations	5.8	Moosa Zameer Hassan	Maldives Ministry of Tourism	zameer@maldivestourism.gov.mv	www.maldivestourism.gov.mv
Colombia enforcement	5.9	Richard Tapper	-	rtapper@dircon.co.uk	www.bfn.de/09/tayrona.pdf
Belize Trust	5.11	-	Protected Areas Conservation Trust	-	www.pactbelize.org
Madagascar revenues	5.11	-	Association Nationale pour la Gestion des Aires Protégées	-	www.parcs-madagascar.com/angap
Morocco loans	5.12	Myriem Touhami	United Nations Environment Programme	Myriem.touhami@unep.fr	www.uneptie.org/energy/
Catalonia incentives	5.12	Salvador Semitier Marti	Generalitat de Catalunya, Department de Medi Ambient i Habitatage	wsamitier@gencat.net	www.gencat.net/mediamb/qamb/inici.htm
Rimini beaches	5.12	Enzo Finocchiaro	Provincia di Rimini	finocchiaro@provincia.rimini.it	www.turismosostenibile.provincia.rimini.it
UK Carbon Trust	5.12	-	-	-	www.hospitableclimates.co.uk
Barbados offset	5.12	-	Government of Barbados	-	www.barbadostourisminvestment.com
Exploitation code	5.13	-	ECPAT	-	www.thecode.org
Arctic codes	5.14	Miriam Geitz	WWF Arctic Programme	mgeitz@wwf.no	www.panda.org/arctic
Sydney reporting	5.15	Simon McArthur	Q-Station	Simon.McArthur@q-station.com.au	www.q-station.com.au
S Africa trademark	5.16	Jennifer Seif	Fair Trade in Tourism South Africa	info@fairtourismsa.org.za	www.fairtourismsa.org.za
VISIT ecolabels	5.17	-	European Voluntary Initiative for Sustainability in Tourism	-	www.yourvisit.info
Blue Flag	5.18	Finn Bolding Thomsen	Foundation for Environmental Education	blueflag@blueflag.org	www.blueflag.org
Lake District Trust	5.19	Claire Stott	Lake District Tourism and Conservation Partnership	Claire@lakespartnership.org.uk	www.lakespartnership.org.uk

Boxed example	Box #	Contact name	Organization	Email	Website
Austria transport	5.20	Veronika Holzer	Austrian Ministry of Agriculture, Forestry, Environment and Water	veronika.holzer@lebensministerium.at	www.mobilito.at; www.alpsmobility.org
Turkey waste	5.21	-	-	-	www.toinitiative.org/destinations/destination.htm#Side
ODIT France	5.22	Jean-Paul Teyssandier	Observation, Développement et Ingénierie Touristique, France	jean-paul.teyssandier@odit-france.fr	www.odit-france.fr
England manual	5.23	-	The Countryside Agency	-	www.greenauditkit.org
Jamaica EAST	5.24	Hugh Cresser	Environmental Audits for Sustainable Tourism project	east@infochan.com	
Nepal TRPAP	5.25	Rabi Jung Pandey	Tourism and Rural Poverty Alleviation Programme	rjpandey_trpap@ntb.org.np	www.welcomenepal.com/trpap
REDTURS	5.26	-	-	-	www.redturs.org
Tanzania Culture	5.27	-	-	-	www.snvworld.org/cds/rgTUR/documents_1.htm
Leave no Trace	5.28	-	The Leave No Trace Programme	-	www.lnt.org
UK market influence	5.29	-	Foreign and Commonwealth Office, Department for International Development	-	www.fco.gov.uk www.dfid.gov.uk/pubs/files/rough-guide/better-world.pdf

Notes

About the World Tourism Organization

The World Tourism Organization is a specialised agency of the United Nations that serves as a global forum for tourism policy and issues. Its Members include 152 countries and territories as well as over 300 Affiliate Members from the public and private sectors.

WTO generates know-how for its members and the international tourism community. **WTO Sustainable Development of Tourism Department is currently involved in the following main fields of activity**:

> **Policies and planning for the sustainable development of tourism**: WTO has been providing technical assistance on sustainable tourism planning at the national, regional and local levels in all countries.

> **Sustainable tourism at specific destinations**: WTO supports the sustainable development and management of coastal, rural, and urban destinations, cultural heritage sites, protected areas, etc. and of Small Island Developing States.

> **Tourism and poverty alleviation**: at the World Summit on Sustainable Development in 2002, WTO launched the concept of "Sustainable Tourism as an effective tool for Eliminating Poverty" (ST-EP) and is currently implementing projects in this field. WTO is collaborating with Micro-Finance Institutions and governments in the developing world, encouraging them to coordinate efforts and to support micro, small and medium sized tourism enterprises.

> **The Global Code of Ethics for Tourism**, approved by the UN, is a comprehensive set of principles whose purpose is to guide the stakeholders in tourism development, including tourists, towards ethical behaviours.

> **Indicators of sustainable tourism**: WTO encourages the application of sustainability indicators at destinations, as fundamental tools for the planning and monitoring of tourism.

> **Climate change and tourism**: WTO is addressing the complex relations between climate change and tourism.

> **Voluntary initiatives for sustainable tourism**: certification systems, eco-labels and other forms of voluntary regulation represent an effective alternative to direct legislation.

WTO´s mission is to promote and develop tourism as a significant means of fostering international peace and understanding, sustainable economic development and international trade.

For more information,
see **www.world-tourism.org**